EARTHQUAKE DAYS

The 1906 San Francisco Earthquake & Fire in 3-D

DAVID BURKHART

FAULTLINE BOOKS

California-born historian David Burkhart is an honors graduate of Yale. A resident of the Bay Area since 1980, he and his wife live on the San Francisco Peninsula, half a mile from the aptly named San Andreas Lake. Mr. Burkhart is a member of the small staff at San Francisco's renowned Anchor Steam® Brewery. A professional trumpeter, he teaches at the San Francisco Conservatory and performs regularly with the San Francisco Symphony and Opera. He is also a member of the National Stereoscopic Association.

Faultline Books, San Bruno, CA 94066

©2005 by Faultline Books
All rights reserved. Published 2005
Printed in Canada by Hemlock Printers using stochastic screening

ISBN (cloth): 0-977-33056-7

Library of Congress Control Number: 2005934321

Faultline Books
PO Box 849
San Bruno, CA 94066
www.faultlinebooks.com

This book is printed on acid-free paper.

To my wife,
Deborah Shidler,
and my parents,
John and Virginia Burkhart.
And to the thousands who
perished as a result of the
Earthquake and Fire of 1906.

ACKNOWLEDGMENTS

Special thanks to Kirk Amyx and Jack Martin, without whom this book would never have been possible.

Patricia Akre, San Francisco History Room,
    San Francisco Public Library
Kirk Amyx, Amyx Photography, San Francisco
Jeannette Anderson
Matthew Bailey, National Portrait Gallery, London
Stephen Becker, California Historical Society, San Francisco
Gianna Capecci, Society of California Pioneers, San Francisco
Kip Cranna, San Francisco Opera
Reid and Peggy Dennis
Jack von Euw, The Bancroft Library,
    University of California, Berkeley
Joe Evans, North Baker Research Library,
    California Historical Society, San Francisco
Philip L. Fradkin
Bruce French
Don Gibbs, National Stereoscopic Association
Susan Goldstein, San Francisco History Room,
    San Francisco Public Library
Herbert Hamrol, 1906 Earthquake Survivor
Richard Hansen, San Francisco History Room,
    San Francisco Public Library
James S. Holliday
Allen Johnson
Patricia Keats, Society of California Pioneers, San Francisco
Frits Kouwenhoven, Hemlock Printers, Burnaby, B.C.
Michael D. Lampen, Grace Cathedral, San Francisco
Ann Longknife

Richard Marino, San Francisco History Room,
    San Francisco Public Library
Jack Martin, Jack Martin Design, San Francisco
John Martin, JFM Digital Imaging, San Rafael
Fritz Maytag, Anchor Brewing Company, San Francisco
Karen Mead, Piedmont Editorial, Piedmont
Mary Morganti, North Baker Research Library,
    California Historical Society, San Francisco
Erica Nordmeier, The Bancroft Library,
    University of California, Berkeley
Larry and Jane Rosen
Tricia Roush, San Francisco Performing Arts
    Library & Museum
Janet Sakai, Department of Special Collections,
    Stanford University Libraries
Erika Schmidt, Mechanics' Institute Library, San Francisco
Wolfgang Sell, Oliver Wendell Holmes Research Library,
    National Stereoscopic Association, Cincinnati
Marc André Singer, Mechanics' Institute Library, San Francisco
Susan Snyder, The Bancroft Library,
    University of California, Berkeley
Kevin Starr
K. D. Sullivan, Creative Solutions Editorial, San Francisco
Kirsten Tanaka, San Francisco Performing Arts
    Library & Museum
Steve Thomas, UCR/California Museum of Photography,
    University of California, Riverside
Roberto Trujillo, Department of Special Collections,
    Stanford University Libraries
Grace Woo

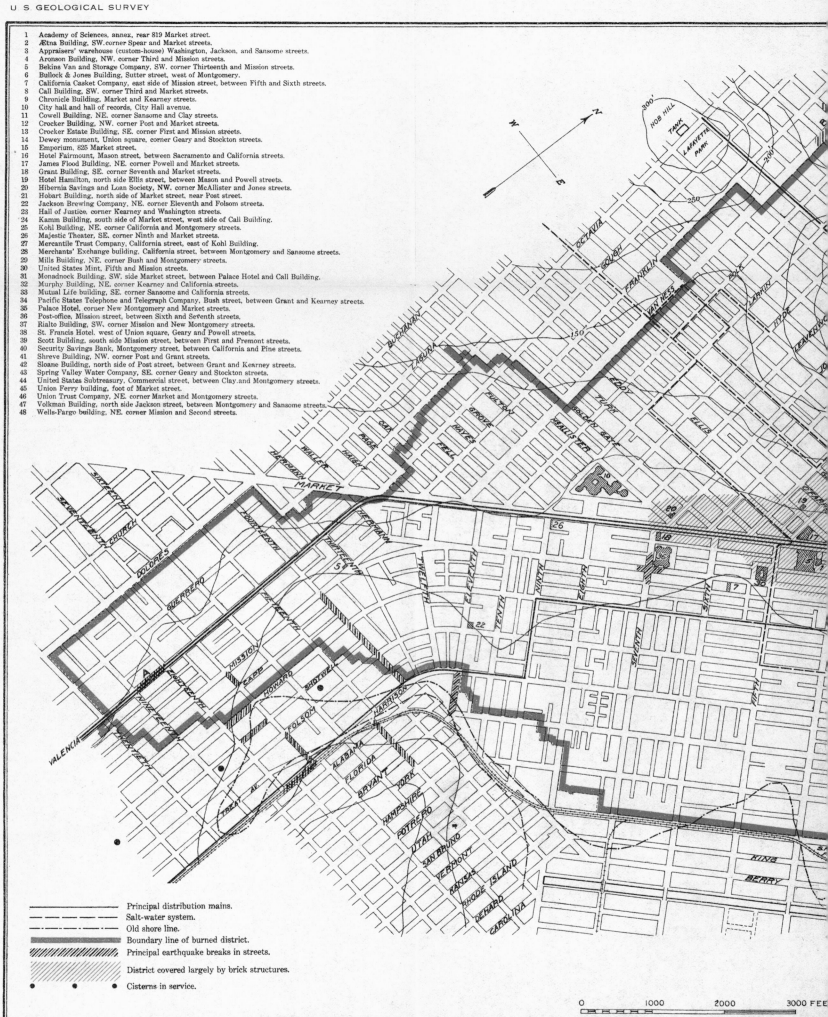

1   Academy of Sciences, annex, rear 819 Market street.
2   Aetna Building, SW. corner Spear and Market streets.
3   Appraisers' warehouse (custom-house) Washington, Jackson, and Sansome streets.
4   Aronson Building, NW. corner Third and Mission streets.
5   Bekins Van and Storage Company, SW. corner Thirteenth and Mission streets.
6   Bullock & Jones Building, Sutter street, west of Montgomery.
7   California Casket Company, east side of Mission street, between Fifth and Sixth streets.
8   Call Building, SW. corner Third and Market streets.
9   Chronicle Building, Market and Kearney streets.
10 City hall and hall of records, City Hall avenue.
11 Cowell Building, NE. corner Sansome and Clay streets.
12 Crocker Building, NW. corner Post and Market streets.
13 Crocker Estate Building, SE. corner First and Mission streets.
14 Dewey monument, Union square, corner Geary and Stockton streets.
15 Emporium, 825 Market street.
16 Hotel Fairmount, Mason street, between Sacramento and California streets.
17 James Flood Building, NE. corner Powell and Market streets.
18 Grant Building, SE. corner Seventh and Market streets.
19 Hotel Hamilton, north side Ellis street, between Mason and Powell streets.
20 Hibernia Savings and Loan Society, NW. corner McAllister and Jones streets.
21 Hobart Building, north side of Market street, near Post street.
22 Jackson Brewing Company, NE. corner Eleventh and Folsom streets.
23 Hall of Justice, corner Kearney and Washington streets.
24 Kamm Building, south side of Market street, west side of Call Building.
25 Kohl Building, NE. corner California and Montgomery streets.
26 Majestic Theater, SE. corner Ninth and Market streets.
27 Mercantile Trust Company, California street, east of Kohl Building.
28 Merchants' Exchange building, California street, between Montgomery and Sansome streets.
29 Mills Building, NE. corner Bush and Montgomery streets.
30 United States Mint, Fifth and Mission streets.
31 Monadnock Building, SW. side Market street, between Palace Hotel and Call Building.
32 Murphy Building, NE. corner Kearney and California streets.
33 Mutual Life building, SE. corner Sansome and California streets.
34 Pacific States Telephone and Telegraph Company, Bush street, between Grant and Kearney streets.
35 Palace Hotel, corner New Montgomery and Market streets.
36 Post-office, Mission street, between Sixth and Seventh streets.
37 Rialto Building, SW. corner Mission and New Montgomery streets.
38 St. Francis Hotel, west of Union square, Geary and Powell streets.
39 Scott Building, south side Mission street, between First and Fremont streets.
40 Security Savings Bank, Montgomery street, between California and Pine streets.
41 Shreve Building, NW. corner Post and Grant streets.
42 Sloane Building, north side of Post street, between Grant and Kearney streets.
43 Spring Valley Water Company, SE. corner Geary and Stockton streets.
44 United States Subtreasury, Commercial street, between Clay and Montgomery streets.
45 Union Ferry building, foot of Market street.
46 Union Trust Company, NE. corner Market and Montgomery streets.
47 Volkman Building, north side Jackson street, between Montgomery and Sansome streets.
48 Wells-Fargo building, NE. corner Mission and Second streets.

——————— Principal distribution mains.
- - - - - Salt-water system.
-·-·-·-·- Old shore line.
▆▆▆▆▆▆ Boundary line of burned district.
▨▨▨▨▨▨ Principal earthquake breaks in streets.
▨▨▨▨ District covered largely by brick structures.
•   •   • Cisterns in service.

0   1000   2000   3000 FEE

MAP OF SAN FRANCISCO SHOWING BURNED DISTRICT; ACCOMPANYING RE

1907

"ON WEDNESDAY MORNING, April 18, 1906, at twelve minutes past five o'clock, San Francisco, this city of wonderful setting, suffered an earthquake whose sensible duration was about one minute. The shock left her powerless to supply light, heat, water, drainage, to convey her people or to carry their messages; but it would not have paralyzed her activities had it not been that because of the breaking of the main water conduits, the fires, thirty of which were said to have started immediately, could not be controlled.

"The fires started on both sides of Market Street, and within three hours after the earthquake, made a continuous line of flame from north of Market Street, along the water front, past the Ferry Building, south of Market Street and along Mission Street to beyond Third Street, where was the main station of the only railroad that ran out of the city. As the fire spread to the southwest and the north, the whole population seemed cut off from escape except by going west and south within the city. Comparatively few knew during the first two days that there was a narrow but safe way around the fire to the Ferry Building from which the boats were running…. On the second and third days small supplies of water were brought to play upon the fire, but not until the morning of Saturday the twenty-first, by the use of dynamite, was the advance of the flames stopped.

"The burned area, the very heart and vitals of the city, covered 4.7 square miles, on which were located 521 blocks, 13 of which were saved, 508 burned. The number of buildings destroyed was 28,188, the number of persons made homeless about 200,000 of San Francisco's estimated population of 450,000. The loss of real and personal property has been estimated at $500,000,000,—about $1,100 per capita of the city's population…. The loss of life as a result of both earthquake and fire was reported by General Greely, after careful inquiry, to be: known dead, 304; unknown dead, 194; total, 498; number seriously injured, 415."–*San Francisco Relief Survey*, Charles O'Connor et al, ©1913 Russell Sage Foundation, NY, NY. Reprinted with permission.

"The loss of life attending the great disaster is officially recorded at 478. Whether more than this, or how many more, can never be told."–*San Francisco Municipal Reports*, 1906

Today, historians estimate San Francisco's death toll to be between six and ten times its contemporaneous enumerations.

*Down Market Street
From 4th., Showing Sky Scrapers
of America's Most Cosmopolitan
City, San Francisco.*

*After the greatest of modern
catastrophes—Market St. N.E.
past the Call Bldg., San
Francisco.*

For in the immediate world, everything is to be discerned, for him who can discern it, and centrally and simply, without either dissection into science, or digestion into art, but with the whole consciousness, seeking to perceive it as it stands: so that the aspect of a street in sunlight can roar in the heart of itself as a symphony, perhaps as no symphony can: and all the consciousness is shifted from the imagined, the revisive, to the effort to perceive simply the cruel radiance of what is.

–James Agee, in *Let Us Now Praise Famous Men*, 1941 (courtesy of the Houghton Mifflin Company)

CONTENTS

COPYRIGHT 1906 BY P. F. COLLIER & SON

RELIEF MAP OF SAN FRANCISCO, AS THE CITY APPEARED BEFORE THE EARTHQUAKE AND FIRE

The heavy dotted line "▬▬▬▬▬▬" indicates the boundaries of the district destroyed by fire. Three little unburned oases remain within the general area of devastation—one along the water-front by the ferry building, one on the side of Telegraph Hill, and one between these two. The ruined region includes practically all that was known as San Francisco—all the business, financial, amusement, and most of the residence sections. There is little outside of it but scattered dwellings, isolated manufacturing plants, and open spaces. The burned district is a solid bulk over three miles long and two miles wide. The value of the property destroyed within it must have been at least $300,000,000, and may have reached $400,000,000, about half-covered by insurance. The principal landmarks and buildings of the city were:

1 City Hall	7 The Chronicle Building	14 Portsmouth Square	22 St. Ignatius Church	30 Russian Church	35 Olympic Club
2 Post-Office	8 The Flood Building	15 Chinatown	23 St. Mary's Cathedral	31 St. Dominick's Church	36 California Theatre, where
3 United States Mint (saved)	9 The Examiner Building	16 Union Square	24 Majestic Theatre	32 Telegraph Hill	Fire Chief Sullivan was
4 Grand Opera House	10 The Palace Hotel	17 St. Francis Hotel	25 Mechanics' Pavilion	33 Wells Fargo Express Com-	killed
5 The Call Building	11 The Grand Hotel	18 Bush Street Synagogue	26 Jefferson Square	pany's Building	37 The Emporium, the largest
6 The Crocker-Woolworth	12 The Merchants' Exchange	19 Mark Hopkins Institute	27 Masonic Cemetery	34 Unburned District around	department store in San
Bank	13 Hall of Justice	20 Fairmount Hotel	28 Alamo Square	Telegraph Hill	Francisco
		21 Southern Pacific R.R. Station	29 St. Patrick's Cathedral		

COLLIER'S, MAY 5, 1906

"To those in the East, and all persons who live without the limits of earthquake disturbances, the thought of the ground itself being unstable and liable at any moment to be convulsed by some mighty hidden power, inspires more real terror than the ordinary shocks that are frequently felt in California. Visitors to this coast feel much solicitude on account of the 'shaky' condition of the country, until they have been made acquainted with the phenomenon, by feeling a few smart shakes. Familiarity with danger subdues fear and dread; and a year's residence in San Francisco will quiet any fearful apprehensions from earthquakes."
—B. E. Lloyd, *Lights and Shades in San Francisco*, 1876

DANCING ON THE BRINK

"Did you feel that?" Californians have been asking and answering that question for centuries, and no earthquake survivor—from ancient Alexandria to modern San Francisco—ever forgets where they were or what they were doing when "the big one" struck.

William Shakespeare's "big one" may have been the London earthquake of April 6, 1580. And he may have been writing *Romeo and Juliet* at the time. An earthquake certainly plays an important role in Act I, Scene 3. Shakespearean scholars disagree on virtually everything, however, especially dates. Perhaps the bard was simply trying to add verisimilitude to his play—a significant earthquake did occur in Verona in 1348. Or maybe he was attempting to rekindle his London audiences' own memories of the quake of April 6, 1580—or some other contemporaneous seismic event in London or Verona. In any case, Juliet's nurse's earthquake recollections help her convince Lady Capulet of Juliet's precise and tender age:

> On Lammas-eve at night shall she be fourteen;
> That shall she, marry; I remember it well.
> 'Tis since the earthquake now eleven years;
> And she was wean'd—I never shall forget it—
> Of all the days of the year, upon that day....
> Shake quoth the dove-house: 'twas no need, I trow,
> To bid me trudge.
> And since that time it is eleven years.

San Francisco's earthquake memories are particularly vivid. Along with "the jargon of the mining camp" and the "*patois* of the frontier," her earthquake experiences shaped San Francisco's unique language. The City-By-The-Bay has always been "shaky on her pins," and the colloquial concept of "earthquake weather" is still prevalent today. According to the July 1875 *Scribner's Monthly*, San Franciscans even had their own localism for "getting at the character of a man." It was, "coming down to the bedrock."

Within a few frenzied years of millwright James Marshall's January 24, 1848, discovery of gold, the geological folklore of the Bay Area's original inhabitants became inextricably bound up with San Francisco's own historical record. *The Annals of San Francisco* was published in 1855, as much to promote California's "Great City," as to record its history. Authors Soulé, Gihon, and Nisbet recount the "tradition among the Indians of California, that San

Francisco Bay originally formed a fresh water lake. An earthquake, however, suddenly opened the line of mountains along the coast, when the sea rushed in, and changed the region to what it now is. The surplus fresh waters of the old lake were supposed to have been discharged into the Bay of Monterey, by a great river flowing through the valley of San José and Santa Clara."

San Francisco was Robert Louis Balfour Stevenson's adopted home, and the Bohemian his adopted lifestyle. Stevenson (1850–1894) came to California in August 1879 to be with his Indianapolis-born sweetheart, Frances Matilda Vandegrift (better known as Mrs. Fanny Osbourne). He married her in San Francisco the following May. Having penned three books and numerous shorter works during his California sojourn, Stevenson departed the "big jostling city" of San Francisco on August 7, 1880, one year to the day after leaving his native Scotland. *Treasure Island*, inspired in part by his time in the Golden State, was published in 1883.

Stevenson's essay, *San Francisco*, was first published in 1882. In describing California's "changeful and insecure" geology, he, too, alludes to Native American legend:

"I have dined, near the 'punctual centre' [as on a compass] of San Francisco, with a gentleman (then newly married), who told me of his former pleasures, wading with his fowling-piece in sand and scrub, on the site of the house where we were dining. In this busy, moving generation, we have all known cities to cover our boyish playgrounds, we have all started for a country walk and stumbled on a new suburb; but I wonder what enchantment of the Arabian Nights can have equalled this evocation of a roaring city, in a few years of a man's life, from the marshes and the blowing sand. Such swiftness of increase, as with an overgrown youth, suggests a corresponding swiftness of destruction. The sandy peninsula of San Francisco, mirroring itself on one side in the bay, beaten on the other by the surge of the Pacific, and shaken to the heart by frequent earthquakes, seems in itself no very durable foundation. According to Indian tales, perhaps older than the name of California, it once rose out of the sea in a moment, and sometime or other shall, in a moment, sink again. No Indian, they say, cares to linger on that doubtful land."

Indians, of course, did linger on California lands—as long as they could. In 1542, Portuguese navigator Juan Rodríguez Cabrillo (d. 1543) commanded a Spanish expedition, sailing along California's coast. But the San Francisco Bay Area's Coast Miwok and Ohlone (Spanish explorers called the Ohlone the "Costanoan Indians") had their homeland pretty much to themselves until the late eighteenth century. According to historian Zoeth S. Eldredge, "From the time of Cabrillo, Spain had claimed the coasts of the Pacific up to forty-two degrees north latitude by right of discovery, but more than two hundred years had passed and she had done nothing towards making good this right by settlement."

Enter Father Junípero Serra (1713–1784), founder of nine missions in Upper California: "The popular mind accepts the oft-repeated statement that the settlement of California was due to the pious zeal of a devoted priest, eager to save the souls of the heathen," Eldredge asserts. "Radient [sic] as is the priestly figure of Junípero… the careful investigator will find that the impelling factor in the occupation of California was stern military necessity, not missionary zeal…. The country was open to colonization by any nation strong enough to maintain and protect its colonies."

In 1775, the *San Carlos*, under Lieutenant Juan Manuel de Ayala (1745–1797), became the first ship to sail into San Francisco Bay. But it was the party of Catalonian Gaspar de Portolá (1723–1826), six years earlier, that "discovered" San Francisco for Spain.

On July 14, 1769, explorer/adventurer Portolá, accompanied by a small band of soldiers and missionaries, set out from San Diego. They were in search of a land route to the already-discovered Monterey Bay. What they discovered—quite by accident—was an immense "estero o brazo del mar." It was the bay of what would one day be known as San Francisco.

En route, just two weeks and 32 leagues (the Spanish "legua" was equivalent to 5000 varas, about 2.6 miles) out of San Diego, the party camped near a river now known as the Santa Ana. There, they met a tribe of quite hospitable Indians, who offered them food and even land. The Tongva (also called Gabrieleño or Gabrielino because of their later association with Mission San Gabriel) were the first Los Angelinos. Sebastián Vizcaíno had encountered them in 1602, as had Cabrillo before him.

Tongva means "People of the Earth," and the peaceful tribe's cosmogony included earthquakes. According to A. L. Kroeber, their creator "fixed the earth on seven giants whose stirrings caused earthquakes." Their word for earthquake was Yí-tōk-e-ŭr-hur (one of several pronunciations). Portolá expedition member Miguel Costansó must have heard it uttered on July 28, 1769:

"Friday, July 28.—From Santiago we went to another place of which the scouts gave us particulars. It was not far, in truth, as we arrived after an hour's march. It is a beautiful river [the Santa Ana River], and carries great floods in the rainy season, as is apparent from its bed and the sand along its banks. This place has many groves of willows and very good soil, all of which can be irrigated for a great distance.

"We pitched our camp on the left bank of the river. To the right there is a populous Indian village; the inhabitants received us with great kindness. Fifty-two of them came to our quarters, and their captain or cacique asked us by signs which we understood easily, accompanied by many entreaties, to remain there and live with them. [He said] that they would provide antelopes, hares, or seeds for our subsistence, that the lands which we saw were theirs, and that they would share them with us.

"At this place we experienced a terrible earthquake [un horroroso terremoto], which was repeated four times during the day. The first vibration or shock [movimiento ó temblor] occurred at one o'clock in the afternoon, and was the most violent; the last took place at about half-past four. One of the natives who, no doubt, held the office of priest among them, was at that time in the camp. Bewildered, no less than we, by the event, he began, with horrible cries and great manifestations of terror, to entreat the heavens, turning in all directions, and acting as though he would exorcise the elements [conjuraba los tiempos]. To this place we gave the name of Río de los Temblores."

The expedition's more laconic leader, Portolá, described the earthquake in his diary:

"The 28th, we proceeded for two hours on a good road and we halted by a stream about eight yards wide and about sixteen inches deep which flowed with great rapidity. Here, at twelve o'clock, we experienced an earthquake [temblor de tierra] of such violence . . . supplicating Mary Most Holy. It lasted about half as long as an Ave Maria and, about ten minutes later, it was repeated though not so violently."

Portolá's supplication enabled him to accurately "measure" the quake's duration. It was California's first recorded temblor.

San Francisco's first recorded earthquakes occurred almost forty years later. Historian Hubert Howe Bancroft (1832–1918) described them—and their effect on morale at the Presidio:

"In June and July 1808 there came the most severe earthquakes that San Francisco had ever experienced. On July 17th [Comandante of the Presidio Luis Antonio de] Argüello wrote to the governor [José Joaquin de Arrillaga]: 'I notify you that since the twenty-first day of June there have been felt at this presidio some earthquakes, eighteen shocks to date, and among them some so violent that as a result of them the walls of my house have been cracked, being badly built, so that one of its rooms was ruined; and if the shocks have done, until now, no further damage, it is because they found no chance for lack of dwellings. The quarters of Fort San Joaquin [the Castillo de San Joaquin was the Royal Spanish fort near where San Francisco's Fort Point is today] threaten ruin, and I fear that if the shocks continue there may happen some unfortunate accident to the troops stationed there.' Arrillaga, who was accustomed to an earthquake country, is said to have replied to this report and to Luis Argüello's verbal account of the *temblores* by advising the commandant to go home and repair his house for winter and not mind such trifles as earthquakes, sending also a box of dates as a consolation."

The Annals of San Francisco chronicles subsequent shocks in 1812, 1829, and 1839. "Since these dates," however, "no serious occurrences of this nature have happened at San Francisco, though almost every year slight shocks, and occasionally smarter ones have been felt. God help the city if any great catastrophe of this nature should ever take place! Her huge granite and brick palaces, of four, five and six stories in height, would indeed make a prodigious crash, more ruinous both to life and property than even the dreadful fires of 1849, 1850 and 1851. This is the greatest, if not the only possible obstacle of consequence to the growing prosperity of the city, though even such a lamentable event as the total destruction of half the place, like another Quito or Caraccas, would speedily be remedied by the indomitable energy and persevering industry of the American character. Such a terrible calamity, however, as the one imagined, may never take place. So 'sufficient for the day is the evil thereof.'"

The reference is to Jesus's Sermon on the Mount, Matthew 6:34: "Take therefore no thought for the morrow: for the morrow shall take thought for the things of itself. Sufficient unto the day is the evil thereof." The *Annals* concludes, "This maxim abundantly satisfies the excitement-craving, money-seeking, luxurious-living, reckless, heaven-earth-and-hell-daring citizens of San Francisco."

Significant earthquakes did occur, in 1865, 1868, and in 1906. After the latter, some proposed that the "wicked city" had finally reaped what it had sown. San Francisco's May 19, 1906, *Argonaut* cited an editorial in the eastern press, *The Naked Truth About San Francisco*: "Physically and morally San Francisco was built on mud…. Leaving the theologians to quarrel over the proposition that this catastrophe was a vengeful visitation of divine wrath, it is a fact that no modern city better deserved the fate of Gomorrah than beautiful San Francisco." A more Californian notion of Fate was voiced by gold rush romanticist Bret Harte (1836–1902):

FATE
"The sky is clouded, the rocks are bare,
The spray of the tempest is white in air;
The winds are out with the waves at play,
And I shall not tempt the sea to-day.

"The trail is narrow, the wood is dim,
The panther clings to the arching limb;
And the lion's whelps are abroad at play,
And I shall not join in the chase to-day."

But the ship sailed safely over the sea,
And the hunters came from the chase in glee;
And the town that was builded upon a rock
Was swallowed up in the earthquake shock.

According to another, more famous, Harte poem, San Francisco was "serene, indifferent of Fate." Rudyard Kipling (1865–1936), who visited "the great city of San Francisco" in 1889, disagreed. He found in the fin de siècle metropolis "neither serenity nor indifference." After the Earthquake and Fire of 1906, however, Harte's line was dusted off and invoked by journalists, authors, and university presidents. Stanford president David Starr Jordan (1851–1931) wrote of "the most cosmopolitan of all American towns, the one fullest of the joy of living, the one least fearful of future disaster, 'serene, indifferent to [sic] fate,' thus her own poets have styled her, and on no other city since the world began has *fate, unmalicious, mechanical and elemental*, wrought such a terrible havoc." [italics added]

Indeed, Fate has dealt San Francisco many blows throughout the City-By-The-Bay's colorful history. More often than not, San Francisco has been unprepared for her. But each time—even in the aftermath of the Earthquake and Fire of 1906—San Francisco's indomitably pioneering spirit has prevailed.

O · GLORIOUS · CITY · OF · OUR
HEARTS · THAT · HAST · BEEN
TRIED · AND · NOT · FOUND
WANTING · GO · THOU · WITH
LIKE · SPIRIT · TO · MAKE
THE · FUTURE · THINE

−Inscription in the rotunda of San Francisco's new City Hall, which rose from the ashes of 1906

3

MIRROR WITH A MEMORY

CLOSE ONE EYE and try threading a needle. Now open both eyes and try again. This simple experiment demonstrates the distinct advantage of binocular over monocular vision: the facilitation of the ability to perceive depth.

Until the 1830s, students of optics believed that two eyes were better than one because, they speculated, two eyes enabled a person to see *more* of an object—"around it" as some theorized. Over the next thirty years, three men—Sir Charles Wheatstone, Sir David Brewster, and Oliver Wendell Holmes—pushed the study of optics and binocular vision into modernity. Each came to the field from a different perspective, and each would be better remembered for something other than stereoscopy.

The word stereoscope was coined by Charles Wheatstone (1802–1875) in the 1830s from the Greek στερεός (stereos: solid) + σκοπείν (skopein: to look at, examine). Today, Sir Charles is better known for the eponymous "Wheatstone bridge," a "differential resistance measurer," as he called it. Wheatstone did not take credit for its invention. In 1837, with William Fothergill Cooke (1806–1879), he began work on the electric telegraph, for which each deserves both credit and fame.

Charles was born near Gloucester in 1802. His father, William, was a successful musical instrument maker. Through music, young Charles first took an interest in acoustics, electricity, and optics. Charles patented his best-known musical invention, the concertina, in 1829. Seventy years later, its most famous San Francisco practitioner would be McTeague, the literary creation of novelist Frank Norris (1870–1902). McTeague was a "poor crude dentist of Polk Street, stupid, ignorant,

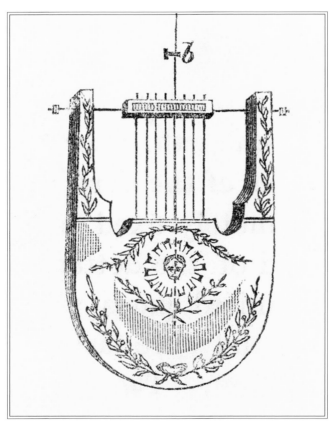

The Enchanted Lyre (Wheatstone)

vulgar, with his sham education and plebeian tastes, whose only relaxations were to eat, to drink steam beer, and to play upon his concertina."

Young Charles's most charming musical invention was the enchanted lyre—the acoucryptophone, as he christened it. Wheatstone, ever the wordsmith, created this intimidating moniker from the Greek ακούειν (akouein: to hear, as in acoustics) + κρυπτός (kryptos: hidden, secret, as in cryptography) + φωνή (phone: voice, sound, as in gramophone or telephone). Like his later kaleidophone (Wheatstone's "phonic kaleidoscope," as he called it), the acoucryptophone was a scientific instrument as popular in the parlor as the laboratory.

While still in his teens, Charles began experimenting with sympathetic vibration and "the transmission of the modulated sounds of musical instruments." By 1821, those experiments flowered into his brief but critically acclaimed concert career, as a virtuoso on his mysterious invention. The enchanted lyre was suspended from a brass wire—"about the thickness of a goose-quill"—in the ceiling. As if by magic, haunting refrains emanated from the apparently player-less instrument. His rapt audience was unaware that the wire ran through the ceiling into the room above, where it was attached to the sounding board of a piano, played by Wheatstone himself. The sound of his piano was transmitted through the wire, exciting the strings of its enchanted counterpart below.

His experiments in the transmission of sound led Wheatstone to the study of the transmission of both electricity and light. It is through the latter that he came to the study of binocular vision and the birth of

5

The Wheatstones (stereoscopic daguerreotype, circa 1851–1852, by Antoine Claudet (1797–1867)). Charles Wheatstone married Emma West at Christchurch Marylebone on February 12, 1847. The first of their five children, Charles Pablo, was born on May 2. Clockwise, from left: Arthur William Frederick (b. 1848), Charles (b. 1802), Charles Pablo, Emma (b. circa 1813), and Florence Caroline (b. 1850). Daughters Catharine Ada and Angela (not pictured) were born in 1853 and 1855 respectively. On the table is Sir Charles's wave model, by which he is demonstrating the wave properties of light.

stereoscopy. Wheatstone began his groundbreaking stereoscopic experiments in the early 1830s. Had he kept them a secret, his claim that they were the first such experiments might have been successfully challenged. But he told Herbert Mayo, Professor of Anatomy at King's College, London. In 1833, the third edition of Mayo's *Outlines of Human Physiology* contained a chapter entitled, "Of the Organ of Vision." Buried within its exhaustive analysis is a startling optical revelation:

"One of the most remarkable results of Mr. Wheatstone's investigations respecting binocular vision is the following. A solid object being placed so as to be regarded by both eyes, projects a different perspective figure on each retina; now if these two perspectives be accurately copied on paper, and presented one to each eye so as to fall on corresponding parts, the original solid figure will be apparently reproduced in such a manner that no effort of the imagination can make it appear as a representation on a plane surface. This and numerous other experiments explain the cause of the inadequacy of painting to represent the relief of objects, and indicate a means of representing external nature with more truth and fidelity than have yet been obtained. It would require too much space to enter upon the physiological views to which these experiments have led their author."

It would be another five years before Charles Wheatsone announced his discovery to the world, in his seminal *Contributions to the Physiology of Vision.—Part the First. On some remarkable, and hitherto unobserved, Phenomena of Binocular Vision.* (Philosophical Transactions of the Royal Society, 1838). By then, he had already been appointed Professor of Experimental Philosophy at King's College. The shy Wheatstone often relied on his friend and colleague Michael Faraday to do his lecturing and deliver his papers.

In his 1838 paper, Wheatstone—as well-read as any scholar of his time—admits that he was able to find but one author who had remarked on the subject of binocular vision, Leonardo da Vinci (1452–1519). In fact, several others had done so—including Euclid (from earthquake-prone Alexandria) in *Optics*, his essay on the mathematics of optics (circa 300 BC) and Galen of Pergamon, in his anatomical treatise, *On the Usefulness of the Parts of the* Body (175 AD)—but all had arrived at similar conclusions.

Wheatstone refers to a passage in the "great artist and ingenious philosopher" Leonardo da Vinci's *Tratatto della Pittura* (A Treatise on Painting—I. and J. Taylor's 1796

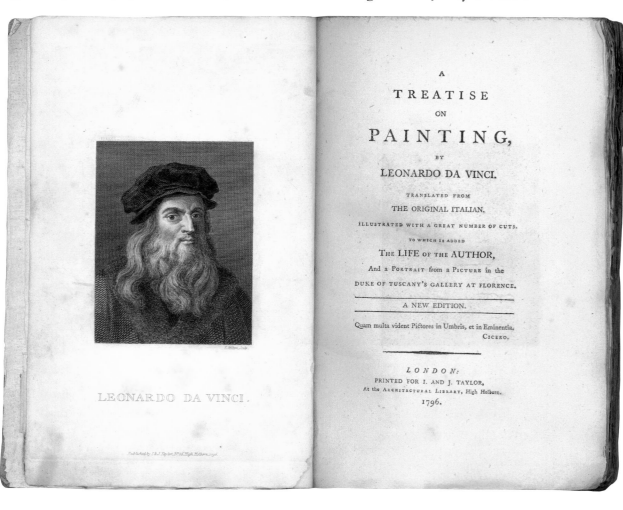

London edition is quoted here), where Leonardo describes "why a painting, though imitated with the greatest perfection from nature, does not appear with as much relievo [relief] as the natural objects whence it is copied." A painting, Leonardo explains, "though conducted with the greatest art, and finished to the last perfection, both with regard to it's [sic] *contour,* it's lights, it's shadows, and it's colours, will never show a *relievo* equal to that of the natural objects, unless these be viewed at a distance, and with a single eye; as may be thus demonstrated." Leonardo continues,

"Suppose the two eyes *A B* viewing the object *C*, at the concourse of the two central lines, or visual rays, *A C, B C*. In this case, I say, that the lines or sides of the visual angle, including those two central lines, will see the space *G D* beyond and behind the said object; and the eye *A* will see the space *F D*, and the eye *B* the space *G E*; so that the two eyes will see behind the object *C* the whole space *F E*. By which means, that object *C* becomes, as it were, transparent, according to the usual definition of transparency, which is that beyond which nothing is hidden. Now, this can never happen

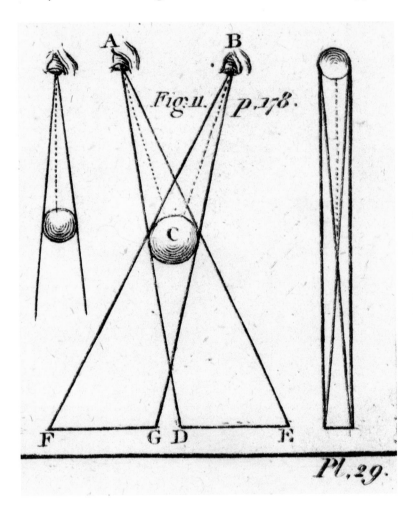

where the object is only viewed with a single eye; and where that eye is less in extent than the object which it views; whence the truth of our proposition is fairly evinced; a painted figure intercepting the whole space behind it; so that the eye is precluded from the sight of any part of the *ground* found behind the circumference of that figure."

Leonardo wrestled with the challenge of re-creating a three-dimensional world in a two-dimensional medium.

Painters, according to Leonardo, are "apt to lament themselves, and quarrel with their own performances" because, linear perspective notwithstanding, "the relievos in painting can never be so bold, as those in nature." Galen had used spheres and columns in his experiments. Leonardo, like Euclid, also used spheres. Wheatstone's genius lay in his ability to think outside the sphere, as it were, enabling him to transcend Leonardo's optical premise. Wheatstone posits,

"had Leonardo da Vinci taken, instead of a sphere, a less simple figure for the purpose of his illustration, a cube for instance, he would not only have observed that the object obscured from each eye a different part of the more distant field of view, but the fact would also perhaps have forced itself upon his attention that the object itself presented a different appearance to each eye. He failed to do this, and no subsequent writer within my knowledge has supplied the omission; the projection of two obviously dissimilar pictures on the two retinæ when a single object is viewed, while the optic axes converge, must therefore be regarded as *a new fact in the theory of vision* [italics added]."

In other words, when a two-dimensional painting is seen with both eyes, "two *similar* pictures are projected on the retinæ." When the three-dimensional subject of that painting—a solid object—is seen with two eyes, "the pictures are *dissimilar.*" Wheatstone then posed a rhetorical question, "What would be the visual effect of simultaneously presenting to each eye, instead of the object itself, its projection on a plane surface as it appears to that eye?"

To find the answer, Wheatstone proposed, draw an object as seen by the right eye only. Then draw an object as seen by the left eye only. Place the drawings side by side. Look at the right drawing with the right eye, while simultaneously looking at the left drawing with the left eye. In the words of Herbert Mayo, "some extraordinary illusions may be produced," the brain convinced that one is viewing the object itself, in all its three-dimensional glory.

Photography was still under development in 1838, when Wheatstone published his crude but groundbreaking stereoscopic illustrations. Today, these historic images may be viewed with a stereoscope, or by simply holding a stiff sheet of paper vertically between any pair, such that the left eye sees only the left image and the right eye only the right image. Position your head about 18˝ directly

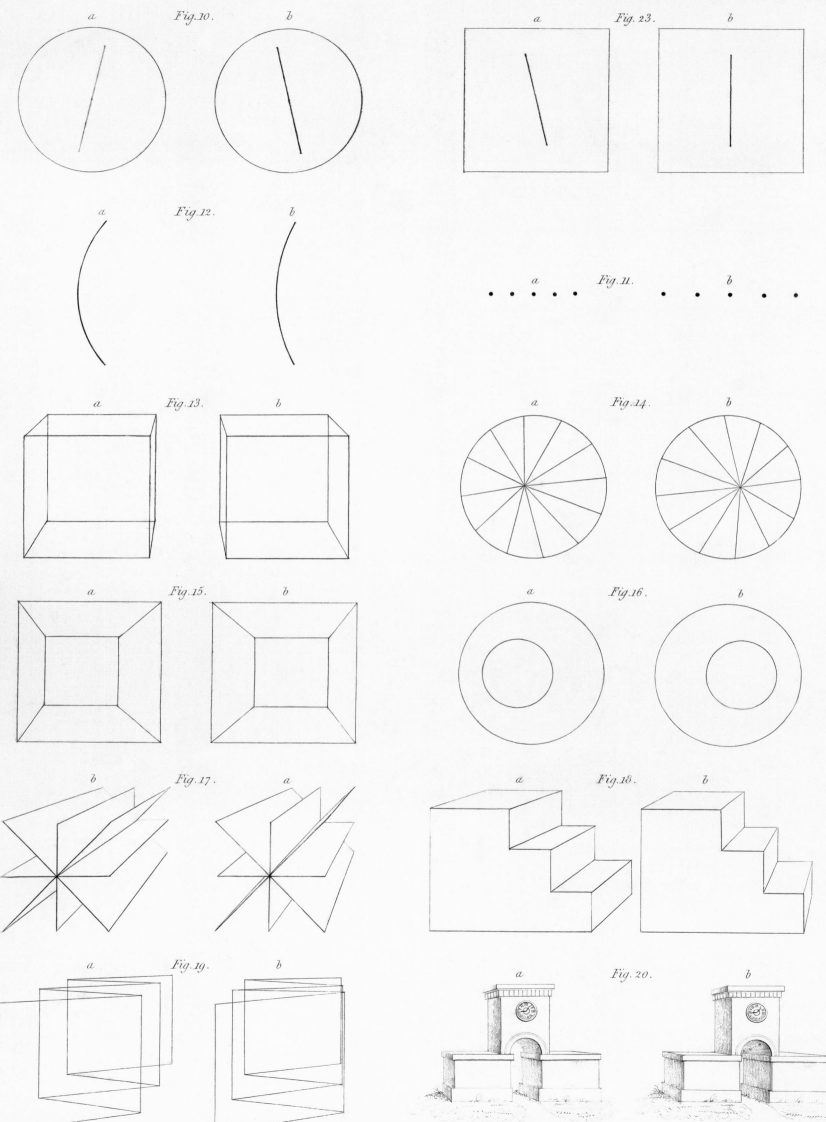

Phil. Trans. MDCCCXXXVIII. Plate XI. p. 3.

Fig.10.

a   b

Fig.23.

a   b

Fig.12.

a   b

Fig.11.

a   b

Fig.13.

a   b

Fig.14.

a   b

Fig.15.

a   b

Fig.16.

a   b

Fig.17.

b   a

Fig.18.

a   b

Fig.19.

a   b

Fig.20.

a   b

above the images. Relax your eyes, looking past rather than at the images. Try moving your head slowly toward the page until the two monocular images merge into one binocular image. With practice, it is possible to do this without the aid of the sheet of paper. Stereo view enthusiasts call this "freeviewing."

Wheatstone described his illustrations as follows:

"Fig. 10. A line in the vertical plane, with its lower end inclined toward the observer.

Fig. 11. A series of points all in the same horizontal plane, but each towards the right hand successively nearer the observer.

Fig. 12. A curved line intersecting the referent plane, and having its convexity towards the observer.

Fig. 13. A cube.

Fig. 14. A cone, having its axis perpendicular to the referent plane and its vertex towards the observer.

Fig. 15. The frustum of a square pyramid; its axis perpendicular to the referent plane, and its base furthest from the eye.

Fig. 16. Two circles at different distances from the eyes, their centres in the same perpendicular, forming the outline of the frustum of a cone.

The other figures need no explanation."

Wheatstone, himself able to freeview, saw the need for an instrument that would facilitate the viewing of stereo pairs of images. He proposed that his invention "be called a Stereoscope, to indicate its property of representing solid figures." It later became known as the reflecting stereoscope, because of its use of mirrors.

"The [reflecting] stereoscope is represented by figs. 8 and 9; the former being a front view, and the latter a plan of the instrument [from above].... E E' are pannels, to which the pictures are fixed in such manner that their corresponding horizontal lines shall be on the same level; these pannels are capable of sliding backwards and forwards in grooves on the upright boards D D'.... The observer must place his eyes as near as possible to the mirrors [A A'], the right eye before the right-hand mirror, and the left eye before the left-hand mirror, and he must move the sliding pannels E E' to or from him until the two reflected images coincide

at the intersection of the optic axes, and form an image of the same apparent magnitude as each of the component pictures.... There is only one position in which the binocular image will be immediately seen single, of its proper magnitude, and without fatigue to the eyes, because in this position only the ordinary relations between the magnitude of the pictures on the retina, the inclination of the optic axes, and the adaptation of the eye to distinct vision at different distances are preserved."

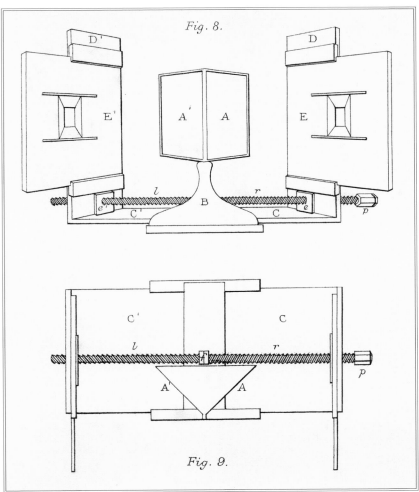

The Reflecting Stereoscope (Wheatstone)

Wheatstone presented "Part the Second" of his paper on binocular vision to the Royal Society in 1852. By that time, he had conducted numerous experiments utilizing stereoscopic daguerreotypes, like the portrait Antoine Claudet took of Wheatstone's family, and stereoscopic talbotypes, an invention of William Henry Fox Talbot (1800–1877). "What the hand of the artist was unable to accomplish," Wheatstone self-deprecatingly remarked, "the chemical action of light, directed by the camera, has enabled us to effect."

THREE YEARS EARLIER, in 1849, competitive and cantankerous Sir David Brewster (Sir David was knighted in 1832; Sir Charles Wheatstone was knighted in 1868) invented his own version of Wheatstone's instrument, the refracting, or "lenticular stereoscope," as Sir David called it.

Born in Jedburgh, Scotland, David Brewster (1781–1868) was educated for the ministry. His early interest in astronomy led him to the study of optics, which he defines in his 1831 treatise on the subject as "that branch of knowledge which treats of the properties of *light* and of *vision*, as performed by the human eye." A biographer of Newton, Kepler, and Galileo, Brewster is also familiar to science as the Brewster in brewsterite, a zeolitic mineral, Brewster's angle, the optimal angle of incidence for the polarization of light by reflection, and the brewster (B), a physical unit used in the measurement of the refraction of light.

To the layman, Brewster is best remembered for the invention of the early 19th century's most popular scientific toy, the kaleidoscope. In his 1819 *A Treatise on the Kaleidoscope*, Brewster explains that the name kaleidoscope, "which I have given to a new Optical Instrument, for creating and exhibiting beautiful forms, is derived from the Greek words καλος, *beautiful*; ἐιδος, *a form*; σκοπεω, to see. The first idea of this instrument presented itself to me in 1814, in the course of a series of experiments on the polarisation of light by successive reflections between plates of glass." Some time afterwards, the idea occurred to Brewster "*of giving motion to objects, such as pieces of coloured glass, &c. which were either fixed or placed loosely in a cell at the end of the instrument.* When this idea was carried into execution [in 1816], and the reflectors placed in a tube, and fitted up on the preceding principles, the Kaleidoscope, in its *simple form*, was completed."

Brewster's daughter/biographer, Margaret Maria

Gordon, describes how "this beautiful little toy, with its marvelous witcheries of light and colour, spread over Europe and America with a *furor* which is now scarcely credible. Although he took out a patent, yet, as it often has happened in this country, the invention was quickly pirated, and thousands of pounds of profit went into other pockets than those of the inventor, who never realized a farthing by it."

Sir David Brewster. Calotype, 1843, by David Octavius Hill (1802–1870) and Robert Adamson (1821–1848). NATIONAL PORTRAIT GALLERY, LONDON.

In 1849, inspired by—if not a little jealous of—the success of Charles Wheatsone and his stereoscope, natural philosopher Sir David Brewster invented his own stereoscope. But not before impugning the primacy of Wheatstone's discovery.

Even Brewster's good friend the Reverend Dr. James Taylor called Sir David "irascible and pugancious to an unusual degree." In his papers, Brewster sought to punch holes in Wheatstone's theories on binocular vision. And, though he never claimed the title for himself, Brewster paraded before the scientific community a host of other pretenders to the stereoscopic throne. In his 1856 book, *The Stereoscope, Its History, Theory, and Construction*, Brewster assailed Wheatstone, as "obviously halting between truth and error, between theories which he partly believes, and ill-observed facts which he cannot reconcile with them," devoting several pages to "the defects" of Wheatstone's reflecting stereoscope. That same year, he even sent an anonymous letter to *The Times*, in which he stakes a stereoscopic claim on behalf of a Mr. James Elliot.

Elliot, it seems, had conducted stereoscopic experiments as early as 1834. Since Wheatstone had not presented his paper on the subject until four years later, Brewster asserted that Elliot was the true father of stereoscopy. How could that be, Wheatstone replied in *The Times* three days later, if Herbert Mayo had published reports of Wheatstone's preliminary findings in *1833*?

This did not end the controversy. Brewster revealed his identity in his next letter to *The Times*, citing other purported progenitors of stereoscopy. Their public binocular battle raged for nearly a month. In Wheatstone's final parry, he replies to his "disputatious" antagonist, "I have always thought myself more usefully employed in investigating new facts, than in contending respecting errors which time will inevitably correct."

The Polyangular Kaleidoscope (Brewster)

The aging but unrelenting writer of *A Treatise on Optics* continued his attempts to dethrone Charles Wheatstone. Finally, in 1867, Sir David approached Charles, saying, "We have had much disagreeable discussion together, but I hope it is all forgotten now." They shook hands cordially. Later, Wheatstone asked of a colleague, "Do you really think he was sincere?"

By the mid-19th century, the nascent art of stereophotography had led to the development of the binocular camera, a single camera with two lenses, separated by a distance approximating the distance between the pupils of the eyes (about 2½ inches). Some preferred to take their stereophotographs with one single-lens camera from two positions, the time lag between the resulting left and right images often resulting in inadvertently ghostly effects. Others utilized a pair of synchronized cameras mounted side by side. In any case, Brewster eschewed a distance greater than 2½ inches between lenses, which added "an artificial relief" that was "but a trick which may startle the vulgar, but cannot gratify the lover of what is true in nature and in art."

Brewster's most valuable contribution to stereoscopy was his invention of the lenticular stereoscope in 1849. Using refraction, rather than reflection, it filled an emerging need for a relatively inexpensive, more portable, means of viewing stereo photographs and daguerreotypes.

Brewster's *The Stereoscope, Its History, Theory, and Construction* carried a London Stereoscopic Company advertisement for "Sir David Brewster's Lenticular Stereoscopes." The top-loading wooden Brewster stereoscope, with which Sir David chose to be stereophotographed,

S ir David Brewster and his
lenticular stereoscope.
Hand-tinted stereo view, circa 1856.
Blind-embossed: "The London
Stereoscopic Company
54. Cheapside."

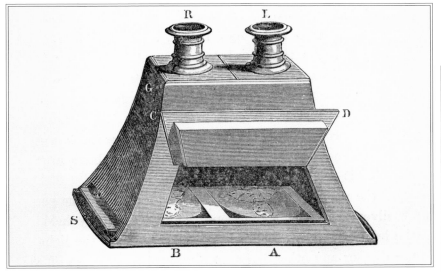

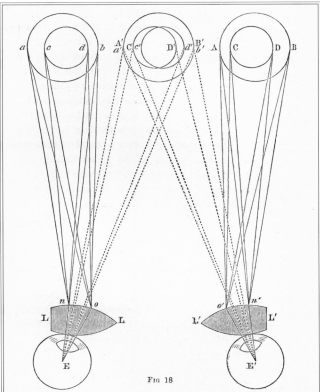

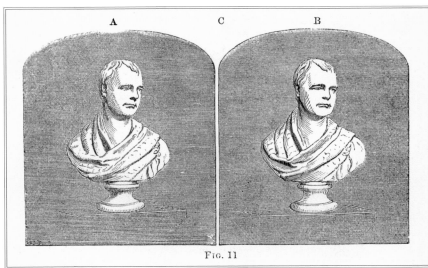

The lenticular stereoscope, a stereoscopic illustration, and the optical principles of the lenticular stereoscope (note the lenses). –Sir David Brewster, *The Stereoscope, Its History, Theory, and Construction,* 1856

was made by Antoine François Jean Claudet (1797–1867). This expensive model was covered with maroon-colored leather. To reduce reflection, the inside was lined with velvet. Its special lenses, patented by George Cooke on July 26, 1856, featured, according to stereoscope expert Paul Wing, "supplementary lenses in hinged mounts behind the principal lenses. These lenses could be rotated in and out of position by means of external levers. The lenses could be either negative or positive to suit near- or far-sighted persons, or even colored filters, similarly

hinged, could be used to 'throw a tint over the pictures, thus subduing the snowy appearance so common to photographs.'"

In his spare time, Sir David Brewster enjoyed a good séance—the more spirit-rapping and table-turning the better. In 1855, Lord Brougham invited Brewster to attend one, "in order to assist in finding out the trick." They sat with two others at a "moderately-sized table, the structure of which we were invited to examine. In a short time the table shuddered, and a tremulous motion ran up

The reverse of the stereo view of Brewster features a label listing his academic achievements.

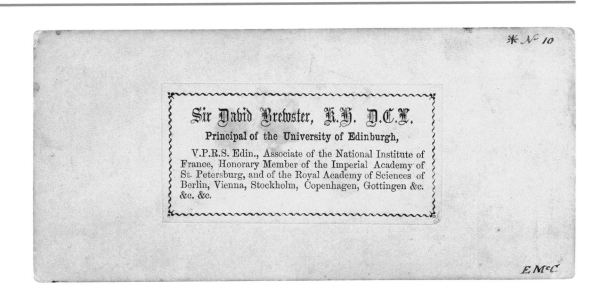

all our arms; at our bidding these motions ceased and returned. The most unaccountable rappings were produced in various parts of the table, and the table actually rose from the ground when no hand was upon it. A larger table was produced, and exhibited similar movements. An accordion was held in Lord Brougham's hand and gave out a single note, but the experiment was a failure; it would not play either in his hand or mine." They could not explain the strange occurrences of the evening, "and could give not conjecture how they could be produced by any kind of mechanism." The skeptical Sir David concluded that "the object of asking Lord Brougham and me seems to have been to get our favourable opinion of the exhibition, but though neither of us can explain what we saw, we do not believe it was the work of idle spirits."

Such events may have inspired Brewster to suggest *The Ghost in the Stereoscope* to the London Stereoscopic Company. He alludes to it in his 1856 book:

"For the purpose of amusement, the photographer might carry us even into the regions of the supernatural. His art… enables him to give a spiritual appearance to one or more of his figures, and to exhibit them as 'thin air' amid the solid realities of the stereoscopic picture. While a party is engaged with their whist or their gossip, a female figure appears in the midst of them with all the attributes of the supernatural. Her form is transparent, every object or person beyond her being seen in shadowy but distinct outline…. In order to produce such a scene, the parties which are to compose the group must have their portraits nearly finished in the binocular camera, in the attitude which they may be supposed to take, and with the expression which they may be supposed to assume, if the vision were real. When the party have nearly sat the proper length of time, the female figure, suitably attired, walks quickly into the place assigned her, and after standing a few seconds in the proper attitude, retires quickly, or takes as quickly, a second or even a third place in the picture…. If this operation has been well performed, all the objects immediately behind the female figure, having been, previous to her introduction, impressed upon the negative surface, will be seen through her, and she will have the appearance of an aerial personage, unlike the other figures in the picture."

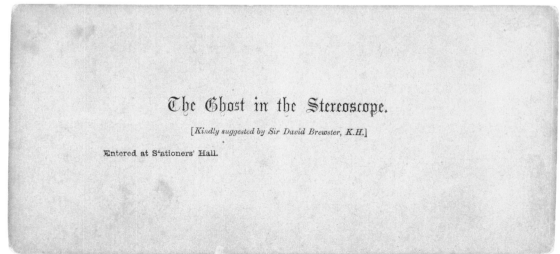

The Ghost in the Stereoscope.

[Kindly suggested by Sir David Brewster, K.H.]

Entered at Stationers' Hall.

14

HARPER'S WEEKLY.

JOURNAL OF CIVILIZATION.

VOL. XXX.—No. 1537.
Copyright, 1886, by Harper & Brothers.

NEW YORK, SATURDAY, JUNE 5, 1886.

TEN CENTS A COPY.
WITH A SUPPLEMENT.

OLIVER WENDELL HOLMES.—Photographed by Notman, Boston.

"The stereograph, as we have called the double picture designed for the stereoscope, is to be the card of introduction to make all mankind acquaintances."—Oliver Wendell Holmes, *Atlantic Monthly*, 1859

His son, Oliver Wendell Holmes, Jr. (1841–1935), also Harvard educated, was a U.S. Supreme Court justice. President Theodore Roosevelt made his recess appointment of the estimable jurist in the summer of 1902.

Holmes, Sr., made two significant contributions to stereoscopy: the Holmes-Bates model stereoscope and his eloquent prose on the stereographic art: "The first effect of looking at a good photograph through the stereoscope is a surprise such as no painting ever produced. The mind feels its way into the very depths of the picture. The scraggy branches of a tree in the foreground run out at us as if they would scratch our eyes out. The elbow of a figure stands forth so as to make us almost uncomfortable. Then there is such a frightful amount of

THE AMERICAN MEMBER of the binocular triumvirate was a Harvard man. Two years before Sir David Brewster invented his lenticular stereoscope, Cambridge, Massachusetts, Brahmin Oliver Wendell Holmes (1809–1894) became dean of Harvard Medical School. The urbane physician and poet was also an essayist on diverse subjects, including stereoscopy.

15

detail, that we have the same sense of infinite complexity which Nature gives us."

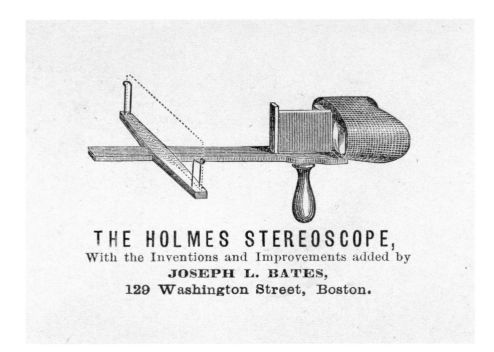

THE HOLMES STEREOSCOPE,
With the Inventions and Improvements added by
JOSEPH L. BATES,
129 Washington Street, Boston.

Holmes's *Atlantic Monthly* (Holmes is credited with naming the celebrated periodical) essays on stereoscopy were reprinted in *Soundings from the Atlantic* in 1864. He praises the daguerreotype as having "fixed the most fleeting of our illusions." The photograph, he continues, "has completed the triumph, by making a sheet of paper reflect images like a mirror and hold them as a picture." A man, he writes, "beholdeth himself in the glass, and goeth his way, and straightaway both the mirror and the mirrored forget what manner of man he was." But the photograph, especially the stereograph, is *"the mirror with a memory."*

To Holmes, if photography was "sun-painting," then, surely, stereophotography was "sun-sculpture," the apotheosis of the photographic art.

The London Stereoscopic Company's motto was, "A stereoscope in every home." When Sir David presented one of his Brewster-model stereoscopes to an enthusiastic Queen Victoria, it created a groundswell of interest in the new invention. But Brewster's design, originally created for stereoscopic daguerreotypes, seemed overpriced, complex, and impractical compared to the revolutionary 1861 creation of Oliver Wendell Holmes and Joseph L. Bates. By 1869, when Holmes described his elegantly simple invention in *The Philadelphia Photographer,* it was ubiquitous:

16

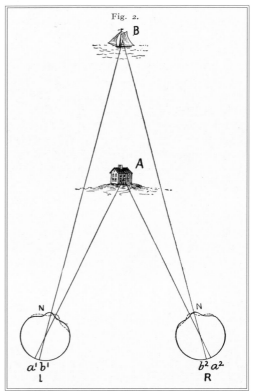
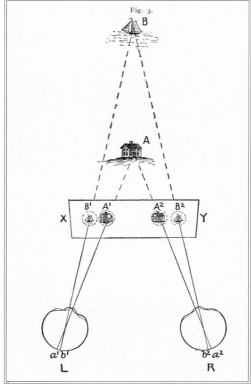
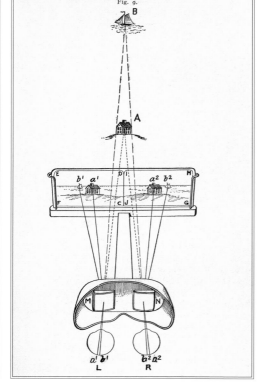

The optical principles of the Holmes-Bates stereoscope (Osborne)

The optical properties of the Holmes-Bates stereoscope are illustrated in a curious little book by Albert E. Osborne. Published in 1909 by stereoscope and view manufacturer Underwood & Underwood, it promotes the stereoscope as an educational tool. Part history, part promotional tool, part religious tract, it exalts the stereograph as capable of transcending its ability to serve as a "remarkable *representation* of places and objects, something non-material and unreal in itself, standing out before us in all the space dimensions and proportions of the places and objects themselves." Osborne boldly asserts, "The traveler seeks experiences of places, not places themselves." Therefore, he concludes, "if we seek the real place only as a means of giving us the experience of it, then we are prepared to see, that, if a substitute for the place can give us the experience, the place itself is not essential to us. Now the claim is that a stereograph of a place *can* serve as such a substitute."

At first, no one was interested in Holmes's stereoscopic contraption, and Holmes never patented it. "I wished no pecuniary profit from it, and refused to make any arrangement by which I should be a gainer. All I asked was, to *give* it to somebody who would manufacture it for sale to the public." He had no takers in Boston— "No prophet is accepted in his own country"—and, so, took his stereoscope to Philadelphia. There, though he "offered it freely and without price.... I might as well have offered my stereoscope to an undertaker." But Holmes persevered; his stereoscope became the kaleidoscope of the Victorian era.

"Two lenses were necessary, and a frame to hold them.... A partition was necessary, which I made short, but wedge-shaped, widening as it receded from the eye. A handle was indispensable... A hood for the eyes was needed for comfort, at least.... This primeval machine, parent of the multitudes I see all around me, is in my left hand as I write, and I have just tried it and found it excellent." Bates's contributions were "the sliding arrangement for adjusting the focus, in place of the original slots, or narrow grooves, and the method of holding the pictures."

Passion in the Parlor

THE GIFTED CANVASSER, or door-to-door stereo-view salesman, was the consummate multitasker, capable of demonstrating the ins and outs of stereoscopy, whilst romancing his customer's wife. The canvassing cards and descriptions below were published by Underwood & Underwood—brothers Bert and Elmer's stereo view and stereoscope manufactory—in 1904. Until April 18, 1906, its San Francisco offices were located in the Phelan Building, on Market Street. After the Earth-quake and Fire, the Monadnock Building, across the street from Lotta's Fountain, became its home. By that time, only the stereoscopic cognoscenti would have credited Sir Charles Wheatstone as inspiration for the illustrations on Underwood & Underwood's instructive cards.

Globe Diagram A.

Examine the diagram on this card carefully, both with and without the stereoscope. Can you see foreground and background; that is, is there any perspective or depth either with or without the instrument?

Both the diagrams on this card are left diagrams (intended for the left eye only), and that is the reason the stereoscope has no effect. That is why there is no binocular (two eye) perspective. It is not stereoscopic. It is like looking at an ordinary, flat photograph, or like two ordinary photographs, taken from the same position with a single camera, mounted on a card and viewed through the stereoscope.

By looking first at this and then at diagram B, a person will more fully appreciate the great difference between a single photograph or representation and a true stereoscopic photograph.

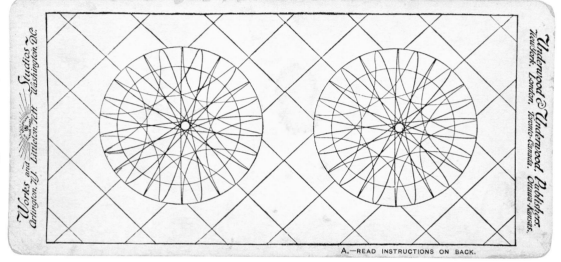

Globe Diagram B.

This diagram will be found useful when canvassing. Show it in the hand first, explaining that these curved and straight lines have a perfectly flat appearance, with no depth whatever to the eyes.

Now place the diagram in the stereoscope and immediately the globe stands out full size in front of the straight diagonal lines. Now there is actual depth for the eyes as though you were looking at a wire globe suspended before a screen. This demonstrates without doubt that properly made stereographs when seen in the stereoscope become actual spaces to the mind. Other kinds of illustrations give only an appearance of depth.

Now taking a stereoscopic photograph we notice that our sight does not rest on the surface of the card, but extends through it as through an open window. The two prints are joined together by the stereoscope and everything in the scene stands out in natural size and proper space relation.

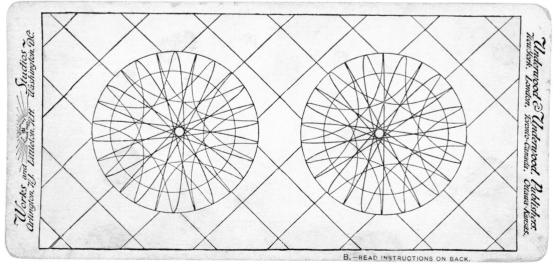

19

The Fresh View Agent Soliciting. The unwitting husband (note ring) is using a Holmes-style stereoscope. The canvasser (note absence of ring) is using a married woman.

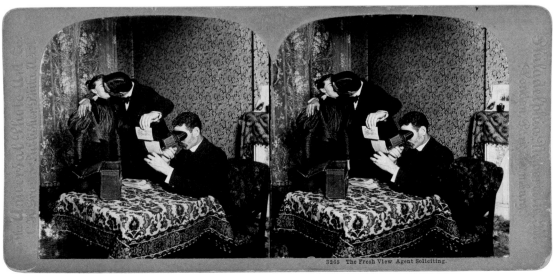

3268 The Fresh View Agent Soliciting.

PRELUDE I
CAUTIONARY TALES

*According to the Seismological Society of America,
San Francisco experienced more than 460 earthquakes
between June 21, 1808, and April 18, 1906*

HERE, INDEED, all is new, nature as well as towns. The very hills of California have an unfinished look; the rains and the streams have not yet carved them to their perfect shape. The forests spring like mushrooms from the unexhausted soil; and they are mown down yearly by the forest fires. We are in early geological epochs, changeful and insecure; and we feel, as with a sculptor's model, that the author may yet grow weary of and shatter the rough sketch.

–Robert Louis Stevenson, *San Francisco* (essay), 1882

FEARS WERE ENTERTAINED that there would be a serious decline of real estate and a decrease of population, but the scare passed off in a few weeks; and since that time earthquakes have been less frequent and severe than before.

–John S. Hittell, on the 1868 San Francisco Earthquake, *A History of the City of San Francisco and Incidentally of the State of California*, 1878

View of San Francisco, formerly Yerba Buena, in 1846-7 ▶

FUR TRADER/PIONEER William F. Swasey (b. Bath, Maine, 1823; d. San Francisco, 1896) journeyed overland to California from Fort Laramie, arriving at Yerba Buena in 1845. Over the next half century, he would witness and participate in "the wonderful rise of a great city from the sand dunes of 'Yerba Buena Cove.'" Based on Captain Swasey's recollection of pre–gold rush San Francisco, his View and its accompanying key were lithographed by the Clay Street firm of Edward Bosqui (b. Montreal, 1832; arrived San Francisco by ship 1850; d. San Francisco, 1917 (see page 32)), and copyrighted by Swasey in 1884.

VIEW OF SAN FRANCISCO, FORMERLY YERBA BUENA, IN 1846-7
BEFORE THE DISCOVERY OF GOLD

WE THE UNDERSIGNED HEREBY CERTIFY THAT THIS PICTURE IS A FAITHFUL AND ACCURATE REPRESENTATION OF SAN FRANCISCO AS IT REALLY APPEARED IN MARCH 1847

A—U. S. S. "Portsmouth."
B—U. S. Transports Ships, "Loo Choo," "Susan Drew" and "Thomas H. Perkins." They brought the 1st Regiment of New York Vols., Col. J. D. Stevenson commanding.
C—Ship "Vandalia"—merchantman consigned to Howard & Mellus.
D—Coasting Schooner.
E—Launch "Luce", belonging to James Lick.
1—Custom House.
2—Calaboose.

3—School House.
4—Alcalde's Office.
5—City Hotel owned by Wm. A. Leidesdorff.
6—Portsmouth Hotel.
7—Wm. H. Davis' Store.
8—Howard & Mellus Store. The old Hudson Bay Co's building.
9—W. A. Leidesdorff's Warehouse.
10—Samuel Brannan's Residence.
11—W. A. Leidesdorff's Cottage.
12—First Residence of the Russ family.

13—John Sullivan's Residence.
14—Peter T. Sherback's do.
15—Juan C. Davis' do.
16—G. Reynolds do.
17—A. J. Ellis Boarding House.
18—Fitch & McKurley's building.
19—Capt. Vioget's Residence.
20—John Fuller's Residence.
21—Jesus Noe's do.
22—Juan N. Pidilla's do.
23—A. A. Andrew's do.
24—Capt. Antonio Ortega's Residence.
25—Francisco Cacerez's Residence.
26—Capt. Wm. Hinckley's do.

Capt. H. Fremsey
A CONTINUOUS RESIDENT SINCE 1845
27—Gen. M. G. Vallejo's building.
28—C. L. Ross' building.
29—Mill.
30—Capt. John Paty's Adobe building.
31—Doctor E. P. Jones' Residence.
32—Robert Ridley's Residence.
33—Los Pechos de la' Choco.
34—Lone Mountain.
35—Sill's Blacksmith Shop.
Trail to Presido.
Trail to Mission Dolores.

J. D. Stevenson
COMMANDING 1ST REGT. OF N.Y. VOLS. IN THE WAR WITH MEXICO.

Gen'l M. G. Vallejo

George Hyde
FIRST ALCALDE DIST. OF SAN FRANCISCO 1846-7

EXECUTED BY THE BOSQUI ENG & PRINT CO.   COPYRIGHTED   DESIGNED & COPIED FROM VIEWS TAKEN AT THE TIME AND PUBLISHED BY

"The villagers saw their little settlement fast approaching the dignity of a new town, and cast about to find a name. Nature caused it to spring out of the ground for them in the form of a species of aromatic mint, which, surrounding their dwellings, perfuming the morning air and supplying frequent and varied medicinal needs, had proved indeed, as the Spaniards called it, 'Yerba Buena,' the Good Herb. So the herb named the town, and the name *stuck*, as the Californians say, for nearly a dozen years."–*Bancroft's Tourist's Guide*, 1871

Diggers of Roots and Gold

"I T IS HEREBY ORDERED that the name of *San Francisco*, shall hereafter be used in all official communications, and public documents, or records appertaining to the town. Wash'n A. Bartlett. *Chief Magistrate.*" –The *California Star*, January 23, 1847

One year and one day later, millwright James W. Marshall (1810–1885) discovered gold near Sutter's Mill. Soon, the tools of the "digger" would become what photographer Carleton E. Watkins (1829–1916) called the "weapons of the argonauts," forever altering Californians' relationship with the earth.

Digger Indians, at Ten Mile River.—Mendocino Co.

T HE WORD "DIGGER" was often used pejoratively by trappers and miners (themselves diggers!) to describe any of a number of Native American tribes in the West, including the Bay Area's Ohlone and Coast Miwok. Fur trapper Zenas Leonard, who journeyed overland to California in 1832, first encountered "Shuckers, or more generally termed, Diggers and Root eaters" west of Salt Lake. In *The World Rushed In*, J. S. Holliday elucidates the popular epithet: "The goldseekers, like the trappers before them, had no tribe in mind; they used the term Diggers to identify any of the skulking marauders who killed or stampeded their animals…. Except for the torment of dust, no subject received more repetitious attention from diarists than the Diggers and their depredations."

Celestial Diggins, Mongolian Flat, in 1849.

A RE-CREATION by stereo-photographer Eadweard Muybridge (1830–1904), who did not arrive in California until 1855. The number of Chinese "Celestials" in California increased from 54 in 1848 to 791 in 1849. "Nearly the whole population of Upper California became infected with the mania, and flocked to the mines.… Within three months after the [January 24, 1848] discovery [of gold], it was computed that there were near four thousand persons, including Indians, who were mostly employed by the whites, engaged in washing for gold. Various modes were adopted to separate the metal from the sand and gravel—some making use of tin pans, others of close-woven Indian baskets, and others still, of a rude machine called the cradle, six or eight feet long, and mounted on rockers, with a coarse grate, or sieve, at one end, but open at the other."

–John Frost, *Frost's Pictorial History of California*, 1850

22

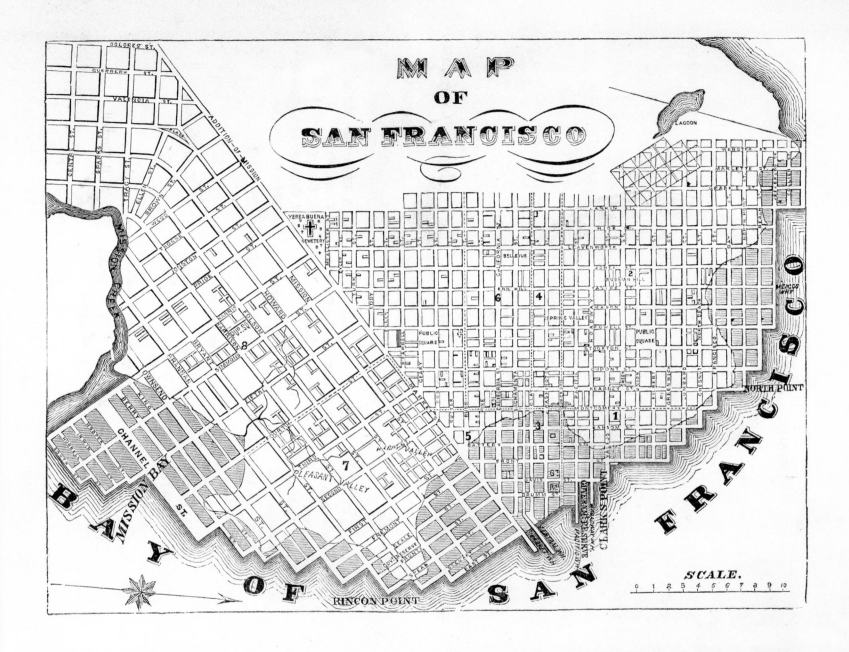

B Y 1855, AS THIS MAP from Soulé, Gihon, and Nisbet's *The Annals of San Francisco* shows, San Francisco's original shoreline was already undergoing a radical transformation.

"Stand at the Ferry Building, looking up Market street, and imagine the beginning of the city that spreads before you. First of all you must realize that this point of observation would, in those days, have been offshore, on the shallow water of Yerba Buena Cove. To the right is the scarp of Telegraph Hill, from which ships coming through the Golden Gate were sighted, and to the left is the lesser Rincon Hill, which is being cut away to provide a light manufacturing district. These marked the headlands of the cove, and the waterfront curved inland as far as…Market and Battery streets."

–Fred Brandt and Andrew Y. Wood, *Fascinating San Francisco*, 1924

*T*HE ANNALS OF SAN FRANCISCO, published in 1855, enumerated six "Great Fires" between December 24, 1849, and June 22, 1851. Hence, a phoenix rising above the Bay on San Francisco's first city seal (adopted on November 4, 1852, and reproduced here from *The Annals*). The imagery would be frequently invoked after April 18, 1906, and the legendary bird still appears on the city and county seal, adopted on March 1, 1859. Bayard Taylor (1825–1878) was an eyewitness to the first of the "Six Great Fires," which began in a gambling saloon known as Dennison's Exchange:

"I went on deck, in the misty daybreak, to take a parting look at the town and its amphitheatric hills. As I turned my face shoreward, a little spark appeared through the fog. Suddenly it shot up into a spiry flame, and at the same instant I heard the sounds of gongs, bells, trumpets and the shouting of human voices. The calamity, predicted and dreaded so long in advance that men ceased to think of it,

had come at last—San Francisco was on fire! The blaze increased with fearful rapidity. In fifteen minutes it had risen into a broad, flickering column, making all the shore, the misty air, and the water ruddy as with another sunrise. The sides of new frame houses, scattered through the town, tents high upon the hills, and the hulls and listless sails of vessels in the bay gleamed and sparkled in the thick atmosphere. Meanwhile the roar and tumult swelled, and above the clang of gongs and the cries of the populace I could hear the crackling of blazing timbers, and the smothered sound of falling roofs."

After the smoke cleared, the *California Star* made the case for a professional fire department: "The disastrous fire which has recently occurred in our town, jeopardizing so large an amount of property, as well as perilling human life, should awaken our citizens to the importance of the adoption of a fire department of some character.—There has not been a solitary individual since San Francisco commenced its rapid growth, who has not predicted a fire at some period or another and dreaded the event." Even "one or two hook and ladder companies," they editorialized, "would have been of an incalculable advantage." San Francisco began paying its fire department in 1866.

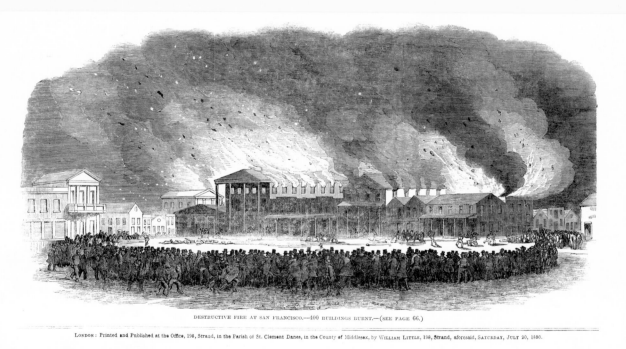

DESTRUCTIVE FIRE AT SAN FRANCISCO.—400 BUILDINGS BURNT.—(SEE PAGE 66.)

LONDON: Printed and Published at the Office, 198, Strand, in the Parish of St. Clement Danes, in the County of Middlesex, by WILLIAM LITTLE, 198, Strand, aforesaid, SATURDAY, JULY 20, 1850.

The second "Great Fire" began May 4, 1850, in the United States Exchange, consuming most of an area bordered by Montgomery, Clay, Dupont (now Grant), and Jackson streets. With property damage of nearly four million dollars, it was international news. *The Illustrated London News* published this dramatic image of Portsmouth Square on July 20, 1850.

"*S*AN FRANCISCO IS A CITY beleaguered with alarms. The lower parts, along the bay side, sit on piles; old wrecks decaying, fish dwelling unsunned, beneath the populous houses; and a trifling subsidence might drown the business quarters in an hour. Earthquakes are not only common, they are sometimes threatening in their violence; the fear of them grows yearly on a resident; he begins with indifference, ends in sheer panic; and no one feels safe in any but a wooden house."

–Robert Louis Stevenson, *San Francisco* (essay), 1882

25

Eureka Hose Co.—Mason St. between Sutter and Post Sts. Hand-labeled Carleton E. Watkins (1829–1916) card.

"Hence it comes that, in that rainless clime, the whole city is built of timber—a woodyard of unusual extent and complication; that fires spring up readily, and served by the unwearying trade-wind, swiftly spread; that all over the city there are fire-signal boxes; that the sound of the bell, telling the number of the threatened ward, is soon familiar to the ear; and that nowhere else in the world is the art of the fireman carried to so nice a point."

–Robert Louis Stevenson, *San Francisco* (essay), 1882

The 1865 Earthquake

IN MAY 1864, the reporter formerly known as Samuel Langhorne Clemens arrived in San Francisco, by way of Virginia City, Nevada. Soon after, the young Mark Twain landed a job as an "ink-slinger," as San Franciscans called reporters in those days, with the *Daily Morning Call*, where he wryly opined on July 22, 1864,

"When we contracted to report for this newspaper, the important matter of two earthquakes a month was not considered in the salary. There shall be no mistake of that kind in the next contract, though. Last night, at twenty minutes to eleven, the regular semi monthly earthquake, due the night before, arrived twenty-four hours behind time, but it made up for the delay in uncommon and altogether unnecessary energy and enthusiasm."

In fact, there were *two earthquakes* in San Francisco that *day*, one at 10:40 p.m., and one, much earlier, at 2:07 a.m. By October 1865, Twain was busy drafting the tale he entitled *Jim Smiley and His Jumping Frog.* Another, far more severe earthquake interrupted this endeavor on October 8. Nevertheless, ten days later, his story of the anuran amphibian from Angel's Camp was complete, just in time for him to get it in the mail. It traveled to New York by side-wheel steamer, the *Golden City*. The *Saturday Press* published it on November 18, 1865, to critical acclaim. Twain penned several accounts of the Great Earthquake of 1868, the most polished of which was included in *Roughing It*, published in 1872:

[On October 8, 1865,] I enjoyed my first earthquake. It was one which was long called the "great" earthquake, and is doubtless so distinguished till this day. It was just after noon, on a bright October day. I was coming down Third street. The only objects in motion anywhere in sight in that thickly built and populous quarter, were a man in a buggy behind me, and a street car wending slowly up the cross street. Otherwise, all was solitude and a Sabbath stillness. As I turned the corner, around a frame house, there was a great rattle and jar, and it occurred to me that here was an item!—no doubt a fight in that house. Before I could turn and seek the door, there came a really terrific shock; the ground seemed to roll under me in waves, interrupted by a violent joggling up and down, and there was a

heavy grinding noise as of brick houses rubbing together. I fell up against the frame house and hurt my elbow. I knew what it was, now, and from mere reportorial instinct, nothing else, took out my watch and noted the time of day; at that moment a third and still severer shock came, and as I reeled about on the pavement trying to keep my footing, I saw a sight! The entire front of a tall four-story brick building in Third street sprung outward like a door and fell sprawling across the street, raising a dust like a great volume of smoke! And here came the buggy—

THE "ONE-HORSE SHAY" OUT-DONE.

overboard went the man, and in less time than I can tell it the vehicle was distributed in small fragments along three hundred yards of street. One could have fancied that somebody had fired a charge of chair-rounds and rags down the thoroughfare. The street car had stopped, the horses were rearing and plunging, the passengers were pouring out at both ends, and one fat man had crashed half way through a glass window on one side of the car, got wedged fast and was squirming and screaming like an impaled madman. Every door, of every house, as far as the eye could reach, was vomiting a stream of human beings; and almost before one could execute a wink and begin another, there was a massed multitude of people stretching in endless procession down every street my position commanded. Never was solemn solitude turned into teeming life quicker.

Of the wonders wrought by "the great earthquake," these were all that came under my eye; but the tricks it did, elsewhere, and far and wide over the town, made toothsome gossip for nine days. The destruction of property was trifling—the injury to it was wide-spread and somewhat serious.

Raconteur, author, and former San Francisco newspaper reporter Mark Twain (1835–1910) ponders his next shot at his Connecticut home.

FROM AN UNDERWOOD & UNDERWOOD GLASS-PLATE NEGATIVE IN THE KEYSTONE-MAST COLLECTION. COURTESY, UCR/CALIFORNIA MUSEUM OF PHOTOGRAPHY, UNIVERSITY OF CALIFORNIA, RIVERSIDE.

The "curiosities" of the earthquake were simply endless. Gentlemen and ladies who were sick, or were taking a siesta, or had dissipated till a late hour and were making up lost sleep, thronged into the public streets in all sorts of queer apparel, and some without any at all. One woman who had been washing a naked child, ran down the street holding it by the ankles as if it were a dressed turkey. Prominent citizens who were supposed to keep the Sabbath strictly, rushed out of saloons in their shirt-sleeves, with billiard cues in their hands. Dozens of men with necks swathed in napkins, rushed from barber-shops, lathered to the eyes or with one cheek clean shaved and the other still bearing a hairy stubble. Horses broke from stables, and a frightened dog rushed up a short attic ladder and out on to a roof, and when his scare was over had not the nerve to go down again the same way he had gone up. A prominent editor flew down stairs, in the principal hotel, with nothing on but one brief undergarment—met a chambermaid, and exclaimed: "Oh, what *shall* I do! Where shall I go!" She responded with naive serenity: "If you have no choice, you might try a clothing-store!"

A certain foreign consul's lady was the acknowledged leader of fashion, and every time she appeared in anything new or extraordinary, the ladies in the vicinity made a raid on their husbands' purses and arrayed themselves similarly. One man who had suffered considerably and growled accordingly, was standing at the window when the shocks came, and the next instant the consul's wife, just out of the bath, fled by with no other apology for clothing than—a bath-towel! The sufferer rose superior to the terrors of the earthquake, and said to his wife: "Now *that* is something *like*! Get out your towel my dear!"

The plastering that fell from ceilings in San Francisco that day, would have covered several acres of ground. For some days afterward, groups of eyeing and pointing men stood about many a building, looking at long zig-zag cracks that extended from the eaves to the ground. Four feet of the tops of three chimneys on one house were broken square off and turned around in such a way as to completely stop the draft. A crack a hundred feet long gaped open six inches wide in the middle of one street and then shut together again with such force, as to ridge up the meeting earth like a slender grave. A lady sitting in her rocking and quaking parlor, saw the wall part at the ceiling, open and shut twice, like a mouth, and then drop the end of a brick on the floor like a tooth. She was a woman easily disgusted with foolishness, and she arose and went out of there. One lady who was coming down stairs was astonished to see a bronze Hercules lean forward on its pedestal as if to strike her with its club. They

both reached the bottom of the flight at the same time,—the woman insensible from the fright. Her child, born some little time afterward, was club-footed. However—on second thought,—if the reader sees any coincidence in this, he must do it at his own risk.

The first shock brought down two or three huge organ-pipes in one of the churches. The minister, with uplifted hands, was just closing the services. He glanced up, hesitated, and said: "However, we will omit the benediction!"—and the next instant there was a vacancy in the atmosphere where he had stood.

EARTHQUAKE IN SAN FRANCISCO, CAL., October 8, 1865—VIEW ON THE CORNER OF THIRD AND MISSION STREETS.
[Sketched by C. L. Bugbee.]

After the first shock, an Oakland minister said: "Keep your seats! There is no better place to die than this"—And added, after the third: "But outside is good enough!" He then skipped out at the back door.

Such another destruction of mantel ornaments and toilet bottles as the earthquake created, San Francisco never saw before. There was hardly a girl or a matron in the city but suffered losses of this kind. Suspended pictures were thrown down, but oftener still, by a curious freak of the earthquake's humor, they were whirled completely around with their faces to the wall! There was great difference of opinion, at first, as to the course or direction the earthquake traveled, but water that splashed out of various tanks and buckets settled that. Thousands of people were made so sea-sick by the rolling and pitching of floors and streets that they were weak and bed-ridden for hours, and some few for even days afterward.—Hardly an individual escaped nausea entirely.

–Mark Twain, *Roughing It*, 1872

28

Jewish Synagogue, Sutter street, front view. Congregation Emanu-El's majestic temple (Bancroft's 1871 *Tourist's Guide* called it "'The Synagogue' par excellence"), built at a cost of $185,000, was dedicated on March 23, 1866. Located on Sutter Street, between Stockton and Powell, construction was already well underway by the October 8, 1865, San Francisco Earthquake. The onion-domed synagogue would remain a part of San Francisco's skyline for forty years. Already slated for demolition in 1906, the sturdy structure withstood the April 18 earthquake, but not the fire that followed.

235. Jewish Synagogue, Sutter street, front view.

COURTESY OF THE SOCIETY OF CALIFORNIA PIONEERS, SAN FRANCISCO.

EARTH QUAKEY TIMES,

SAN FRANCISCO, OCT. 8, 1865.

E. Jump

MARK TWAIN'S FRIEND, artist Edward Jump (1832–1883), was to pictures what Twain was to words. The itinerant French artist spent much of the 1850s and '60s in the Paris of the West. Not long after the 1865 Earthquake, Jump caricatured his departure from San Francisco in *The Last Jump*, depicting himself in a hot-air balloon over The City, bidding a cartoon adieu to his adopted home. By 1883, he was living in Chicago, a destitute alcoholic in an unhappy marriage. On April 20, Jump chose to end his life, selecting a gunshot to the head for his final farewell. He died the following morning. Jump's last words: "Give all my mail to my wife."

An accomplished illustrator, Edward Jump was well-known to San Franciscans for his re-creation of the bedlam of the 1865 Quake in *Earth Quakey Times*, which included a Dali-esque Temple Emanu-El.

The little dog in the foreground is Bummer, San Francisco's favorite and most gifted rat-catcher. Bummer had outlived his poisoned canine partner, Lazarus, by two years, but was already on his last four legs by the afternoon of October 8. In fact, reports of Bummer's death—somewhat exaggerated—had begun to surface in September. Bummer finally "passed in his checks" in early November. Mark Twain's eulogy:

> The old vagrant "Bummer" is really dead at last; and although he was always more respected than his obsequious vassal, the dog "Lazarus," his exit has not made half as much stir in the newspaper world as signalised the departure of the latter. I think it is because he died a natural death: died with friends around him to smooth his pillow and wipe the death-damps from his brow, and receive his last words of love and resignation; because he died full of years, and honor, and disease, and fleas. He was permitted to die a natural death, as I have said, but poor Lazarus "died with his boots on"—which is to say, he lost his life by violence; he gave up the ghost mysteriously, at dead of night, with none to cheer his last moments or soothe his dying pains. So the murdered dog was canonized in the newspapers, his shortcomings excused and his virtues heralded to the world; but his superior, parting with his life in the fullness of time, and in the due course of nature, sinks as quietly as might the mangiest cur among us. Well, let him go. In earlier days he was courted and caressed; but latterly he has lost his comeliness—his dignity had given place to a want of self-respect, which allowed him to practice mean deceptions to regain for a moment that sympathy and notice which had become necessary to his very existence, and it was evident to all that the dog had had his day; his great popularity was gone forever. In fact, Bummer should have died sooner: there was a time when his death would have left a lasting legacy of fame to his name. Now, however, he will be forgotten in a few days.

–Mark Twain, *Territorial Enterprise*, Virginia City, Nevada, November 8, 1865

Twain's prophecy did not come true. Ironically, the attention paid by the likes of Twain and Jump guaranteed Bummer and his "obsequious vassal," Lazarus, canine immortality.

31

The 1868 Earthquake

MONTREAL-BORN Edward Bosqui (1832–1917) arrived in San Francisco on his eighteenth birthday, June 23, 1850. His print shop produced some of San Francisco's finest early books and lithographs, including *Yerba Buena in 1846-7* (see page 21). Bosqui's *Memoirs*, containing his insightfully timely cautionary tale of the 1868 Earthquake, was self-published in October 1904. Two and a half years later, Bosqui's business was completely destroyed by earthquake and fire.

At about eight o'clock in the morning of the 21st of October, 1868, an earthquake shock visited San Francisco and was felt throughout the borders of the bay, filling the people with terror, and causing considerable loss of property. At Oakland, chimneys were thrown down, dwellings were badly wrecked, and the earth rent open in many places. [Unlike 1865 and 1906, this quake originated in the East Bay, along the Hayward Fault, which many 21st century geologists believe will be the likely origin of the Bay Area's next "Big One."] Our family were seated at the breakfast table on Lombard street, when we became suddenly alarmed by a deep rumbling noise like a park of artillery going over the ground. Then came a terrific jar, and an undulating motion which set everything moving, swinging, or creaking. Glasses, dishes and decanters were shaken from the sideboard and thrown to the floor. We all rushed out into the street, where crowds of people could be seen, like ourselves, seeking safety in the open air, with horror and consternation depicted in their faces. Hurrying down town to my office I found everything there in the wildest disorder. Heavy printing presses and machinery had been moved bodily from where they had firmly stood. Piles of paper and binders board had toppled over; type was pied, and type cases were scattered about and mixed up in such confusion that the place could scarcely be recognized. Thirty or forty men and women were employed at our office at the time, but when I reached there at nine o'clock only two or three men were found. John Mitchell and David Coleman were the only ones remaining. The shock seemed to have shattered their nerves, and their pale, anxious faces indicated the terrible ordeal which they had undergone. At the first shock, Morrill, the foreman of the office, was by the side of Mitchell; confronting each other, and feeling that death was near, they grasped hands and bade each other farewell. At the same moment another severe shock was felt, when Morrill

rushed for a bridge which connected the Commercial street and Clay street buildings; and still the shocks continued, while Morrill hesitatingly ran back and forth on the bridge, asking Mitchell which building he thought the safer. This predicament struck Mitchell as so ridiculous that notwithstanding the terror of the situation he burst into a fit of laughter.

The walls of the building on Commercial street were thrown from six to twelve inches out of plumb. We could see the sky between the walls and edge of the roof, which merely held the beams and joists supporting the roof and floors. Only a few inches of the beam ends were precariously supported by the tottering walls. Piles of bricks which had fallen from the top of the fire-wall encumbered the book-binders' benches. Slighter shocks kept recurring at short intervals. One at ten o'clock was so severe, however, that it caused a general stampede of all those who had returned to their posts and were busy endeavoring to put things in order. All now abandoned work, and did not return until the next morning.

A few hours after the great shock Captain Thomas, our landlord, rigged Spanish windlasses with heavy ropes fastened to both side-walls in order to bind them together and prevent their further separation. This device saved the building until permanent iron rods could be put in their place.

Two dead bodies were discovered under the débris of the coping and fire-walls which had fallen on them on Clay street, nearly opposite our office; and farther down the street, between Sansome and Battery, another body was found under similar circumstances.

A feverish state of excitement prevailed all over the city for many days after the earthquake. Not a house in San Francisco or Oakland escaped some visible traces of damage more or less severe; and there was not a brick or stone wall that was not rent from top to bottom. Many people were so frightened by the shocks that they were ill for days afterwards. The prevailing feeling was nausea, with loss of sleep and appetite.

Some were so situated that they saw and felt more of the earthquake than others. Mr. Perkins, the postmaster of San Francisco, described to me the next day his sensations and what he saw, being on the steps at the entrance of the postoffice when the shock occurred. He felt the undulating motion under his feet, which almost threw him down. Gaining his equilibrium, and casting his eyes toward Battery street, he saw toppling walls and clouds of dust arising in every direction. Horror-stricken, he thought every building in sight would be destroyed, and that his career on earth was ended. He soon

COFFEY & RISDON'S BUILDING.

RAILROAD HOUSE & ROSENBAUM'S TOBACCO WAREHOUSE.

THE GAS WORKS   CALIFORNIA STREET BELOW SANSOME

EARTHQUAKE IN SAN FRANCISCO, CALIFORNIA, October 21, 1868.—[SEE PAGE 759.]

recovered from his mortal terror, but felt so deathly sick that he immediately went home, and did not recover his normal condition of health for weeks afterwards. As soon as his health permitted, he arranged his business affairs and went back East, never to return to San Francisco. It was the same with a number of other prominent citizens. Captain J. B. Thomas, our landlord, who owned a large estate, hastily wound up his business affairs and returned to Boston. I might cite other cases of those who, owing to the fact that they saw more of the terrors of the earthquake than the ordinary observer, were so much more frightened. It was estimated that several millions loss was occasioned in the city and about San Francisco Bay; but the newspapers, with one accord, were very wise and prudent in making little account of the disasters, or no doubt many more people would have left the country.

Slight shocks recurred at intervals for several weeks after the great one, but strong enough to make everyone feel anxious and uncomfortable. However, in a short time everything was put in order by the masons, plasterers, carpenters and glaziers, who had plenty to do for months afterwards. For greater safety, many three-story buildings that were badly shattered, and

some that might have been repaired, were taken down and reduced to two stories. Brick and stone buildings became unpopular and were avoided, and none were built for several years after the earthquake of 1868.

As time passed the fears and terrors of the earthquake were forgotten; but General Vallejo remarked to me one day: "They forget, but I do not; for I never come to San Francisco and feel safe when I pass by those tall brick buildings. I am never so happy as when I am about to leave the city, feeling that I have escaped the risk of a *temblor*. Some day one may come, only a little more severe than the one of 1868, when every tall building in the city will be destroyed, to say nothing of the loss of life which may ensue."

I have often thought how strange and incomprehensible it is that such a terrible visitation and its consequences should be almost forgotten in less than one generation. This is shown in the utter folly and recklessness of imitating New York, Chicago and other cities in building lofty structures such as are now being erected in our midst.

—Edward Bosqui, *Memoirs*, October 1904

33

Effects of the Earthquake, Oct 21, 1868, Market and First sts. Oneonta, New York–born Carleton E. Watkins (1829–1916) became the official photographer for the California State Geological Survey in 1865. His early Yosemite and San Francisco views are unrivalled, with the exception of some of the work of Eadweard Muybridge (1830–1904). Muybridge issued his early stereo views under the name "Helios." He is best known today for his panoramas of San Francisco and for photographically capturing a horse in motion with all four hooves off the ground.

*E*ffects of the Earthquake, Oct. 21, 1868, Railroad House, Clay St. Carleton Watkins, stereophotographer. This view was originally released by Watkins himself, as a "Pacific Coast" yellow-mount card. Watkins, never a good businessman, lost most of his negatives to Isaiah West Taber (1830–1912) in the mid-1870s. Before becoming a professional photographer, Taber was a whaler, gold miner, farmer, and dentist. After establishing his own Montgomery Street gallery, Taber began reissuing many of Watkins best views—including this one—uncredited. Taber lost his gallery and negatives to the 1906 Earthquake and Fire.

PACIFIC COAST VIEWS.
No. 8 MONTGOMERY STREET
Opposite Palace and Grand Hotels, SAN FRANCISCO.

Photographic Views of California, Oregon, and the Pacific Coast generally—embracing Yosemite, Big Trees, Geysers, Mount Shasta, Mining, City, etc., etc. Views made to order in any part of the State or Coast.

Effects of the Earthquake, Oct. 21, 1868, Railroad House, Clay st.   984.

36

Effects of the Earthquake, Oct 21, 1868, Cal. St., South side. Oliver Wendell Holmes called the stereo-scopic views of Carleton Watkins "perfection of art." Watkins, who sold them for $1.50 per dozen at his Yosemite Art Gallery, was unable to compete with the business acumen of Taber—or the stereopublishing enterprise of optician Thomas Houseworth. He continued to compete photographically, however, reestablishing himself as manager of what once was his Yosemite Art Gallery in San Francisco. He re-photographed many of his early subjects and photographed many new ones, including silver mines and railroads.

Uncaptioned 1868 Carleton Watkins stereo view. By 1906, Watkins was almost completely blind. He lost his Market Street studio and most of his life's work to the 1906 Earthquake and Fire. In 1910, California's preeminent stereophotographer was committed to the Napa State Asylum for the Insane. He died there six years later.

Watkins first photographed Yosemite in 1861. Three years later, inspired in part by those images, Abraham Lincoln signed the Yosemite Bill. It secured Yosemite's pristine lands from encroachment and, for Watkins, a worthy and enduring legacy.

COURTESY OF THE SOCIETY OF CALIFORNIA PIONEERS, SAN FRANCISCO.

Market Street, San Francisco, Cal. Webster & Albee had a reputation for selling pirated stereo views. Pirated or not, this view provides a marvelous pre-Earthquake glimpse down Market toward the Ferry Building. The large building on the near right is the Parrott Building, home of The Emporium. The 310-foot, 19-story Claus Spreckels (Call) Building is at Third Street. Across the street, the clock tower of the Chronicle Building is visible. Before April 18, 1906, the district below Market Street was known as "South-of-the-Slot." After the Earthquake, when overhead trolley wires were installed on Market, it became simply "South-of-Market."

Webster & Albee, Publishers, Rochester, N. Y.

Sold Only by Canvassers.

3067 Market Street, San Francisco, Cal.

From an Underwood & Underwood glass-plate negative in the Keystone-Mast Collection. Courtesy, UCR/California Museum of Photography, University of California, Riverside.

recorded Caruso singing the famous "Flower Song" from *Carmen* (*La fleur que tu m'avais jetée*) on February 27, 1905. He sang it again at a complete performance of Georges Bizet's opera at the Met on March 5. The next morning, the *New York Times* made no mention of the Italian tenor's French. He had struggled to learn it for the role, but had mastered it, according to Caruso himself, "sufficiently at least for the purposes of opera." But, the *Times* quipped, "after his flower song, his ingrained Italian impulse to acknowledge applause even in the most affecting situations brought him the tribute of a burst of laughter from the audience." Soon after, the Met began its westward sojourn. Caruso would reprise the role of Carmen's jealous suitor in San Francisco—to critical acclaim—on April 17, 1906. But not before meeting President Theodore Roosevelt (1858–1919), who heard him sing in Washington, DC, in late

40

B Y 1906, NEAPOLITAN TENOR Enrico (baptized Errico) Caruso (1873–1921) was a superstar. Having made his Metropolitan Opera debut in 1903, he began recording in New York the following year. Thanks, in part, to Caruso's musical charisma, the gramophone would be to the early-20th-century living room what the stereoscope had been to the mid-19th-century parlor. By the time he arrived in San Francisco in April 1905, many San Franciscans had already experienced Caruso's magnificent voice on 78 rpm gramophone records. On tour with the Met that year, he appeared in *Rigoletto, Pagliacci, Lucia di Lammermoor,* and *La Gioconda* at the Grand Opera House on Mission, between 3rd and 4th streets. The Victor Talking Machine Company

March. In a backstage turnabout, Caruso asked Roosevelt for *his* autograph. TR complied, sending a large, framed photo of himself, signed, "to Enrico Caruso." Caruso carried it with him—through Pittsburgh, Chicago, St. Louis, and Kansas City—all the way to San Francisco.

Ethan Mordden, in his Opera Anecdotes (1985), describes the "phonogenic" tenor's ascendancy:

"There is, in the word 'Caruso,' an awesome renown of entitlement never challenged. His time was the beginning of the century, when recordings carried singers' fame into the home, acculturating opera as a middle-class institution, a marker of status, a collectible; and his place was the Met at its peak of glory. Why was Caruso so great? Because he was the first to exploit a spectacular voice on a spectacular level."

Birdseye view (east) of Naples and Vesuvius, Italy. Unlike San Francisco, Caruso's hometown features a perpetual reminder of nature's destructive potential, Mount Vesuvius: "The sea seemed to roll back on itself, and to be driven from its banks by the convulsive motion of the earth.... I looked back; a dense, dark mist seemed to be following us, spreading itself over the country like a cloud."– Pliny the Younger, 79 AD. In April 1906, as the Met's touring company made its way west, Caruso's "Vesuvio" began a new series of eruptions.

(47)-2011-Birdseye view (east) of Naples and Vesuvius, Italy
© Underwood & Underwood.

Wade's Opera House.

AND

ART GALLERY,

Mission Street, above Third.

FREDERICK W. BERT, - Lessee and Manager.

OPENING NIGHT.

Monday Evening, January 17th, 1876,

Will be presented, for the first time in America, the Grand Spectacular and Dramatic Romance, produced under the direction of MR. JAMES J. BARTLETT, Stage Manager, entitled

SNOWFLAKE!

And the Seven Pigmies!

Queen Envidiaso........................MISS WINNETTA MONTAGUE
Princess Snowflake (her step-daughter)....MISS ANNIE PIXLEY
Lady Sipho................................MISS MARY GRAY
Baroness Antenna..........................MISS HAMILTON
Prince of Goldland........................MISS MATTIE DANIEL
Minister Monticello.......................MR. F. CLEAVES
Otto, companion to the Prince.............MR. W. RYDER
Chamberlain...............................MR. D. C. ANDERSON
Lord Vervex...............................MR. G. GALLOWAY
Master of Ceremonies......................MR. C. ALLEN
Berthold, Court Huntsman..................MR. R. FULFOR
Prince Sting of Beeland...................MISS LAGRET
Prince of Rosemound.......................MISS HENS
King of Diamond Isle......................MR. ROBERT FULFO
Blick   MR. WILLIE SIN
Pick   The   MISS MAUD ES
Dick   Seven   MISS RELLIE DA
Klick   Pigmies   MAST. CHS. DA
Knick   MAST. CHS. DA
Slick   MAST. HARRY DA
Striok

Preceding the piece the Fabbri Opera Troupe will sing the Na___
Anthem, THE STAR SPANGLED BANNER.

SOUVENIR PROGRAMME

PRESENTED BY

SHERMAN & HYDE.

Matinee on Wednesday and Saturday Afternoons.

Sunday Evening, January 23d, Fabbri Opera Company,
In Meyerbeer's Grand Opera, The Hugenots.

▲ COURTESY OF THE SAN FRANCISCO
PERFORMING ARTS LIBRARY & MUSEUM.

- 153 -

OPERA HOUSE

AND Art Building Asso___

CAPITAL STOCK
$300,000
3000 SHARES
100 DOLL. EACH

INCORPORATED AUG. 26, 1873.

This is to Certify that ___
to Five ___ Shares of ___

OF THE Opera House & Art Building Associati___

Transferable on the books of the Association by endorsement hereon, and surrende___

J. F. Garvey SECRETARY

▲ COURTESY OF THE SOCIETY OF CALIFORNIA PIONEERS, SAN FRANCISCO.

The Company

NAMES OF THE ARTISTS ARE IN ALPHABETICAL ORDER

SOPRANI

Mmes.
BESSIE ABOTT   MARIE RAPPOLD
BELLA ALTEN   MARCELLA SEMBRICH
EMMA EAMES   MARION WEED
PAULA RALPH

TENORI

Messrs.
JACQUES BARS   ANDREAS DIPPEL
ALOIS BURGSTALLER   GIOVANNI PAROLI
ENRICO CARUSO   ALBERT REISS

MEZZO-SOPRANI and CONTRALTI

Mmes.
OLIVE FREMSTAD   HELEN MAPLESON
LOUISE HOMER   FLORENCE MULFORD
JOSEPHINE JACOBY   JOHANNA POEHLMANN
                      EDYTH WALKER

BARITONI

Messrs.
BERNARD BÉGUÉ   OTTO GORITZ
GIUSEPPE CAMPANARI   ADOLPH MÜHLMANN
EUGENE DUFRICHE   TAURINO PARVIS
TONY FRANKE   ANTONIO SCOTTI
                      ANTON VAN ROOY

BASSI

Messrs.
ROBERT BLASS   POL PLANÇON
MARCEL JOURNET   ANCANGELO ROSSI

CONDUCTORS

Messrs.
NAHAN FRANKO   ALFRED HERTZ
ARTURO VIGNA

TECHNICAL DIRECTOR
Mr. EUGÈNE CASTEL-BERT

CHORUS MASTER
Mr. PIETRO NEPOTI

STAGE DIRECTOR
Mr. EUGÈNE DUFRICHE

PREMIÈRE DANSEUSE
Mlle. BIANCA FROEHLICH

STAGE MANAGER
Mr. FRANK RIGO

LIBRARIAN
Mr. LIONEL MAPLESON

SCHOOL OF OPERA
Pupils of the Conried Metropolitan Opera School will appear in several of the Operas to be presented.

42

GRAND OPERA
IN
SAN FRANCISCO
BY THE
ENTIRE COMPANY
FROM THE
METROPOLITAN OPERA
HOUSE ~ NEW YORK
UNDER THE DIRECTION
OF
MR. HEINRICH CONRIED
SECOND
TRANS-CONTINENTAL
TOUR
SPRING 1906

GRAND OPERA HOUSE
SIXTEEN PERFORMANCES
TWELVE EVENINGS   FOUR MATINEES
APRIL 16 TO 28, 1906

CHARLES W. STRINE
MANAGER SAN FRANCISCO SEASON

To help finance the construction of his opera house, dentist Thomas Wade sold shares to Irish silver barons John W. Mackay and James C. Flood, among others. Built on Mission, between 3rd and 4th, Wade's Opera House was just a few doors down from St. Patrick's Church. The cavernous 105- by 245-foot auditorium sat 3,200, and had a standing-room-only capacity of nearly 4,000. Its crystal chandelier alone had over 250 gas burners. On January 17, 1876, it opened (ill-fated William C. Ralston's equally titanic Palace Hotel had opened the previous October) with *Snowflake!*, a musical based on *Snow White and the Seven Dwarfs*. Meyerbeer's *Les Huguenots* was its first operatic event.

VIEWS OF MOROSCO'S GRAND OPERA HOUSE.

Anton Van Rooy · Enrico Caruso · Heinrich Conried · Alois Burgstaller · Antonio Scotti
Andreas Dippel · Pol Plancon
Marcel Journet · Giuseppe Campanari · Otto Goritz · Robert Blass

Promoter Walter Morosco took over the "magnificent temple of drama and the song" (as the San Francisco Chronicle reportorially christened it in 1876) on March 26, 1894. By then, the aging theater in a declining neighborhood had found itself home to more melodrama than grand opera. In April of 1905 and 1906, however, the Grand Opera House welcomed the touring company of New York's Metropolitan Opera. The Met opened its 1906 run on April 16 with Goldmark's *The Queen of Sheba*—but without Enrico Caruso. He was not scheduled to appear until the next evening. During the perfomance of *The Queen of Sheba*, the Italian tenor was sighted both at the Grand Opera House and at a nearby performance of *Babes in Toyland*.

The Casts

MONDAY EVENING, APRIL 16, AT 8 O'CLOCK
Goldmark's Opera
Die Koenigin von Saba
(in German)
MMES. WALKER, RAPPOLD, ALTEN; MM. DIPPEL, VAN ROOY, BLASS, MÜHLMANN.
CONDUCTOR .. ..Mr. ALFRED HERTZ

TUESDAY EVENING, APRIL 17, AT 8 O'CLOCK
Bizet's Opera
Carmen
(in French)
MMES. FREMSTAD, ABOTT, RALPH, JACOBY; MM. CARUSO, JOURNET, BEGUÉ, PARVIS, DUFRICHE, REISS.
CONDUCTOR .. ..Mr. ARTURO VIGNA

WEDNESDAY AFTER'N, APRIL 18, AT 2 O'CLOCK
Mozart's Opera
Le Nozze di Figaro
(The Marriage of Figaro)
(in Italian)
MMES. EAMES, ALTEN, POEHLMANN and SEMBRICH; MM. SCOTTI, CAMPANARI, ROSSI, DUFRICHE, REISS, PAROLI.
CONDUCTOR .. ..Mr. NAHAN FRANKO

WEDNESDAY EVENING, APRIL 18, AT 8 O'CLOCK
Richard Wagner's Opera
Lohengrin
(in German)
MMES. RAPPOLD, HOMER; MM. BURGSTALLER, GORITZ, BLASS, MÜHLMANN.
CONDUCTOR .. ..Mr. ALFRED HERTZ

THURSDAY EVENING, APRIL 19, AT 8 O'CLOCK
Puccini's Opera
La Boheme
(in Italian)
MMES. ABOTT, ALTEN ; MM. CARUSO, CAMPANARI, JOURNET, PARVIS, DUFRICHE, ROSSI, PAROLI, FOGLIA.
CONDUCTOR .. ..Mr. ARTURO VIGNA

FRIDAY EVENING, APRIL 20, AT 7.45 O'CLOCK
Richard Wagner's Music Drama
Die Walkuere
(in German)
MMES. WALKER, FREMSTAD, HOMER, ALTEN, BAUERMEISTER, JACOBY, CALL, MULFORD, RALPH, WEED; MM. BURGSTALLER, VAN ROOY, BLASS.
CONDUCTOR .. ..Mr. ALFRED HERTZ

SATURDAY MATINEE, APRIL 21, AT 2 O'CLOCK
GRAND DOUBLE BILL
Donizetti's Opera
Don Pasquale
(in Italian)
MME. SEMBRICH; MM. DIPPEL, SCOTTI, ROSSI, FOGLIA.
CONDUCTOR .. ..Mr. ARTURO VIGNA
FOLLOWED BY
Humperdinck's Fairy Opera
Haensel und Gretel
(in German)
MMES. ALTEN, FREUND, HOMER, WEED, MULFORD, GLANVILLE; MR. GORITZ.
CONDUCTOR .. ..Mr. NAHAN FRANKO

Weber Pianos used exclusively

Louise Homer · Olive Fremstad · Edyth Walker · Marion Weed
Marie Rappold · Bella Alten
Bessie Abott · Emma Eames · Marcella Sembrich · Josephine Jacoby
Paula Ralph · Jeanne Jomelli

Caruso as Don José

Fremstad as Carmen

CARMEN was Georges Bizet's Sistine Chapel. The French composer's operatic masterpiece premiered in Paris on March 3, 1875—to mixed reviews. Tchaikovsky predicted that it would become the world's favorite opera. Alexandre César Léopold (Georges) Bizet (1838–1875) did not live long enough to witness its international success. Sung in French, the opera is set in Seville in the 1820s. It synergistically—and fierily—combines all the elements of great story-telling and great music, including no less than three "hit songs": bullfighter Escamillo's "Toreador Song," Carmen's "Habanera," and Don José's "Flower Song." The stars of the Met's 1906 New York and San Francisco productions were Olive Fremstad, in the title role, and Enrico Caruso, as Don José.

45

"On a night in April, 1906, I was sitting in a box in the Grand Opera House, Mission Street, San Francisco, hearing a performance of Carmen sung by Caruso, Madame Fremstad and others of the Metropolitan Opera Company of New York. Carmen, the first opera of what was intended to be only a short season [it was Caruso's first, but the Company's second, *Queen of Sheba* having been performed April 16] and turned out to be but an engagement for one night, drew a marvelous and appre- ciative audience; all of San Francisco and his wife was there. Most people perhaps have forgotten that Fremstad sang Carmen. It was not one of her great rôles, like her Isolde, but it was a competent performance, and because Fremstad, a blonde, did not wear a dark wig, there had been a good deal of advance advertising. But within a few hours, however, not even a blonde Carmen was a topic for talk. Man's affairs suddenly became very unimportant."

–John Barrymore, *Confessions of an Actor,* 1925

ACT I
LIKE THE CRATER OF A VOLCANO

On April 18, 1906, at 5:12 a.m., San Francisco shook itself like a wet dog. It was a terremoto —as Caruso would have called it—of biblical proportions. George W. Brooks, founder (in 1905) of the reorganized California Insurance Company, wrote of that frightful dawn:

"In common with the other half million citizens of San Francisco on that fateful morning, I was awakened from a sound sleep by a continuous and violent shaking and oscillation of my bed. I was bewildered, dazed, and only awakened fully when my wife suddenly screamed, 'Earthquake!' It was a whopper, bringing with it a ghastly sensation of utter and absolute helplessness and an involuntary prayer that the vibrations might cease. Short as was the period of the earth's rocking, it seemed interminable, and the fear that the end would never come dominated the prayer and brought home with tremendous import the realization of our insignificance....

"The first natural impulse of a human being in an earthquake is to get out into the open, and as I and those who were with me were at that particular moment decidedly human in both mould and temperament, we dressed hastily and joined the group of excited neighbors gathered on the street. Pale faced, nervous and excited, we chattered like daws until the next happening intervened, which was the approach of a man on horseback who shouted as he 'Revere-d' past us the startling news that numerous fires had started in various parts of the city, that the Spring Valley Water Company's feed main had been broken by the quake, that there was no water and that the city was doomed."

Boom! The earth shook shudderingly. Crash! Doomed 'Frisco was in the throes of the earthquake. Buildings toppled down like houses of cards! "Save me!" screamed Lena, then fainted. "If there's safety anywhere!" panted Bob rushing out with mother and child.

46

*U*nion Street [west of Steiner], *rent by the great earthquake —San Francisco, Cal.*

"From the time when Nero played the violin accompaniment to the burning of Rome, down, through the ages, to 5:15 [sic] a.m., April 18, 1906, and up to the present date, the San Francisco disaster is the most prominent recorded in history. It was the greatest spectacular drama ever staged and produced the biggest heap of the 'damn'dest, finest ruins' the world has ever seen."

—George W. Brooks, *The Spirit of 1906*, 1921

GRAND OPERA HOUSE N. SIDE MISSION ST. BET. 3RD & 4TH. 1881.

48

HOME OF GRAND OPERA—ONCE THE CENTER OF GAIETY, NOW AS SILENT AS A TOMB

*R*uins of Scott-Van Arsdale Bldg.
and St. Patrick's Church—west
on Mission St.

Built in 1872, St. Patrick's served
the needs of the City's working-class
Irish, many of whom lived South-of-
the-Slot. The church would be
rebuilt. The Grand Opera House—
pictured but not named here—would
have no such encore.

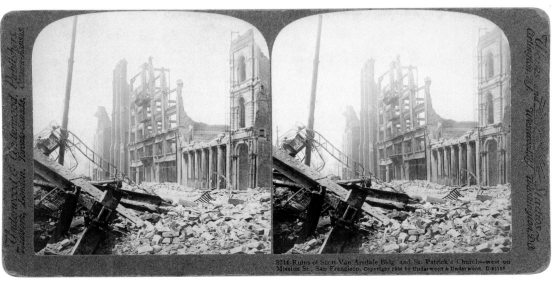

"'Ell of a place! I never come back here."
– Enrico Caruso, April 18, 1906

ON APRIL 24, Caruso arrived in New York by train from San Francisco. He still carried the autographed picture of Teddy Roosevelt, which he had used as "a passport to get around." His reminiscences:

You ask me to say what I saw and what I did during the terrible days which witnessed the destruction of San Francisco? Well, there have been many accounts of my so-called adventures published in the American papers, and most of them have not been quite correct. Some of the papers said that I was terribly frightened, that I went half crazy with fear, that I dragged my valise out of the hotel into the square and sat upon it and wept; but all this is untrue. I was frightened, as many others were, but I did not lose my head. I was stopping [staying] at the St. Francis [actually, the Palace] Hotel, where many of my fellow-artists were staying, and very comfortable I was. I had a room on the fifth floor, and on Tuesday evening, the night before the great catastrophe, I went to bed feeling very contented. I had sung in "Carmen" that night, and the opera had gone with fine *éclat*. We were all pleased, and, as I said before, I went to bed that night feeling happy and contented.

But what an awakening! You must know that I am not a very heavy sleeper—I always wake early, and when I feel restless I get up and go for a walk. So on the Wednesday morning early I wake up about five o'clock, feeling my bed rocking as though I am in a ship on the ocean, and for the moment I think I am dreaming that I am crossing the water on my way to my beautiful country. And so I take no notice for the moment, and then, as the rocking continues, I get up and go to the window, raise the shade and look out. And what I see makes me tremble with fear. I see the buildings toppling over, big pieces of masonry falling, and from the street below I hear the cries and screams of men and women and children.

I remain speechless, thinking I am in some dreadful nightmare, and for something like forty seconds I stand there, while the buildings fall and my room still rocks like a boat on the sea. And during that forty seconds I think of forty thousand different things. All that I have ever done in my life passes before me, and I remember trivial things and important things. I think of my first appearance in grand opera, and I feel nervous as to my reception, and again I think I am going through last night's "Carmen."

And then I gather my faculties together and call for my valet. He comes rushing in quite cool, and, without any tremor in his voice, says: "It is nothing." But all the same he advises me to dress quickly and go in the open, lest the hotel fall and crush us to powder. By this time the plaster on the ceiling has fallen in a great shower, covering the bed and the carpet and the furniture, and I, too, begin to think it is time to "get busy." My valet gives me some clothes; I know not what the garments are but I get into a pair of trousers and into a coat and draw some socks on and my shoes, and every now and again the room trembles, so that I jump and feel very nervous. I do not deny that I feel nervous, for I still think the building will fall to the ground and crush us. And all the time we hear the sound of crashing masonry and the cries of frightened people.

Then we run down the stairs and into the street, and my valet, brave fellow that he is, goes back and bundles all my

Dead Cattle on Mission Street. Lithographic stereo view, from a photographic stereo view by Tom M. Phillips. "Litho views" were ubiquitous in fin de siècle America, enabling thousands to tour the world vicariously and inexpensively.

On Mission, only a few blocks from the Grand Opera House, where the "Toreador Song" had been sung the night before, "lay a dozen steers, in a neat row stretching across the street, just as they had been struck down by the flying ruins of the earthquake. The fire had passed through afterward and roasted them."

–Jack London, *Collier's,* May 5, 1906

things into trunks and drags them down six flights of stairs and out into the open one by one. While he is gone back for another and another, I watch those that have already arrived, and presently some one comes and tries to take my trunks, saying they are his. I say, "No, they are mine"; but he does not go away. Then a soldier comes up to me; I tell him that this man wants to take my trunks, and that I am Caruso, the artist who sang in "Carmen" the night before. He remembers me and makes the man who takes an interest in my baggage "skiddoo," as Americans say.

SIGNOR CARUSO'S SKETCH OF HIMSELF DRIVING TO OAKLAND FERRY AFTER THE DISASTER

Then I make my way to Union Square, where I see some of my friends, and one of them tells me that he has lost everything except his voice, but he is thankful that he has still got that. And they tell me to come to a house which is still standing; but I say houses are not safe, nothing is safe but the open square, and I prefer to remain in a place where there is no fear of being buried

away, but the soldiers will not let us pass. We can find no vehicle to take our luggage, and this night we are forced to sleep on the hard ground in the open. My limbs ache yet from so rough a bed.

Then my valet succeeds in getting a man with a cart, who says that he will take us to the Oakland Ferry [the Ferry Building was and still is at the foot of San Francisco's Market Street] for a certain sum, and we agree to his terms. We pile the luggage in the cart and climb in after it, and the man whips up his horse and we start. We pass terrible scenes on the way: buildings in ruins, and everywhere there seems to be smoke and dust. The driver seems in no hurry, which makes me impatient at times, for I am longing to return to New York, where I know I shall find a ship to take me to my beautiful Italy and my wife and my little boys.

When we arrive at Oakland we find a train there which is about to start, and the officials are very polite, take charge of my luggage, and tell me to get on board, which I am very glad to do. The trip to New York seems very long and tedious, and I sleep very little, for I can still feel the terrible rocking which made me sick. Even now I can only sleep an hour at a time, for the experience was a terrible one.

SIGNOR CARUSO'S SKETCH OF HIMSELF WATCHING THE BURNING OF SAN FRANCISCO

by falling buildings. So I lie down in the square for a little rest, while my valet goes and looks after the luggage, and soon I begin to see the flames and all the city seems to be on fire. All the day I wander about, and I tell my valet we must try and get

51

–Enrico Caruso, *The Theatre Magazine* (from *The Sketch*, London), 1906

On duty "amid the encircling gloom" of their city's certain destruction. Magnificent fire scene near Union Ferry Building. NB: It appears that the negative used to produce this stereo view was retouched. "The Harbor Emergency Hospital on the water-front (long a factor in the city's care of the victims of accidents and broils) was filled from the first. The injured and sick and dying were taken there in large numbers from the charnel-house south of Market. While the fire was burning hottest all around, the attendants worked away, unmindful of the danger. [continued]

EARTHQUAKE INVESTIGATION COMMISSION

MT. HAMILTON, CAL. Ewing Three-Component Seismograph.
(From hand-tracing; reduced 1:2.)

CHARLES FRANCIS RICHTER (1900–1985) was just five years old in April 1906. In 1935, the California seismologist—having grown weary of questions about the relative size of earthquakes—invented the now-familiar Richter Scale. The USGS estimates that the 1906 San Francisco Earthquake would have registered 8.3 on this logarithmic measurement. By comparison, the 1989 Loma Prieta Earthquake registered 7.1; the 1994 Northridge Earthquake registered 6.4.

Named for pioneer/benefactor James Lick, the Lick Observatory sits atop 4200-foot Mt. Hamilton, in the Diablo Range east of San Jose, California. In 1898, Observatory director Professor Edward S. Holden published his "Catalogue of Earthquakes of the Pacific Coast from 1769 to 1897." According to Holden, "it was necessary at the Lick Observatory to keep a register of the times of occurrence of all earthquake shocks in order to see if the positions of the astronomical instruments were affected. Accordingly, a set of Professor Ewing's instruments was ordered for the Observatory, and they were delivered in 1887. The Lick Observatory began its active work in 1888. A part of this work consisted in the registration of earthquake shocks. Reports of shocks felt elsewhere on the Pacific Coast were diligently collected." Holden was fond of the Rossi-Forel Scale for assessing the comparative magnitude of seismic events, a scale from **I** ("Microseismic shock—recorded by a single seismograph, or by seismographs of the same model, but not putting seismographs of different patterns in motion; reported by experienced observers only.") to **X** ("Great disasters; overturning of rocks; fissures in the surface of the earth; mountain slides."). The earthquake of April 18, 1906, was nearly a perfect **X**. It registered on seismographs at 96 locations around the world, including the three-component Ewing seismograph at Lick Observatory. The quake's epicenter, just off the coast near today's Daly City, was only 53 miles from the Observatory. The Ewing seismograph recorded just ten seconds of April 18's seismic waves before going off scale.

"Ambulances and patrol wagons hurried the patients to the hospital, while others waited to remove them should it become necessary."

–Aitken & Hilton, *A History of the Earthquake and Fire in San Francisco,* 1906

Lick Observatory on Mount Hamilton, California

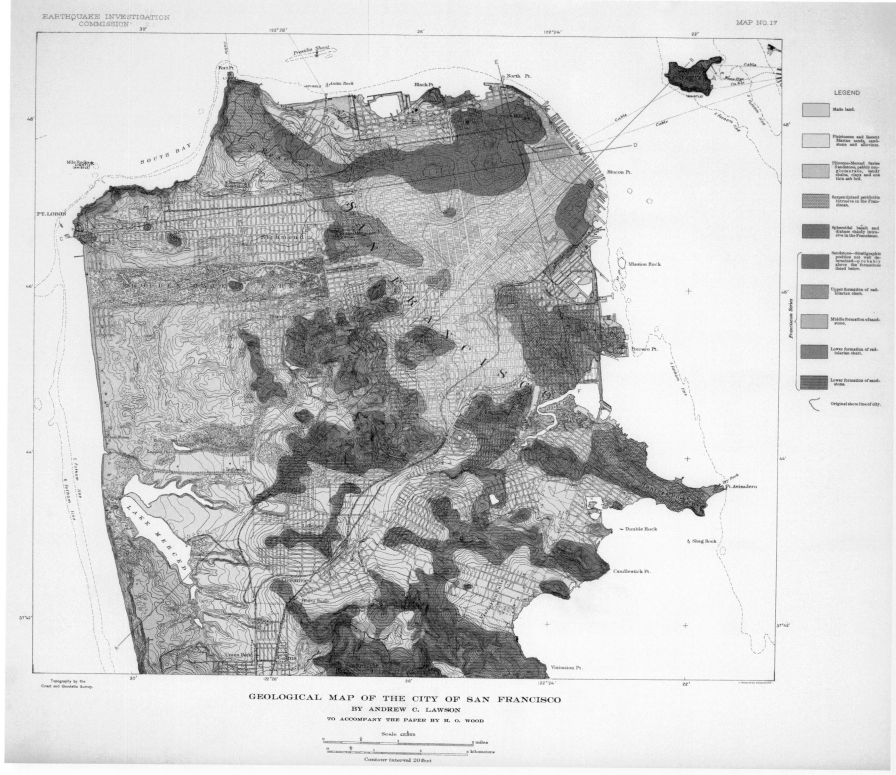

GEOLOGICAL MAP OF THE CITY OF SAN FRANCISCO
BY ANDREW C. LAWSON
TO ACCOMPANY THE PAPER BY H. O. WOOD

Scale

Contour interval 20 feet

"IT IS THE NATURAL and legitimate ambition of a properly constituted geologist to see a glacier, witness an eruption and feel an earthquake. The glacier is always ready, awaiting his visit; the eruption has a course to run, and alacrity only is needed to catch its more important phases; but the earthquake, unheralded and brief, may elude him through his entire lifetime. It had been my fortune to experience only a single weak tremor, and I had, moreover, been tantalized by narrowly missing the great Inyo earthquake of 1872 and the Alaska earthquake of 1899. When, therefore, I was awakened in Berkeley on the eighteenth of April last by a by a tumult of motions and noises, it was with unalloyed pleasure that I became aware that a vigorous earthquake was in progress."–Grove Karl Gilbert, United States Geological Survey, *The Investigation of the California Earthquake of 1906*, 1907

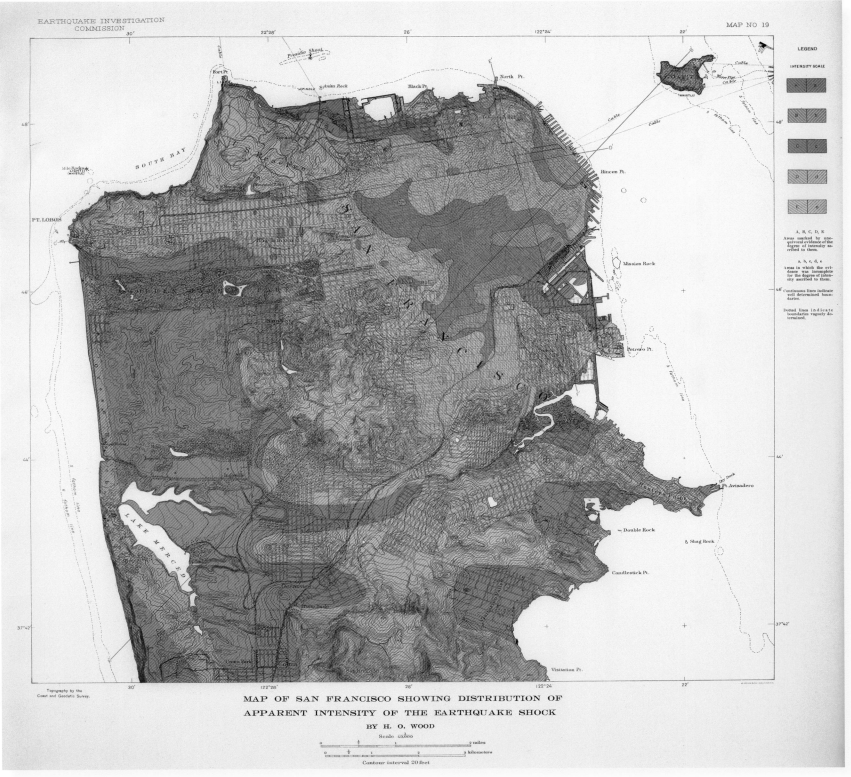

MAP OF SAN FRANCISCO SHOWING DISTRIBUTION OF
APPARENT INTENSITY OF THE EARTHQUAKE SHOCK

BY H. O. WOOD

Scale c.1:500

Contour interval 20 feet

55

"A VERY RESPECTABLE EARTHQUAKE, even from the undisturbed point of view of the geologist."—J. C. Branner.

As the fires smoldered, the USGS's Gilbert and Stanford's Branner joined UC Professor Andrew C. Lawson's geological dream team, which became known as the State Earthquake Investigation Commission. They understood that the so-called San Francisco Earthquake was in reality a *California* Earthquake, having occurred along hundreds of miles of the San Andreas Fault (today, we know that the San Andreas is a 750-mile-long strike-slip fault, from Cape Mendocino to the Salton Sea). A 19″ x 24″ atlas artistically conveyed the results of their exhaustive investigation, as well as the unique *California*-ness of the event. It included this cartographic "before and after" of San Francisco, a telling reminder of the perils of "made ground."

Andrew C. Lawson (University of California), G. K. Gilbert (USGS), H. F. Reid (Johns Hopkins), J. C. Branner (Stanford), A. O. Leuschner (University of California), George Davidson (University of California), Charles Burckhalter (Chabot Observatory), and W. W. Campbell (Lick Observatory, University of California), *Atlas of Maps and Seismograms Accompanying the Report of the State Earthquake Investigation Commission upon the California Earthquake of April 18, 1906*, Carnegie Institution of Washington, DC, 1908

Collier's

SAN FRANCISCO

"San Francisco, at the present time, is like the crater of a volcano, around which are camped tens of thousands of refugees."—From the eyewitness account of

The Call Building in a Maelstrom of Flame —The Great San Francisco Fire completing the devastation of the famous Spreckels' structure.

INTERNATIONAL STEREOGRAPH CO.
Photographers and Publishers

HOME OFFICE AND WORKS
Decatur, Illinois, U.S.A.

20615 The Call Building in a Maelstrom of Flame—The Great San Francisco Fire completing the devastation of the famous Spreckels' structure. Copyright 1906 by C. L. Wasson.

58

38. Postal Telegraph Building.
Copyright by Tom M. Phillips, 1906.

Postal Telegraph Building. 534 Market. "The city practically ruined by fire. It's within half block of us in the same block. The Call Building is burned out entirely, the Examiner building just fell in a heap. Fire all around in every direction and way out in the residence district. Destruction by earthquake something frightful. The City Hall dome stripped and only the frame work standing. The St. Ignatius Church and College are burned to the ground. The Emporium is gone, entire building, also the Old Flood Building. [continued]

"Lots of new buildings just recently finished are completely destroyed. They are blowing standing buildings that are in the path of flames up with dynamite. No water. It's awful. There is no communication anywhere and entire phone system is busted. I want to get out of here or be blown up."

    —Final communication, Postal Telegraph Office, April 18, 2:20 p.m.

An Actual View of The Burning of San Francisco as Seen by An Eye Witness.

13350—An Actual View of The Burning of San Francisco as Seen by An Eye Witness.

THE GREATEST CONFLAGRATION IN THE HISTORY OF

"THE BURNING OF SAN FRANCIS

OVER 450 SQUARE BLOCKS WERE DESTROYED WITH A LOSS OF OV

IN THE ABOVE SCENE THE FIRE LINE IS OVER FIVE MILES IN LENGTH ON

VORLD.

CO" APRIL 18, 19, 20, 1906.

O MILLION DOLLARS.
VENING OF THE FIRST DAY.

SCHMIDT LITHOGRAPH CO., S.F.

"Business was increasing from month to month and everything was running smoothly when the great fire of 1906 laid San Francisco's business and manufacturing district in ruins. On the afternoon of April 18 [Schmidt Lithograph] removed all [their] books, records, [lithographic] stones and the like to the great vaults under Second street, carefully locked up and went home. In the morning when they returned to work there was no plant to work in. Dynamite and fire had destroyed everything. There wasn't a stone, a scrap of paper, a record of any kind left."—Elford Eddy, *The Log of a Cabin Boy*, Schmidt Litho. Co., 1922

The clock tower of Max Schmidt's post-1906 San Francisco print shop at Second and Bryant is familiar to Bay Bridge commuters today. It was built to hold the large water tanks for Schmidt's sprinkler system.

"The Burning of San Francisco"
April 18, 19, 20, 1906; chromolithograph on paper with hand coloring;
Carl A. Beck, artist;
Schmidt Lithograph Company,
San Francisco, lithographers,
c. 1906.

Cast of Characters

"This monster tragedy, a whole city for a stage, 500,000 actors and everyone playing his part."
–Mary Edith Griswold, "Three Days Adrift," *Sunset Magazine*, June-July 1906

"The Yankee Hustler"

"YANKEE" (as defined by Webster) is the popular name applied indiscriminately to "All inhabitants of the United States."

"HUSTLER" is a term generally used in describing "One who is wide-awake, pushing, energetic, progressive and enterprising."

In adopting the name of "THE YANKEE HUSTLER" as the title of this composition, Mayor Eugene E. Schmitz has been very successful in expressing, in appropriate terms, not only his high estimation of the characteristics of the American people, to whom this March is dedicated, but in paying a fitting tribute of honor and respect to their well known progress and enterprise.

E UGENE E. SCHMITZ was born in San Francisco on August 22, 1864. His father, '49er Jos. L. Schmitz, was an orchestra leader, and his uncle, Christopher, taught young Eugene drums, piano, and violin. By the late 1890s, the 205-pound, 6′ 1″ Eugene had become an accomplished violinist, composer, and leader of the pit orchestra at the Columbia Theatre. He had also become the first president of the fledgling San Francisco Musicians Union. In 1901, attorney/political boss Abraham Ruef (1864–1936) saw in Schmitz the ideal candidate for mayor, appealing to the City's disgruntled working class without alienating big business, whose owners were familiar with the well-dressed "Handsome Gene" from the Theatre. San Francisco's new Union Labor Party elected Schmitz to three successive terms as mayor. Although graft and corruption would eventually bring both Schmitz and Ruef toppling down, Schmitz's compassion and resolve in the immediate aftermath of the Earthquake earned him San Francisco's enduring gratitude and goodwill. Despite his municipal malfeasance, he was elected to the Board of Supervisors in 1917, and again in 1921. He died at his Fillmore Street home on November 20, 1928.

Mayor Schmitz in his temporary quarters at Fort Mason. This is the original, 1906 H. C. White Co. glass negative—now broken—upon which a stereo pair of images of his honor were exposed. The camera sees the left image as the right and vice versa.

"As soon as it was realized that a great disaster to the City of San Francisco was imminent, and before the extent of the misfortunes of the people could be ascertained or even prophesied, and while the conflagration was yet incipient, measures for the relief that was soon to be necessary were initiated. Mayor Eugene E. Schmitz hurriedly appointed a committee, known thereafter as the Citizens' Committee of Fifty, and called together such as could be reached, and a meeting was held at the Hall of Justice, on Kearny and Washington streets, on Wednesday afternoon, April 18, 1906, at 3:00 p.m. Mayor Schmitz was elected chairman and Rufus P. Jennings, secretary. The Mayor outlined what had been done for the relief of people in distress and the committee authorized the chief executive to issue orders for supplies to be given to those in need. [Ex-mayor] James D. Phelan was elected chairman of the Finance Committee, with authority to name the other members thereof. It being at that time apparent that the Hall of Justice would soon be destroyed by the approaching conflagration, the committee adjourned to meet the next day at the Fairmont Hotel. [By 10:00 a.m. on April 19, the Fairmont was no longer an option. The meeting took place at the North End Police Station.]"

—The Work of Relief and the Restoration of the City of San Francisco from the Disaster of April, 1906, San Francisco Municipal Reports, Board of Supervisors, 1908

63

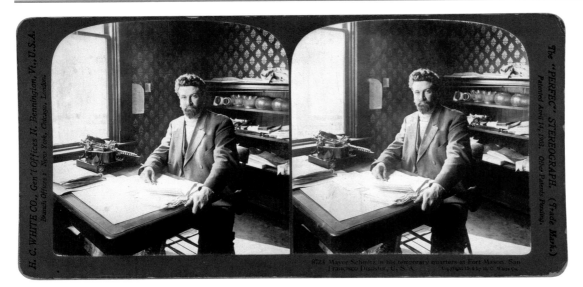

Mayor Schmitz in his temporary quarters at Fort Mason. This is an original, 1906 H. C. White Co. stereo card. The photographic prints on the card were created from the glass negative. During mounting, the left and right images were switched in order that a person viewing the card will see the left image on the left and the right image on the right.

WIRELESS TELEGRAPHY IN OUR NAVY—*See Page 1148*

HARPER'S WEEKLY
JOURNAL OF CIVILIZATION

Vol. XLIII.—No. 2238
Copyright, 1899, by HARPER & BROTHERS
All Rights Reserved

NEW YORK, SATURDAY, NOVEMBER 11, 1899

TEN CENTS A COPY
FOUR DOLLARS A YEAR

BRIGADIER–GENERAL FREDERICK FUNSTON, U.S.V.,
ON BOARD THE TRANSPORT "TARTAR" ON THE DAY OF HIS ARRIVAL AT SAN FRANCISCO FROM MANILA.
SEE PAGE 1143.

"THE HEADQUARTERS of the Pacific Division and of the Department of California were located in office-buildings in the heart of the city [the Grant and Phelan Buildings, respectively—both burned], and the officers on duty thereat lived in the city and not at the army posts near it. Maj.-Gen. A[dolphus] W. Greely, commanding the Pacific Division, had departed from the city on a visit to his home in Washington [DC] only a few days previous to the earthquake, which accounts for the writer, as senior officer, being in command until the return of the division commander. I was living with my family at 1310 Washington Street, near Jones, one of the most elevated parts of the city, and was awakened by the earthquake shock at 5:16 [sic] a.m. on that never-to-be-forgotten eighteenth day of April. The entire street-car system being brought to

a standstill by the damage resulting from the shock, I hastened on foot toward the business section of the city for the purpose of ascertaining what damage had been done to the hotels and other large buildings. At the highest part of California Street, on what is popularly known as 'Nob Hill,' several columns of smoke were seen rising from the region south of Market Street, with others rising apparently from fires in the banking district. Walking rapidly down California to Sansome, I found that several fires were burning fiercely, and that the city fire-department was helpless, owing to water-mains having been shattered by the earthquake. I realized then that a great conflagration was inevitable, and that the city police-force would not be able to maintain the fire-lines and protect public and private property over the great area affected. It was at once determined to order out all available troops, not only for the purpose of guarding federal buildings, but to aid the police- and fire-departments of the city."

—Frederick Funston, "How the Army Worked to Save San Francisco," *Cosmopolitan Magazine*, July 1906

Inscription accompanying this Keystone-Mast Collection glass-plate negative: *General Frederick Funston, Commander of the Presidio, declared martial law in San Francisco following quake.* Despite the pervasive rumors, San Francisco was never under martial law. Remembered fondly by San Franciscans for his decisive action in the aftermath of the 1906 Earthquake and Fire, 5′ 4″ Frederick Funston (1865–1917) became the first person to lie in state in San Francisco's new City Hall.

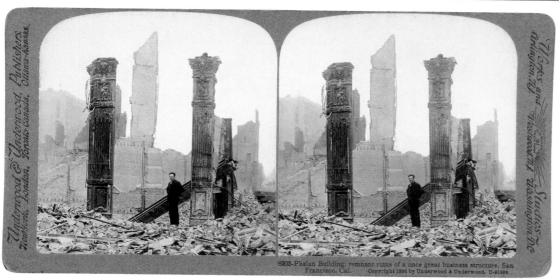

Phelan Building [unidentified man], *remnant ruins of a once great business structure.* James D. Phelan's Irish-born father's first business burned "in the memorable fire of June, 1851." After sustaining a loss of $75,000, "the business rose Phoenix-like from the flames.... As far back as 1854, he had become the owner of the lot upon which stands the magnificent structure which bears his name, and which may be considered an enduring monument to his enterprise and fame. The Phelan Building was erected in 1881–82, at a cost of $500,000, and is among the most prominent edifices on Market street."–W. H. Murray, *The Builders of a Great City*, 1891

"San Francisco has rebounded from the temblors and catastrophes of two weeks ago, and is again on march to prosperity."
-James D. Phelan, *The Present Situation*, 1906

JAMES S. PHELAN (1861–1930) was elected mayor of San Francisco in 1897. Following a bitter and bloody teamster's strike in 1901, the Democratic mayor chose not to seek a third term. After the Earthquake, the former mayor and future United States senator (1915–1921) contributed his time, energy, money—even his automobile—to San Francisco's recovery and rebuilding effort. In *Americans and the California Dream*, historian Kevin Starr elucidates the essence of the man. While his "temperamental Hamiltonianism sometimes led him down ambiguous paths—his advocacy of Oriental exclusion, for instance, his urban bias in the Hetch Hetchy crisis—it also accounted for his effective service to San Francisco and to California. At bottom, Hamiltonianism and Mediterraneanism intersected at a point of dynamic orderliness. Each signified the hope for values of art and life which assuaged the longing for a past and met present need. James Duval Phelan of San Francisco would be both reformer and patrician; the Californian as the newest of new Americans, and the Irish-Californian as having validated his claim to a wider historicity."

Like his mayoral successor, Eugene E. Schmitz, James D. Phelan was born in the city he would one day run. Legend has it that James D.'s father, banker James Phelan, was asked by a local tobacconist why he smoked nickel cigars, while his son smoked only the most expensive kind. His reply: "I do not have a wealthy father." The younger James enjoyed success in banking (serving as chairman of the Mutual Savings Bank on Market, which survived the Earthquake and Fire) and real estate, as well as politics. In 1904, he founded the Association for the Improvement and Adornment of San Francisco. It culminated in architect Daniel H. Burnham's civic beautification plan, which was delivered to City Hall on April 17, 1906. The same day, Phelan and Rudolph Spreckels filed articles of incorporation for the Municipal Street Railways of San Francisco. They had created their streetcar company to demonstrate that Mayor Schmitz's San Francisco did not need to replace its cable railroads with the unsightly overhead trolleys proposed by the bribe-giving United Railroads. A California progressive as well as a reformer, Phelan teamed with Spreckels and newspaper editor Fremont Older to weed out and punish "boodle mayor" Schmitz, boss Abe Ruef, and others of their ilk.

U.S. MINT.

200,000 PEOPLE AT GOLDEN GATE PARK.

CITY HALL.

SEA

BUSINESS DISTRICT IN FLAMES.

REIGN OF MARTIAL LAW, & DISTRIBUTING BREAD.

PIER

CHINATOWN & TELEGRAPH HILL.

VIEW OF RUINS FROM NOB HILL.

VIEW FROM STANFORD RESIDENCE ON NOB HILL.

SUTRO HEIGHTS.

CALIFORNIA ST.

NEWSPAPER ROW.

STANFORD MEMORIAL CHAPEL.

PALACE HOTEL.

APRIL 18TH, 1906.

DESTRUCTION OF SAN FRANCISCO BY EARTHQUAKE

68

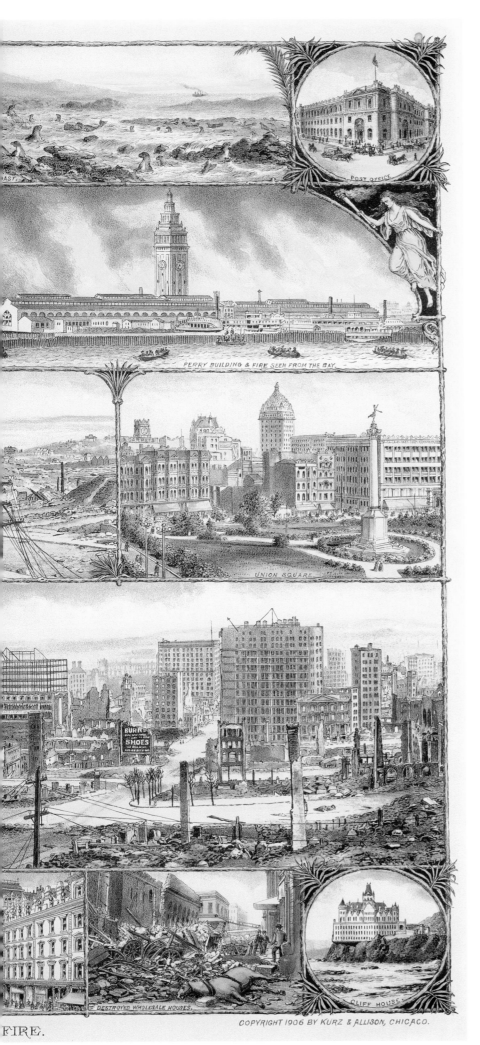

BY 1893, AS THE WORLD FLOCKED to Chicago's lakefront for the Columbian Exposition, Chicago lithographers Louis Kurz and Alexander Allison had already established themselves as the Currier and Ives of the Midwest. Their patriotic prints of Lady Liberty, Abraham Lincoln, and Civil War battle scenes were immensely popular.

Kurz and Allison's 1887 lithograph, *The Miners Pioneer Ten Commandments of 1849*, combined scenes of the California gold rush with a humorous incantation of the miner's credo. Commandment VII:

"Thou shalt not grow discouraged, nor think of going home before thou hast made thy '*pile*,' because thou hast not '*struck a lead*' nor found a rich '*crevice*' nor sunk a hole upon a '*pocket*,' lest in going home thou leave four dollars a day and go to work ashamed at fifty cents a day, and serve thee right; for thou knowest by staying here thou mightest strike a lead and fifty dollars a day, and keep thy manly self-respect, and then go home with enough to make thyself and others happy."

Nineteen years later, Kurz and Allison created another synthesis of California scenes, here shown in a hand-colored version of their before-and-after lithograph, *Destruction of San Francisco by Earthquake and Fire*.

69

EXTRA

Berkeley Reporter

Last Edition

VOL. IV.   BERKELEY, CALIFORNIA, WEDNESDAY, APRIL 18, 1906.   No. 133

CITY A ROARING FURNACE

Palace Hotel Burns---Cliff House Topples Into Ocean

FEARFUL TEMBLOR SHAKES THE ENTIRE PACIFIC COAST

AS THE REPORTER goes to press San Francisco and the entire state face one of the worst calamities that has ever visited the coast---The earthquake of 1868 in point of violence was more severe than the shock of this morning, but the ruin that is following from the fires that have been started as the result of the awful shock is appalling and unprecedented---The Reporter has used every resource that human ingenuity could suggest to get the news from every center and from all over the state---The reports show Los Angeles, San Jose, San Diego and Sacramento have suffered appalling loss---Berkeley passed through disaster comparatively uninjured, and has cause to be thankful---San Francisco is a charnel house---At four o'clock fire had reached northern part of city and spread north to Washington street.

BERKELEY SUFFERS LEAST DAMAGE FROM EARTHQUAKE OF ANY CITY IN CALIFORNIA

HUNDREDS ARE KILLED BY THE FALLING RUINS

San Jose Burns

A correspondent of the Reporter who returned from San Jose this morning, reports that the Garden City is being consumed by fire, which started immediately after the earthquake.

The fire department found that several of the water mains had been crippled and dynamite was resorted to to raze several of the buildings.

It is reported that a number of lives were lost.

Berkeley's escape from the awful violence of this morning's earthquake is one of the inexplicable wonders of the dire catastrophe. Oakland and San Francisco suffered most, and San Francisco is now a roaring furnace along the entire water front and in the factory districts. Buildings are being dynamited to check the fire fiend's progress. At 10 o'clock the Chronicle building was dynamited to save property west of that point.

Among the structures which sustained the greatest amount of damage are the buildings of the State University, the State Institute for the Deaf and Blind, the Berkeley High School, the new Masonic Temple and numerous leading business blocks.

According to the record made by the seismograph at the University of California, the earthquake was of 28 seconds duration, and the oscillation was from north to south. The precise moment at which the first quake started was 5:14:48 a. m.

In an instant the entire population of the city was aroused, and people rushed from the swaying

Continued on Page Eight

DOOM IS CERTAIN

AT 3 O'CLOCK FIRE REACHED MONTGOMERY STREET NORTH OF MARKET AND ANNIHILATION FACES ENTIRE CITY. FLAMES ARE WIPING OUT THE WHOLE COMMERCIAL DISTRICT.

EYE-WITNESS TELLS OF FEARFUL CALAMITY IN SAN FRANCISCO

DEAD INCINERATED BY SWEEPING FLAMES

The following latest report from the scene of ruin and horror in San Francisco was secured by L. B. Littlefield for the Reporter at the risk of his life. He chartered a special boat early this morning and landed at the San Francisco water front, staying in the city until 2 o'clock in gathering news for this paper. Many times he was imperiled and when he arrived in Berkeley this afternoon with his copy he was completely prostrated.

BY L. B. LITTLEFIELD

When I left San Francisco at 2 o'clock this afternoon the entire south side of Market street seemed to be transformed into a furnace of flames. Nothing can save that part of town—in fact, it is already a smoldering heap of ruin. Firemen and citizens, soldiers and police, engineers and volunteer brigades are doing everything possible to save that part of the city north of Market street. Buildings were being dynamited right and left all the morning, and when these heroic measures failed to save the city on the south the workers were transferred to the north of Market to try to save that part of the city.

(Continued on Page Four)

TIDAL WAVE AT SAN DIEGO

It is reported that immediately following the earthquake shock a tidal wave swewt over the San Diego water front, with loss of several lives and great distruction of property.

MILITIA ON GUARD DUTY

A call for militia in Oakland was responded to almost immediately by several companies. The men were immediately detailed to watch buildings that are in imminent danger of falling. Business in this city is entirely stagnated.

MEN LYING DRUNK FROM STOLEN LIQUOR.

The soldiers and police are making heroic efforts to keep back the crowd.

There has been very little carrying away of stuff from buildings yet, though some liquor was taken along the water front. As a result numbers of men are lying drunk about the ferry.

The reaction from the terrible shock has caused many cases of heart failure. In a trip from Market street to the ferry four or five men were seen to drop dead or faint away.

FIVE MEN AND WOMEN BURIED IN OAKLAND BUILDING

In Oakland destruction is spelled by ruin after ruin that line every street. The latest report shows the known dead to be five, but when the wreckage is cleared away the fatalities will far exceed that number. Those whose bodies now lie in the morgue were all taken from the ruins of the Empire Theatre. The unfortunate victims of the early morning horror were actors employed in the Empire Theatre. They were asleep in bed when the earthquake came, bringing sudden calamity.

The dead are:
MR. and MRS. WILLIAM MARNEY.
OTTO WICHER, of New York.
ALMADA WICHER, aged twelve years.
AN UNKNOWN.

The Marneys were man and wife, and were found buried under tons of brick, side by side in bed.

Otto Wicher was the father of Almaca Wicher. His second daughter Friena aged nineteen was sleeping in the same room and escaped with her life.

To a respresentative of the Reporter who was aiding the rescue party she said: "When I felt the first shock I rolled out of bed and under the bedstead to escape the falling bricks. The framework of the bed protected me in some miraculous way. I heard my sister screaming and women and men crying for help then I lost my senses until rescue came.

Frieca Wicher was buried under the ruins an hour until the firemen and willing citizens dug her out and restored der to consciousness. Dr. Radford Fern and a score of others assisted in the work of rescue and displayed remarkable heroism.

Fifteen minutes after the earthquake subsided the power was shut off and now this side of the bay is without light or car service. The water mains are broken and there is no water to fight the dozen or more fires that have started in the residence district, the danger from fire here however has not reached alarming proportions.

According to the record taken at Charbot observatory on the seismograph, the direction of the temblor was from north to south. The vibrations were so numerous that the delicate instruments could keep no record of them. The marks on the black surface of the recording glass resembled a tangle of Neira's hair.

A second shock was felt in Oakland at 8:14 o'clock.

Continued on Page Eight

Cliff House and Seal Rocks W.N.W. from the sea-beach. On April 18, rumors spread like wildfire—faster and farther, indeed, than the fire itself. San Francisco's historic Cliff House was undamaged. A spectacular fire on September 7, 1907, however, completely destroyed it. "In the earlier years, before Golden Gate park was thought of, the Cliff house was the objective of all visitors to the City.... The traveler had to see the seals and all who came saw them. The San Franciscan visited the Cliff for quite a different purpose. A visit to it was usually a punctuating mark in an afternoon drive, refreshments solid and liquid being a specialty."–John P. Young, *San Francisco, A History of the Pacific Coast Metropolis,* 1912

PROCLAMATION
BY THE MAYOR

The Federal Troops, the members of the Regular Police Force and all Special Police Officers have been authorized by me to KILL any and all persons found engaged in Looting or in the Commission of Any Other Crime.

I have directed all the Gas and Electric Lighting Co.'s not to turn on Gas or Electricity until I order them to do so. You may therefore expect the city to remain in darkness for an indefinite time.

I request all citizens to remain at home from darkness until daylight every night until order is restored.

I WARN all Citizens of the danger of fire from Damaged or Destroyed Chimneys, Broken or Leaking Gas Pipes or Fixtures, or any like cause.

E. E. SCHMITZ, Mayor

Dated, April 18, 1906.

ALTVATER PRINT, MISSION AND 22D STS.

"ANTICIPATING THAT looting would take place—I had already seen some of it on my own trip down town—and realizing that we would have no place in which to keep prisoners if we arrested any, and that it was time for firm and decisive action, I told Colonel [Charles] Morris and also the Captain [M. L. Walker] that reported to me from General Funston, to let the news be widely spread that anyone caught looting should not be arrested but should be shot. Colonel Morris asked me if I would be responsible for that order and I told him Yes; that I would be responsible for that order; we could not take prisoners; we must stop looting, and therefore to shoot anyone caught looting. The same order was also issued to the Police Department." –Eugene E. Schmitz, as published in *The Argonaut*, January 15, 1927

A Mission District printer outside the fire lines—their presses turned by hand—printed thousands of copies of Mayor Schmitz's official but illegal edict. Although San Francisco was never under martial law, it is no wonder that her citizens believed that she was.

72

On the watch for looters (valuables lie buried here). Heart of Chinatown where frightful mortality resulted from quake. Old St. Mary's. "San Francisco, no doubt, has, or, at least, had its full share of criminals and equally worthless and dangerous persons, who would have been more than glad to take advantage of the opportunity to loot such a treasure house as the banks, stores and dwellings of the opulent metropolis of the Pacific Coast. These people were overawed by the rifles with fixed bayonets, and the full cartridge belts of one thousand seven hundred regular soldiers and a large force of National Guards in addition to the police force of the city."–Frederick Funston, *San Francisco's Courage*, 1906

Mayor Schmitz's shoot-to-kill order was world news, and the inspiration for this apocryphal scene.

Soldiers at Mess. Company D, 20th U.S. Regulars, stationed in burned district. "The soldiers lacked good sense and judgment, or perhaps it may have been that some incompetent officers gave senseless orders,—for instance, the people occupying the stores on Polk Street, between Clay and Pacific, and the apartments above, were driven out at 8 A.M. of Thursday, and not permitted to re-enter. As the fire did not reach this locality until about 4 P.M., there was abundant time to save many valuable articles which were by this imbecile order lost."–James B. Stetson, *San Francisco During the Eventful Days of April, 1906,* June 1906

The Call=Chronicle=Examiner

SAN FRANCISCO, THURSDAY, APRIL 19, 1906.

EARTHQUAKE AND FIRE: SAN FRANCISCO IN RUINS

DEATH AND DESTRUCTION HAVE BEEN THE FATE OF SAN FRANCISCO. SHAKEN BY A TEMBLOR AT 5:13 O'CLOCK YESTERDAY MORNING, THE SHOCK LASTING 48 SECONDS, AND SCOURGED BY FLAMES THAT RAGED DIAMETRICALLY IN ALL DIRECTIONS, THE CITY IS A MASS OF SMOULDERING RUINS. AT SIX O'CLOCK LAST EVENING THE FLAMES SEEMINGLY PLAYING WITH INCREASED VIGOR, THREATENED TO DESTROY SUCH SECTIONS AS THEIR FURY HAD SPARED DURING THE EARLIER PORTION OF THE DAY. BUILDING THEIR PATH IN A TRIANGUAR CIRCUIT FROM THE START IN THE EARLY MORNING, THEY JOCKEYED AS THE DAY WANED, LEFT THE BUSINESS SECTION, WHICH THEY HAD ENTIRELY DEVASTATED, AND SKIPPED IN A DOZEN DIRECTIONS TO THE RESIDENCE PORTIONS. AS NIGHT FELL THEY HAD MADE THEIR WAY OVER INTO THE NORTH BEACH SECTION AND SPRINGING ANEW TO THE SOUTH THEY REACHED OUT ALONG THE SHIPPING SECTION DOWN THE BAY SHORE, OVER THE HILLS AND ACROSS TOWARD THIRD AND TOWNSEND STREETS. WAREHOUSES, WHOLESALE HOUSES AND MANUFACTURING CONCERNS FELL IN THEIR PATH. THIS COMPLETED THE DESTRUCTION OF THE ENTIRE DISTRICT KNOWN AS THE "SOUTH OF MARKET STREET." HOW FAR THEY ARE REACHING TO THE SOUTH ACROSS THE CHANNEL CANNOT BE TOLD AS THIS PART OF THE CITY IS SHUT OFF FROM SAN FRANCISCO PAPERS.

AFTER DARKNESS, THOUSANDS OF THE HOMELESS WERE MAKING THEIR WAY WITH THEIR BLANKETS AND SCANT PROVISIONS TO GOLDEN GATE PARK AND THE BEACH TO FIND SHELTER. THOSE IN THE HOMES ON THE HILLS JUST NORTH OF THE HAYES VALLEY WRECKED SECTION PILED THEIR BELONGINGS IN THE STREETS AND EXPRESS WAGONS AND AUTOMOBILES WERE HAULING THE THINGS AWAY TO THE SPARSELY SETTLED REGIONS. EVERYBODY IN SAN FRANCISCO IS PREPARED TO LEAVE THE CITY, FOR THE BELIEF IS FIRM THAT SAN FRANCISCO WILL BE TOTALLY DESTROYED.

DOWNTOWN EVERYTHING IS RUIN. NOT A BUSINESS HOUSE STANDS. THEATRES ARE CRUMBLED INTO HEAPS. FACTORIES AND COMMISSION HOUSE'S LIE SMOULDERING ON THEIR FORMER SITES. ALL OF THE NEWSPAPER PLANTS HAVE BEEN RENDERED USELESS, THE "CALL" AND THE "EXAMINER" BUILDINGS, EXCLUDING THE "CALL'S" EDITORIAL ROOMS ON STEVENSON STREET BEING ENTIRELY DESTROYED.

IT IS ESTIMATED THAT THE LOSS IN SAN FRANCISCO WILL REACH FROM $150,000,000 TO $200,000,000. THESE FIGURES ARE IN THE ROUGH AND NOTHING CAN BE TOLD UNTIL PARTIAL ACCOUNTING IS TAKEN.

ON EVERY SIDE THERE WAS DEATH AND SUFFERING YESTERDAY. HUNDREDS WERE INJURED, EITHR BURNED, CRUSHED OR STRUCK BY FALLING PIECES FROM THE BUILDINGS AND ONE OF TEN DIED WHILE ON THE OPOPERATING TABLE AT MECHANICS' PAVILION, IMPROVISED AS A HOSPITAL FOR THE COMFORT AND CARE OF 300 OF THE INJURED. THE NUMBER OF DEAD IS NOT KNOWN BUT IT IS ESTIMATED THAT AT LEAST 500 MET THEIR DEATH IN THE HORROR.

AT NINE O'CLOCK, UNDER A SPECIAL MESSAGE FROM PRESIDENT ROOSEVELT, THE CITY WAS PLACED UNDER MARTIAL LAW. HUNDREDS OF TROOPS PATROLLED THE STREETS AND DROVE THE CROWDS BACK, WHILE HUNDREDS MORE WERE SET AT WORK ASSISTING THE FIRE AND POLICE DEPARTMENTS. THE STRICTEST ORDERS WERE ISSUED, AND IN TRUE MILITARY SPIRIT THE SOLDIERS OBEYED. DURING THE AFTERNOON THREE THIEVES MET THEIR DEATH BY RIFLE BULLETS WHILE AT WORK IN THE RUINS. THE CURIOUS WERE DRIVEN BACK AT THE BREASTS OF THE HORSES THAT THE CAVALRYMEN RODE AND ALL THE CROWDS WERE FORCED FROM THE LEVEL DISTRICT TO THE HILLY SECTION BEYOND TO THE NORTH

THE WATER SUPPLY WAS ENTIRELY CUT OFF, AND MAY BE IT WAS JUST AS WELL, FOR THE LINES OF FIRE DEPARTMENT WOULD HAVE BEEN ABSOLUTELY USELESS AT ANY STAGE. ASSISTANT CHIEF DOUGHERTY SUPERVISED THE WORK OF HIS MEN AND EARLY IN THE MORNING IT WAS SEEN THAT THE ONLY POSSIBLE CHANCE TO SAVE THE CITY LAY IN EFFORT TO CHECK THE FLAMES BY THE USE OF DYNAMITE. DURING THE DAY A BLAST COULD BE HEARD IN ANY SECTION AT INTERVALS OF ONLY A FEW MINUTES, AND BUILDINGS NOT DESTROYED BY FIRE WERE BLOWN TO ATOMS. BUT THROUGH THE GAPS MADE THE FLAMES JUMPED AND ALTHOUGH THE FAILURES OF THE HEROIC EFFORTS OF THE POLICE FIREMEN AND SOLDIERS WERE AT TIMES SICKENING, THE WORK WAS CONTINUED WITH A DESPERATION THAT WILL LIVE AS ONE OF THE FEATURES OF THE TERRIBLE DISASTER. MEN WORKED LIKE FIENDS TO COMBAT THE LAUGHING, ROARING, ONRUSHING FIRE IEMON.

NO HOPE LEFT FOR SAFETY OF ANY BUILDINGS

San Francisco seems doomed to entire destruction. With a lapse in the raging of the flames just before dark, the hope was raised that with the use of the tons of dynamite the course of the fire might be checked and confined to the triangular sections it had cut out for its path. But on the Barbary Coast the fire broke out anew and as night closed in the flames were eating their way into parts untouched in their ravages during the day. To the south and the north they spread; down to the docks and out into the resident section, in and to the north of Hayes Valley. By six o'clock practically all of St. Ignatius' great buildings were no more. They had been leveled to the fiery heap that marked what was once the metropolis of the West.

The first of the big structures to go to ruin was the Call Building, the famous skyscraper. At eleven o'clock the big 18-story building was a furnace. Flames leaped from every window and shot skyward from the circular windows in the dome. In less than two hours nothing remained but the tall skeleton.

By five o'clock the Palace Hotel was in ruins. The old hostelry, famous the world over, withstood the seige until the last and although dynamite was used in frequent blasts to drive

Continued on Page Two

BLOW BUILDINGS UP TO CHECK FLAMES

The dynamiting of buildings in the track of the fire, to stay the progress of the flames, was in charge of John Bermingham, Jr., superintendent of the California Powder Works. Several experienced men from the powder works, assisted by policemen and members of the fire department, did the hazardous work of blowing up the buildings. They were razed in sets of threes, but the open spaces where the shattered buildings fell were quickly turned into holocausts of flame. The work was most effective in the business blocks east of Kearny street.

WHOLE CITY IS ABLAZE

At 10 o'clock last night the Occidental Hotel was destroyed by the flames which swept unchecked across Montgomery street and attacked the block bounded by Montgomery, Sutter, Bush and Kearny, the new Merchants' Exchange building was a mass of flames from basement to tower.

The Union Trust building and Crocker-Woolworth Bank were both ablaze and the Chronicle building and other buildings in the block were threatened by the flames.

Shortly after 10 o'clock the fire had eaten its way southward from Portsmouth Square to Kearny and California streets. The entire section fronting on the west side of Kearny street seemed doomed.

All the buildings adjoining the Hall of Justice were ablaze and the firemen were striving to save the structure by using dynamite. It is almost a certainty that everybuilding contained in the section bounded by Clay, Kearny, Market and East streets will be consumed.

The flames had eaten their way westward in the residence section as far as Gough street. There, by dynamiting blocks ter blocks, the fireman succeeded in hecking the devouring element.

CHURCH OF SAINT IGNATIUS IS DESTROYED

The magnificent church and College of St. Ignatius, on the northwest corner of Van Ness avenue and Hayes street represents in its destruction a material loss of over $1,000,000. The actual cost of the great building was over $900,000, but during the years which have elapsed since its erection the church has been enriched by paintings and frescoes, which were priceless. Some of them were works of art which can never be replaced, however willing those interested in the church might be to meet any expense in the effort.

MAYOR CONFERS WITH MILITARY AND CITIZENS

At 1 o'clock yesterday afternoon 50 representative citizens of San Francisco met the Mayor, the Chief of Police and the United States Military authorities in the police office in the basement of the Hall of Justice. They had been summoned thither by Mayor Schmitz early in the forenoon, the fearful possibilities of the situation having forced themselves upon him immediately after the shock of earthquake in the morning, and the news which at once reached him of the completeness of the diaster. He lost no time in making out a list of citizens from whom to seek advice and assistance, and in summoning them to the conference. It was called at the Hall of Justice, as virtually the first news which reached the Mayor regarding the extent of the disaster was that of the ruin of the City Hall. He did not realize that even while the conference was to be going on cornices would be crashing down and windows falling in fragments in the Hall of Justice also, and that before sunset desperate efforts would be made to blow the structure up in the vain endeavor by this means to check the advance of the flames in the northern section of the downtown district.

All, or nearly all of the citizens summoned to the conference

Continued on Page Two

TELEGRAPH HILL BURNING

*T*elegraph Hill Burning.
A frightening view of the
conflagration from the Bay.

◄ This hastily assembled and uniquely
cooperative reportorial effort was printed
on the presses of the Oakland Tribune and
distributed free of charge. The special
edition was voraciously consumed by San
Franciscans, eager for any and all news.

THE BANCROFT LIBRARY, UNIVERSITY OF CALIFORNIA, BERKELEY.

AT LEAST 500 ARE DEAD

NO HOPE LEFT FOR SAFETY OF ANY BUILDINGS

(Continued From Page 1.)

the fire away from the swept section toward Mission street. they made their way to the point of the hotel until the old place began to crumble away in the blaze

The City Hall is a complete wreck The entire part of the building from Larkin street down City Hall avenue to Leavenworth, down from top of dome tothe steps is ruined. The colossal pillars supporting the arches at the entrance fell into the avenue far out across the car tracks and the thousands of tons of bricks and debris that followed them piled into a mountainous heap.. The west wing sagged and crumbled, caving into a shapeless mass. At the last every vestige of stone was swept away by the shock and the building laid bare nearly to its McAllister street side. Only a shell remained to the north, and the huge steel frame stood gaping until the fire that swept from the Hayes Valley set the debris ablaze and hid the structure in a cloud of smoke. Every document of the City government is destroyed. Nothing remains but a ghastly past of the once beautiful structure. It will be necessary to entirely rebuild the Hall.

Mechanics' Pavilion, covering an entire block, went before the flames in a quarter of an hour. . The big wooden structure burned like tinder and in less time than it takes to write it was flat upon the ground.

The flames had come from the west, this time fanned by a lively wind. Down from Hayes Valley they swooped, destroying residences in entire rows, sending to cinders the business houses and leaping the gaps caused by the dynamiting of homes. They had stolen their way out from the Mission while a dense crowd blocked that street. So quickly did they make their way to the north of Market that their approach was not noticed. When it was realized that the danger had come to this particular residence section, the police and the cavalry drove the crowd back i haste to the north and out of uar way. Down Hayes street playing the cross streets coming on like a demon, the fire swept over St. Ignacious Church, leveled barns and houses, and, as if accomplishing a purpose long desired, blazed down to the front of Mechanics' Pavilion. Only shortly before the patients in this crude hospital had been removed to other hospitals in outlying districts.

From the big shed the flames spread to the north, east, south and west, everywhere. Confusion reigned. Women fainted and men fought their way into the adjoining apartment houses to rescue something from destruction — anything, if only enough to cover their wives and their babies when the cold of the night came on. There was a scene that made big, brave men cry. There were the weeping tots in their mothers' arms wailing with fear of the awful calamity; salesmen and soldiers fighting to get the women out of harm's way through the crowd; heroic dashes in the ambulances and the patrol wagons after the sick and injured and willing men, powerless as the mouse in the cluth of the lion, ready to fight the destroyer, but driven back step by step while their homes went down before them.

It was when the terrible shock of the first big rumbler was passing off, that San Franciscans, sent scurrying into the streets in their nightclothes, turned to the east and south and first saw the pillars of flame that have bred such wicked destruction.

Down in the wholesale district south of the cable and along through the section facing the city's front, the flames appeared. Fire shot into the air from ever corner. Before the first alarm was sent in the fire was beyond control The city was beyond saving from the time that the first blaze broke toward the heavens.

Gradually the flames stole along Mission and Howard streets, and then rapidly they made their way from building to building until Seventh street was reached. Out into the warehouse district bounded by Sansome on the west and the bay on the north and east they went and such structures as the Wellman Peck Building and the Tillman, Bendel building were made into whitened wills, left tottering in the breeze that was blowing. Everywhere were scenes of horror. People rushed frantically through the streets, looking for missing relatives and rescue parties parties were formed to go into the burning blocks to save life. Here and there the grim-faced men dug out the unfortunates who had gone down into the shapeless piles of debris when the big shock came. Man fought to save man and many times did the sickened crowds turn away as they saw the rescuers driven back by the flames that reacheddown through the ruins ti claim their victims.

Steadily the fire found its way into the uptown retail districts. From the sout hand east the south side of Market was attacked. One by one the familiar buildings went down. Levi Strauss and Company, Zellerbach and Company, Holbrook, Merrill and Stetson, Hicks-Judd Company, D. N. and E. Walters, W. W. Montague, the Donohoe estate building, Uhl Brothers, the Bancroft Building,—all the places that have made the San Francisco business district.. Everyone of them went.. They can't be enumerated.. The work of the fire demon was too complete to make that necessary. . From Mission to Market and east to Ninth the many-storied structures were gutted. True, many of these places had crumbled when the earth shook, but evidence of this was remooved in the path ff the flames.

From Second to Third streets Market street held its own until late in the afternoon. The Call Building was ablaze, but the Examiner Building, the Palace Hotel, the Grand, and the other structures toward Second street stood.. Two attempts were made to dynamite the new Monadnock Building when it was seen that the Hearst structure was doomed. And slowly came the blaze from Mission street just below Third, sweeping everything before it and igniting the Examiner Annex. Then the main building took fire and by two o'clock only the Third street wall was standing. Later the Palace took fire in the rear and the flames made quick proogress to Market street. By five o'clock Colonel Kirkpatrick's famous hotel was no more. The Grand went at the same time, and in a few minutes the flames had Market street again. At Sansome they combined with the fire on the north side of the street but the changeable winds kept the fire back from the buildings extending from this point to Kearney street.

At seven o'clock the entire region lying just back of the Hall of Justice was on fire. The dynamite did no good. From the Fairmount Hotel now could be seen the gigantic semicircle of flame extending from the Mission at about Thirteenth street down through the entire southern end of the city proper, along the channel, over the hill, along the waterfront, through the wholesale district and over onto Barbary Coast.

At nine o'clock the Crocker-Woolworth Bank Building was was on fire at the gore. Across from it is the railroad building and Masonic Temple. Only a row of small buildings separate it from the Chronicle Building.

Then the fire fighters prepared for the thing they hoped would not happen. It was certain that the fire would spread northward and join the inferno near the Hall of Justice. Dynamite was placed in the Hall of Justice to be sent into the air at the signal. The flames on lower Kearny street had gained the office buildings on the west side of the street. This means the doom of Chinatown. Thousands on thousands of Celestials scurried over Nob Hill to safety.

PARDEE ISSUES PROCLAMATION

OAKLAND, April 18—Governor Pardee tonight issued a proclamation declaring tomorrow, Thursday, a legal holiday, and that all business be suspended throughout the State. This followed a conference held by the Governor with Mayor Mott, Lieutenant J. Anderson, of the Adjutant General's staff, and Judge Henry A. Melvin at the Mayor's office. Governor Pardee said he had sent Lieutenant Anderson to San Francisco to investigate conditions. The Governor came to Oakland as quickly as possible in order to be in touch at the nearest point with which he could keep in communication with San Francisco.

BUILDINGS ARE ALL RUINED

Fire Chief Nick Ball and Fire Warden MacDonald, are making a tour of the City of Oakland condemning all buildings damaged by the earthquake and left in a menacing condition. The tower of the First Baptist church has been ordered torn down, and other structures throughout the city have also been placed under the official ban.

EFFECTS HEROIC RESCUE

The disaster brought forth hundreds of heroic deeds. About the only persons in the awoke when the trembior occurred were the mechanical workers of the newspapers, policemen and saloonmen. Among the heroes were Emile Dengel, foreman of "The Examiner" stereotyping department, and several of his men. After the first crash, and upon their escape from the building they were passing Krumm's cafe when they heard cries for help coming from beneath the debris of the place. Dengel rushed out to a passing hose cart, seized an axe, and with his great strength began chopping a hole through the structure to release its captive inmates.

A woman's voice kept saying from beneath the ruins, "I'm all right, hurry and get me out." The imprisoned people—Krumm, the proprietor, his wife and a waiter—were finally released, but none too soon for 20 minutes later flames consumed the fallen structure.

Later Dengel caught a vandal looting the body of a dead man; and upon Dengel seizing him the fellow turned and made a vicious cut at Dengel with a key-hole saw. He was finally overpowered and arrested by the police.

NEWSPAPER ROW IS GUTTED

The Examiner and Call buildings gave the inferno of flame that swept up from the district south of Market street a stubborn fight and prevented the fire from sweeping up Kearny street. The two buildings burned slowly, and held out for hours, only to be finally gutted.

When the Winchester Hotel crumbled into ruins at 11 o'clock the cafe in the top of the twenty-story Call building began spouting fire. At that time Market street as far as Seventh street was burning as a single block from the Bohemian Cafe.

As the fire burned out in the top stories of the Call, it descended and turned the building into a fountain of flame.

At 12 o'clock the annex of the Hearst building took fire and a half an hour later the rear wall fell. Shortly afterwards the fire appeared through the frieze on the seventh floor, where the editorial rooms were located, but it was 3 o'clock before the windows of the lower floors began to belch flames.

The fire burned out gradually and the building remained standing, completely gutted.

At 4 o'clock the ground floor of the Call building began to burn again with redoubled fury, but the building stood amid the surrounding ruins, a denuded frame of blackened stone.

MAYOR CONFERS WITH MILITARY

(Continued From Page 1.)

responded. Among those promptly on hand were Hartley and Herbert Law, capitalists, the brothers Magee of Thomas Magee & Sons, real estate men; J. Downey Harvey, of the Ocean Shore Railway Company; ex-Mayor James D. Phelan, Garrett McEnerney, the prominent attorney; ex-Judge C. W. Slack, W. H. Leary, manager of the Tivoli Opera House; J. T. Howell, of Baldwin & Howell, real esate men; former City Attorney Franklin K. Lane, also many others.

No time was lost at the meeting, and almost the first words spoken by the Mayor breathed strongly of the grimness of the disaster and its accompaniments.

"Let it be given out," said the Mayor, sternly, "that three men have already been shot down without mercy for looting. Let it be also understood that the order has been given to all soldiers and policemen to do likewise without hesitation in the cases of any and all miscreants who may seek to take advantage of the city's awful misfortune. I will ask the Chief of Police and the representatives of the Federal military authorities here present if I do not echo their sentiments inthis?"

The uniformed officials to whom the Mayor turned as he spoke signified their acquiescence, and Chief Dinan stated also he would undertake the distribution throughout the city of printed proclamations making public the order.

Then the Mayor told those present of what had already been done t olighten the effects of the disaster. For one thing he had secured 2400 tents which were already in process of erection in Jefferson Square, Golden Gate Park and on the Presidio grounds, for the accommodation of the homeless

Garrett McEnerney, moved, and the large number of other prominent citizens present unanimously voted, that the Mayor be authorized to draw checks for any amount for the relief of the suffering, all of the gentlemen present pledging themselves to make such checks good. Ex-Mayor Phelan was appointed chairman of a Relief Finance Committee with full authority to select his associates.

The Mayor announced that orders had already been given forbidding the burning of either gas or electric currents, even where possible. During the fire citizens must get along with other light, as no chances could be taken of a renewed outbreak of flames. Police Chief Dinan stated that he had also instructed his men to announce all over the city that no fires were to be lighted in stoves or grates anywhere lest the chimneys should be defective as the result of the earthquake.

Then the statement was made that expressmen were charging $30 a load to haul goods—a rate which was prohibitive to poor people. The announcement provoked great indigation, and an immediate order from Mayor Schmitz, in which Dinan heartily concurred.

"Tell your men," said the Mayor, "to seize the wagons of all such would-be extortionists, and make use of them for the public good. The question of recompense will b eseen to later."

Then a further notice was ordered distributed as widely as possibly throughout the city instructing all householders to remain at home at night for protection of their families and property during the continuance of the trouble and excitement

It was at this point that the explosion of a heavy charge of dynamite used in blowing up a building a block away brought glass and cornice work in theHall of Justice crashing down. At once W. H. Leary and J. Downey Harvey urged that the Mayor at least immediately remove from the building. "Your life is too valuable, Mayor," said Mr. Harvey, "at this dreadful juncture for any unnecessary risk to be taken."

To this all present conceded, and a few moments later an adjournment was taken to the center of Portsmouth Square, across Kearney street. There, in close and dangerous proximity to a great pile of dynamite, brought thither to be used for the necessary destruction of buildings, the Mayor and his officials continused for some time longer to discuss the situation. When they finally separated it was with the agreement to meet again this morning at 10 o'clock at the Fairmont.

The Never Ending Search for the Missing in the Earthquake and Fire Devastated Ruins of San Francisco.

"An enumeration of the buildings destroyed would be a directory of San Francisco. An enumeration of the buildings undestroyed would be a line and several addresses. An enumeration of the deeds of heroism would stock a library and bankrupt the Carnegie medal fund. An enumeration of the dead—will never be made."

–Jack London, *Collier's*, May 5, 1906

32C. The Never Ending Search for the Missing in the Earthquake and Fire Devastated Ruins of San Francisco.

ENTIRE CITY OF SAN FRANCISCO IN DANGER OF BEING ANNIHILATED

Big Business Buildings Already Consumed by Fire and Dynamite--30,000 Smaller Structures Swept Out and Remainder Are Doomed

PANIC-STRICKEN PEOPLE FLEE

SAN FRANCISCO April 18.—This city lies in smouldering ruins and total annihilation seems to be its fate. The magnificent business district lying between the water's edge and Tenth street and even still farther west is destroyed, and there is scarcely any hope of saving but a few of the magnificent skyscrapers that have been erected during the last ten years.

Thirty thousand houses were either partially or wholly destroyed by earthquake, and the subsequent fire which started in 100 different places simultaneously has swept the city from one end to the other. Hundreds of buildings are burning without any effort being made to check the fire By tonight it is estimated that there will be 180,000 homeless people.

NUMBER OF DEAD.

The number of the dead cannot be roughly estimated One hundred bodies about have been recovered, but hundreds perished miserably in the broken down wooden houses along the water front, in the Mission and along Market street

Falling walls pinned many victims fast and they were compelled to suffer untold agonies while the fiery flames crept toward them. Some believe that the number of deaths will reach the appalling figure of 5000, but from the number of bodies thus far recovered the figure may be excessive.

PEOPLE IN PANIC.

The entire city presents a scene of indescribable confusion. The fire zone is so large that it takes two and one-half hours to go around it Every automobile vehicle and wagon in the city was pressed into service as ambulances

Mayor Schmitz appointed 3000 or more special policeman. It is estimated that aside from the regular fire department there were 25,000 firefighters Marvelous deeds of heroism are reported on all sides

There were many thrilling rescues. The deeds of valor performed by the firemen and police would fill a volume

TURNED INTO HOSPITAL.

The Mechanics' Pavilion was early this morning turned into a hospital for the city injured, and a resting place for the unfortunate dead.

Every physician and nurse in the city volunteered their services. Shortly after noon the flames hedged the pavilion about and the injured and dead were removed in wagons, automobiles to the Presidio, the Children's Hospital and other hospitals which go to the front and assist the police in maintaining order.

Market street at the two extremes

of the fire and all the intervening streets are practically under martial law

Mayor Schmitz to prevent disorder ordered all of the saloons closed. There were but few cases of theft reported.

The Call building is already destroyed utterly and it is probable that the Examiner building and the Chronicle building will also be destroyed.

The Emporium is reduced to ashes as is the Flood building. The magnificent new store of Hale Brothers was dynamited in an effort to stop the progress of the flames which burned with the same uncontrollable intensity that was manifested in the Mission.

CITY HALL GONE.

The City Hall is a grand mass of ruins. It is totally destroyed The surrounding streets are choken with the debris. Several other buildings were destroyed as the huge building tottered to its destruction. In all 150 of San Francisco's best buildings have been destroyed and probably 20,000 others.

STOPS CLOCKS.

The earthquake which did such terrific damage occurred at 5:16 o'clock precisely. The clock on the dome of the Ferry building stopped precisely at that time. The Ferry building itself was cracked and split, but is still in a safe condition Twenty or more wharves and the buildings on them collapsed utterly along the water front

STEAMER SUNK.

The steamer San Pablo was struck and sunk by a huge girder which fell on it How many lives were lost is not known

Some of the crew are missing but owing to the great confusion nothing definite could be ascertained Another vessel is reported to have been sunk by the walls of a building falling on it. The name of the vessel is not known. After the work of demolition had been accomplished by the earthquake fires in twenty places started up along the water front

It is assumed that the twistings and turnings of the earth broke the electric wires and caused the fires to break out.

MANY ALARMS

In twenty minutes' time alarms to the number of several hundred had been turned in

The fire department responded but the extent of the conflagration made the streams of water poured on them seem like toy streams

On the water front the hose was connected with the bay and a fair showing made.

Owing to the fact that the mains of the Spring Valley Water Company were

broken by the earthquake during the early progress of the fire nothing could be done to stay the hungry blaze.

BUILDINGS DYNAMITED.

More than 100 buildings were dynamited with hope that the fire could be kept within a certain district.

In the business district, at Sansome and Bush streets, the flames are supposed to be under control. Twenty buildings were dynamited in this district.

One of the particularly sad features of the catastrophe was the drowning of a score or more persons in the Mission. Apparently the earthquake was more violent at this point than anywhere else in the city Depressions of ten feet were made.

MAINS BROKEN.

The mains of the Spring Valley were broken at this point and flooded the tenements. Many of the victims were pinned in the basements by falling walls and had no recourse but to await their fate by drowning.

BIG FIRE IN MISSION

SAN FRANCISCO, April 18.—A great fire is raging in the Mission district and is utterly beyond control. Before night, it is estimated, that in this particular section of the city 50,000 persons will be homeless.

RESIDENCES BURNING

SAN FRANCISCO, April 18.—An intense fire broke out late this afternoon immediately west of the Mechanics' Pavilion, threatening to destroy one of the most thickly populated residence districts of the city. As there were no fire apparatus on hand the flames are raging unchecked.

750 ARE TREATED

SAN FRANCISCO, April 18.—Up to half-past two this afternoon, more than 750 persons who were seriously injured by the earthquake and the fire, had been treated at the various hospitals throughout of the city. The proportion or dead is not as large as it might be expected. Only twenty of those admitted to the hospitals have died since their admission.

DEAD IN STREET

SAN FRANCISCO April 18.—The front of the Bailey and La Coste building on Clay near Montgomery fell in. Three men and seven horses were killed and seven horses were still lying there at 9 o'clock.

Captain Gleason of the Police Department was seriously injured at noon today by the falling of tiling.

EMPORIUM IN RUINS

SAN FRANCISCO, April 18.—The Emporium is a mass of ruins, with nothing but the walls of this magnificent store standing. The buildings immediately adjoining it are doomed to destruction.

DYNAMITE BUILDINGS

SAN FRANCISCO, April 18.—At 2:30 o'clock this afternoon the firemen are dynamiting one of the most imposing structures on Market street. Buildings in the vicinity of the United States Mint and the United States Postoffice were blown up in the hope that they would be saved. Both of them are in grave danger, and while standing the shock of the earthquake, will probably fall victims of the uncontrollable conflagration raging in that vicinity.

RUINS 20 COMPANIES

SAN FRANCISCO April 18.—From the present appearance of things, it is probable that twenty or more insurance companies will be ruind. The managers of the larger companies are of the opinion that they will be able to meet the losses. In any event all the insurance companies doing business in this city have been hit a staggering blow, from the effects of which many will never recover

SAN FRANSICO, April 18.—The United States bonded warehouse where liquor is stored before the duties are collected is destroyed

DOCTOR'S BRAVERY

SAN FRANCISCO, April 18.—Dr. McGinty of the Central Emergency Hospital while attempting to rescue some persons who had been buried by the falling wall was himself pinned to the ground by additional debris that fell. He was rescued and insisted on resuming his duties of attending the wounded and injured.

FATEFUL BUILDING

SAN FRANCISCO, April 18.—The scene at the Mechanics' pavilion during the early hours of the morning and up until noon, when all the injured and dead were removed, because of the threatened destruction of the building by fire, was one of indescribable sadness. Sisters, brothers, wives and sweethearts searched eagerly for some missing dear ones. Thousands of persons hurriedly went through the building inspecting the cots on which the sufferers lay in the hope that they would locate some loved one that was missing.

The dead were placed in one portion of the building, and the remainder was devoted to hospital purposes. After the fire forced the nurses in positions to desert the building, the eager crowds followed them to the Presidio and Children's Hospital, where they renewed their search for missing relatives.

WITHOUT A NEWSPAPER

SAN FRANCISCO, April 18.—The buildings occupied by the San Francisco Post and the San Francisco Bulletin are threatened with fire and may be consumed. This will leave the city without a single daily newspaper.

DAMAGE A BILLION

SAN FRANCISCO, April 18.—Market street which has been the pride of San Francisco since 1849 is simply one black mass of ruin. It is estimated that up to the present time the fire and earthquake have done at least $150,000,000 worth of damage to the thoroughfare alone. The damage to the entire city will probably aggregate $1,000,000,000. There is, however, no accurate means by which the loss can be ascertained.

THEATERS RUINED

All of San Francisco's best playhouses, including the Majestic, Columbia and Grand Opera House, are a mass of ruins. The earthquake demolished them for all practical purposes, and at the present time it appears the fires will complete the work of demolition. The Rialto and Casserly buildings were burned to the ground, as was everything in that district.

The Terminal Hotel at the foot of Market street fell this morning and buried twenty persons under the debris. These were incinerated, and there is no possibility of learning their identity.

NARROW ESCAPE

SAN FRANCISCO, April 18.—The stereotypers and pressmen of the Examiner and Call, as soon as the temblor was felt, rushed out of their buildings and found that the coffee house at Stevenson and Third street had collapsed.

They immediately set to work with axes and anything in the way of an implement they could arm themselves with and set to work to rescue those inside.

SAN FRANCISCO, April 18.—Every available conveyance is pressed into service and is used in hauling explosives from the Presidio for the blowing up of buildings in the center of the city.

Pacific Mutual Building and the Italian–American Bank Building, San Francisco, Wrecked by Earthquake. Corner of Montgomery and Sacramento streets. "The streets in places had sunk three or four feet, in others great humps had appeared four or five feet high. The street car tracks were bent and twisted out of shape. Electric wires lay in every direction. Streets on all sides were filled with brick and mortar, buildings either completely collapsed or brick fronts had just dropped completely off…. Warehouses and large wholesale houses of all descriptions either down, or walls bulging, or else twisted, buildings moving bodily two or three feet out of a line and still standing with walls all cracked."–Jerome B. Clark, in *The San Francisco Calamity*, Charles Morris, 1906

LOSS IS $200,000,000

HEARTBREAKING SCENES AT THE PAVILION

The immense Mechanics' Pavilion, the former scene of many pleasures and sports, was utilized as a huge morgue and hospital, and soon its space was filled with dead, dying and injured, and its vaulted ceiling echoed their cries and groans. Fully 300 persons were treated. Doctors and nurses by the score hurried to the scene and volunteered their much-needed aid. Drug stores were broken into for medical supplies, and the department stores ransacked for pillows and mattresses for the injured.

The scenes and cries were fearful to behold and hear. The operating tables were filled all the time. Infants were brought in in their mothers' arms, burned and bleeding. Men and women had been caught by falling walls and horribly mangled, in many cases the broken bones protruding through the flesh.

At 1 o'clock in the afternoon the flames, which had been gradually creeping nearer and nearer to this improvised hospital, finally reached it.

Dr. Charles Millar, chief surgeon of the Emergency Hospital, immediately ordered all patients removed.

Every sort of vehicle was pressed into service, and the dead and injured removed. The wounded were taken to Golden Gate Park, for there was no other haven of refuge not in the danger zone, and were laid upon the grass. Many were taken into near by houses by kind-hearted people and cared for.

At the Harbor Hospital fully 100 injured persons had been treated up to 10 o'clock in the morning.

Upon the receipt of the news of the disaster torpedo boats and tugs loaded with navy and army doctors, nurses and sailors, were dispatched from the Mare island Navy Yard and Goat Island, and rendered great aid to the injured in the Harbor hospital.

Never was there such a scene in San Francisco as was there in Mechanics' Pavilion yesterday. Too much praise cannot be given the doctors and the nurses who gave their aid to the injured. Their work was beyond praise. As assistants to Dr. Millar, Doctors Pinkham, Herzog, Tillman, Roche, Goodale and fifty or more volunteers performed the surgical work.

And the nurses. Well, their efforts will long be remembered. Young women from the hospitals, graduates in the nurses' homes, neighbor women and those who drove to the door of the Mechanics' Pavilion in their private automobiles, all took a hand in the work. Catholic sisters worked by the side of Salvation Army lasses, and the priests and ministers made their way among the cots, giving the comfort of their cloth.

MAYOR MOTT OF OAKLAND SENDS MESSAGE

The following message was sent last evening to Mayor Schmitz by Mayor Frank K. Mott, of Oakland:

Oakland, April 18th.

Hon. E. E. Schmitz:

Mayor of San Francisco:

Large committee formed tonight ready to go to San Francisco and render whatever assistance you need in caring for the injured and helpless. Los Angeles has wired me offering similar help. Let me know at once, and will act immediately.

FRANK K. MOTT,

Mayor.

FIVE KILLED IN OAKLAND THEATRE

OAKLAND, April 18.—The earthquake shock began in Oakland at 5:14 a. m., lasting twenty-eight seconds, in which time nearly all the principal business buildings were badly damaged, five people were hurled to death in the ruins of the Empire Theater building, and scarcely a residence in the city escaped without more or less damage. Those who met death amid the ruins of the theater were Otto Witcher, 45 years of age, Amelia Witcher, 13 years of age, Louis Marney, 25 years old, and his wife, aged 25 years, and an unidentified man. J. P. Judge, a locomotive engineer, died from heart failure caused by shock and excitement.

All were caught by the falling walls of the building, and were buried beneath tons of brick and broken timbers, the bodies were removed from the ruins by the firemen, and were removed to the Morgue.

The buildings which suffered most from the terrific shock, were the Physicians' Building on Washington street, between Twelfth and Thirteenth streets, the entire front of the upper floor being torn away and hurled into the street below; the Central Bank Building, the walls of both corners fronting on Broadway being wrecked, the First Baptist Church, a handsome stone building at Telegraph avenue and Hobart street, was so badly wrecked that it will have to be torn down, a three-story building on Thirteenth street between Broadway and Washington streets, a complete wreck; the building occupied by the Crane Company, at Thirteenth and Webster streets; St. Francis de Sales church, one wall of which was torn loose from the building; St. Mary's College, and the First Unitarian church.

Not a brick or stone building in the city escaped damage, in most cases a part of the walls of the upper stories being torn away and thrown into the streets. At the corner o fEleventh and Clay streets, a bakery wagon was caught by the falling debris, being reduced to kindling wood, and the horse killed.

Awful as is the damage to this city, however, it is nothing compared to the appalling calamity which has overtaken San Francisco, and the people of Oakland are thankful that the horrors of fire were not added to those of the earthquake.

Owing to the fact that the entire telephone and telegraph system has been rendered temporarily useless, it is impossible to secure details a sto the amount of damage done in the interior of the county. The newly erected magnasite plant at Fruitvale has been entirely wrecked, and a number of other buildings more or less damaged. Among the Oakland and East Oakland water front a number of warehouses and wharves have been partly demolished and will have to be rebuilt.

At Niles large boulders dislodged from the hill and crashed through the pipe line of the Spring Valley Water Company, and the flood of water released from the big main washed out the tracks of the Southern Pacific Company, delaying trains for several hours, and helping to cripple the water supply of stricken San Francisco. A number of buildings in Niles were badly damaged.

At Centerville the entire front

MARTIAL LAW IS DECLARED

After a conference between Schmitz and Chief of Police Dinan, San Francisco was placed under martial law at 9 o'clock yesterday morning.

All the troops at the Presidio were rushed to the city and mounted couriers were sent out to notify commanding officers of nea.by garrisons that the Federal troops were needed in the stricken city.

In less than an hour more than 2000 regular soldiers were patrolling the streets under orders to shoot thieves and vandals on sight.

Mounted men drove back the frantic crowds by riding into the press of people, and many were injured in trying to escape from the riders.

Disorderly throngs rushing over the fire lines called for quick and effective methods in handling the jam of people.

Many acts of vandalism were committed and during the excitement crooks looted countless damaged stores and office buildings.

Colonel Morris commanding officer of the Presidio, is in command of the troops guarding the city, and Major Brown is in command of the artillery division, comprising the First, Ninth and Twenty-fourth Light Batteries, mounted troops and five companies of heavy artillery, dismounted.

One troop of the Fourteenth Cavalry is acting as mounted couriers.

The Twenty-second Infantry arrived at noon from Fort McDowell.

Drafts of troops were sent from Alcatraz and Angel Islands.

More than 5000 regular soldiers in addition to the militia, police and special officers kept order in the city last night.

◆◆◆◆◆◆◆◆◆◆◆◆

wall of the Centerville Bank collapsed, and other buildings were damaged.

Berkeley escaped with little damage, a few chimnies being thrown down, and the walls of some of the brick buildings slightly damaged. Not one of the buildings of the University of California was affected by the shock.

The Southern Pacific sheds, and the coal bunkers at Long Wharf collapsed into the bay, carrying with them thousands of tons of coal.

Another heavy shock was felt at Martinez at 6 o'clock tonight, which still further wrecked the already tottering buildings, and should there be any further disturbance, many of them will collapse. The damage already done by the earthquake is estimated at $50,000.

SAN JOSE IS RUINED

Passengers arriving on trains from other cities in California bring tales of death and disaster from nearly al of them. The loss of life and property in San Jose was great, it being estimated that nearly 50 people were killed and many more injured. The Vendome Hotel Annex was badly wrecked, between 10 and 15 people being killed there. The St. Francis Hotel there was badly damaged, one aged woman being killed. Hiram Bailey sustained internal injuries. Dr. DeCrow was killed and his wife badly injured. Every business building in the city was demolished to such an extent that nearly all wll have to be torn down. The postoffice building was half demolished, the front of the new Court house fell into the street and the entire building is a wreck. The First Presbyterian Chuch is conpletely demolished. Martial law has been declared, the State miitia guarding property together with 500 special deputies.

From Santa Cruz, Monterey, Gilroy and Hollister come reports that all of these cities have been completely wrecked, the damage at Hollister being greatest, even all of the frame residences at the place being razed to the ground. The death list at Santa Cruz is reported to be very large.

..All of the Stanford University buildings at Palo Alto with one exception, are reported demolished. No loss of life has been reported from there.

The State Insane Asylum at Agnew is reported demolished, the superintendent and his wife being killed and seventeen nurses injured. Two hundred inmates of the asylum escaped and are roaming over the countryside.

..The military academy at Warren was partly demolished and the students are making every effort to get away from there.

MESSAGE COMES TO PARDEE FROM ROOSEVELT

OAKLAND, April 18.—Early this morning Governor Pardee received the following message from President Roosevelt:

"It was difficult to credit the news of the calamity that had befallen San Francisco. I feel the greatest concern for you and the people, not only of San Francisco, but of California in the terrible disaster. You will let me know if there is anything that the givernment can do.

"THEODORE ROOSEVELT."

Governor Pardee also received telegrams of sympathy and offering help from the governors of Louisiana, Washington and Oregon.

The following message was sent by Governor Pardee to Mayor Schmitz of San Francisco:

"Am appalled and overwhelmed by the great calamity to San Francisco, only meager details of which have reached me. I extend sympathy and assurance of my earnest desire to help those in distress in any manner in which I am able.

"GEORGE C. PARDEE."

REFUGEES GO TO OAKLAND

OAKLAND, April 18.—Thousands of refugees, rendered homeless by the terrible calamity which has overtaken San Francisco, have come to this city to escape from the terrors across the bay. On learning of this the Realty Syndicate at once offered Idora Park for the use of those left without shelter by the earthquake. The offer has been gratefully accepted by the Police and Fire Commissioners, and two hundred cots have been placed in the theater for the use of the refugees. Relief stations have also been established at the City Hall, and at the various public parks throughout the city.

Other relief stations have also been established in such of the churches throughout the city as are considered safe for use as such.

Mayor Frank K. Mott has issued the following appeal to the people of Oakland to aiid the authorities in preserving peace and order:

"To the People of Oakland:

"The earthquake this morning visited upon our city a great calamity, yet it is a source of much satisfaction that we were spared from a conflagration and serious loss of life. The officials of the city have the situation well in hand, but I desire to appeal to the people to co-operate with the authorities in maintaining peace and order.

"As many buildings are in an unsafe condition the public are admonished to keep off the streets, and particularly warned against congregating in groups. It is also very essential that precaution be used in the building of fires until the chimneys have been inspected and repaired. Those who have not either gas or oil stoves are advised that danger may be avoided by moving their stoves out of doors.

"FRANK K. MOTT, Mayor."

Chief N. A. Ball, of the Oakland Fire Department, has made the following suggestions to householders regarding fires in houses the chimneys of which have fallen:

"Build no fires in coal stoves, grates or fire places until the interior of the chimneys has been inspected, cleaned out and put in repair. In many places where the chimneys appear to be all right, they may have cracks in the interior or may be stopped up with refuse, which might cause a blind fire.

While the earthquake was at its height, the two smokestacks at the gas works at the foot of Grove street fell, crashing through the roof of the works, crushing the boiler and killing one of the firemen, whose identity has not yet been learned.

The force of the earthquake has caused the Twelfth street dam, opposite the boathouses on Lake Merritt, to sink eighteen inches.

A report comes from Martinez that the Martinez Bank Building, one of the finest structures in the town, has been completely destroyed.

It is at present impossible to estimate the amount of damage to property in this city, owing to the fact that practically no inspection has been made of the buildings, except by Fire Warden George McDonald, and this only for the purpose of condemning those which are unsafe and must be torn down. Many of the structures which from the outside show little apparent damage, on closer examination prove to have been so badly twisted and racked by the shock that it is feared they will have to be torn down.

SANTA ROSA IS A TOTAL WRECK

SANTA ROSA, April 18—This city is a total wreck. There are 10,000 homeless men, women and children huddled together. The loss of life is not to be estimated. It will probably reach the thousands.

As the last great seismic tremor spent its force in the earth the whole business portion tumbled into ruins. The main street is piled many feet deep with the fallen buildings. Not one business building from the California Northwestern Pacific depot, in the ertreme west end of the city, to the Atheneum on the est, is left intact.

This destruction includes all of the county buildings. The four-story court house, with its dome mounting high into the heavens, is merely a pile of broken masonry. Nothing is left.

Identification is impossible.

What was not destroyed by the earthquake has been swept by fire. Until the flames leaped into the heavens there was hope of saving the residence district. It was soon apparent that any such idea, that might have been entertained, was to be abandoned.

This was appreciated by the citizens and they prepared to desert their homes. Not even their household goods were taken. They made for the fields and hills, to watch the destruction of one of the most beautiful cities of the West.

The water system of the municipality was destroyed by the earthquake. Fire fighting was not to be thought of. The city was at the mercy of the elements and crumbled and cracked as the gentle west breeze from the great Pacific blew from the hill to fan the flames to undestroyed localities. Thus the citizens watched from the Rincoon hills their homes erased.

In a few cases some attempted to return to the burning city to rescue valuables. Many of them who ventured too close were overcome by the heat and smoke. They dropped, choked and fainting, in their tracks. In many instances these foolish souls were left to their fate. There were too many injured and dying who needed attendance, and who had been injured in the first awful crash to allow those who had returned o ftheir own free will to be cared for.

Later in the day some water was pumped from Santa Rosa Creek. This was, comparatively, of no use, as the fire-fighting force of the city was limited.

Among other buildings ruined are the three leading hotels: Occidetal, Saint Rose and Grand.

It was in these hostelries that the greatest number of deaths occurred. They were all brick structures, the Saint Rose having a stel frame. They fell as it constructed of playing cards, and in tahe heaps were buried the hundreds of lodgers.

..Relief was immediately dispatched from Petaluma. Carts and wagons loaded with provisions and clothing were brought in from the adjoining city during the day. These supplies were distributed among the homeless.

When the flames allowed, the ruins were searched for dead. The undertaking was far greater than had been imagined. It was found that besides the hotels, the many lodging houses and room-

OFFICER KILLED IN DYNAMITE EXPLOSION

Lieutenant Charles C. Pulis, commanding the Twenty-fourth Company of Light Artillery, was blown up by a charge of dynamite at Sixth and Jessie streets shortly before noon, and was fatally injured. He was taken to the Military Hospital at the Presidio. He had a fractured skull and several bones broken, and internal injuries. He will not recover.

Lieutenant Pulis placed a heavy charge of dynamite in a building on Sixth street. The fuse was imperfect and did not ignite the charge as soon as was expected. Pulis went into the building to relight it and the charge exploded while he was in the building.

The injured officer is a graduate of the Artillery School at Fortress Monrce, Virginia. He is thirty years of age, single, and a native of Chicago.

◆◆◆◆◆◆◆◆◆◆◆◆

ing quarters of the city contained dead.

With the limited number of men, and the mass of ruins, months must necessarily elapse before any kind of an appreciation of the fatalities can be learned. The mangled forms will be found as long as excavations are made.

On the north conditions are fully as shocking as here. There is no communication by wire or railroad between here and Healdsburg. Besides, the wires all being on the ground, the bridges crossing the Russian river at that point are in the stream. This makes all communication by rail from the northern part of Sonoma county impossible.

Many have arrived, however, on horseback and in wagons.

These messengers bring the saddest tidings of the destruction of Healdsburg, Geyserville, Cloverdale, Hopland and Ukiah. This repor takes in the country as far north as Mendocino and Lake couuties, and as far west as the Pacific Ocean. These are frontier counties and have not as large towns as farther south.

In every case the loss of life and property is as shocking as here.

In the country the farmers have converted their spacious homes and outhouses into dwellings for the people left without shelter in the cities. Every man of the country is working to relieve the suffering of their more unfortunate urban brethren.

That the beautiful old summer resort of Skaggs Hot Springs, the second oldest watering place of California, is in ruins, was reported late this afternoon. This place is located far back in the coast range of mountains, and communication with it is cut off. The report carries, however, that many were injured who were registered at the hotel.

West of here seven miles the town of Sebastopol is no more. The bank building is the only structure left standing in the village. This hamlet is located in the most fertile locality and was noted for its prosperity.

Here too many have suffered death and injuries. As here they are being cared for by the country people. The shock, from the condition of the frame buildings at Sebastopol, was even more severe than here. In most cases homes constructed of wood withstood the twisting effect of the disturbance. In this country place buildings of wood were destroyed along with the brick and stone structures.

As the residences are all constructed of wood, the injured will number large. There are not, however, so many dead in the residence section as might be expected. They were saved, in many cases, by the peculiar way in which the buildings fell. The timbers did not give way entirely and the occupants were able to crawl from the tangled mass.

Although the city of Petaluma lies but sixteen miles south of here, it escaped the mere violent shock. But few buildings were totally destroyed. The injured and dead are small.

In view of their escape the citizens of Petaluma are organizing relief parties that are being sent into the neighboring cities and towns.

To the southeast of here, Sonoma, Glen Ellen and a dozen other small towns throughout the Sonoma Valley, are all reported in ruins. The country far and wide, from the meager reports received by horsemen, must be in ruin.

How many are dead and suffering in these outlying districts cannot be ascertained at this writing. It seems that to say, "Some are alive," is the easiest and most accurate report to send to the outside world.

*D*ynamiting the Earthquake and *Fire Wrecked Bldgs on Market St.* "Squads of dynamiters began to appear. Everywhere they hurried; charges were set; the men scurried away, and with a roar and a cloud of dust a building would fall. Unfortunately many charges were set by unskilled hands, and the fire was scattered. At this time, too, most of the 'dynamiting' was done with ordinary black powder, the only explosive available; often it set fire to the ruins it had made, or hurled burning brands in all directions." —Aitken & Hilton, *A History of the Earthquake and Fire in San Francisco,* 1906

63C. Dynamiting the Earthquake and Fire Wrecked Bldgs on Market St., San Francisco.

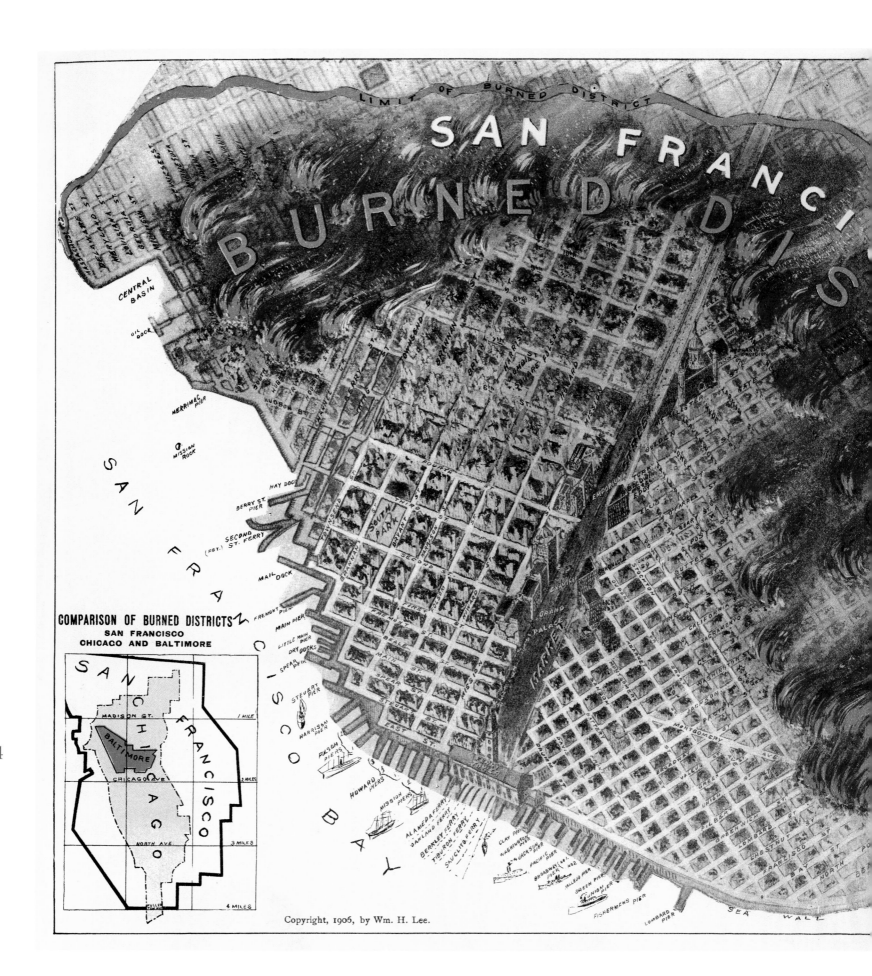

Copyright, 1906, by Wm. H. Lee.

Wᴵᴸᴸᴵᴬᴹ Rᴬɴᴅᴏʟᴘʜ Hᴇᴬʀsᴛ (1863–1951), publisher of the San Francisco *Examiner,* did much to raise awareness of and money for the City's relief and "upbuilding" effort. He returned to San Francisco from his home in New York soon after what civic leaders were already calling the Great Fire of 1906. Perhaps in an effort to inspire investor confidence, he joined with them in portraying the *earthquake* damage as minimal—*fire* was bad for business, but fire could happen to *any* city. Despite his de-emphasis of the earthquake's significance, Hearst's poignant description of his arrival at San Francisco is nonpareil:

I had come to think that the whole disaster had been exaggerated, and when I boarded the ferry for San Francisco I had begun to hope that there was less destruction than I expected.

As the boat drew near the San Francisco side, however, the fearful havoc of the actual destroyer—the fire—began to appear. The destruction was awful, utter, complete.

I looked to compare the burned district with what remained unburned. Practically nothing remained unburned. The burned district was everywhere. I looked for the outlines of the gutted buildings. There were hardly any of those. The city had not only been burned but burned to the ground.

When I landed from the ferry the awfulness of the disaster almost overpowered me. There was nothing to be seen but a desert of tumbled brick, twisted iron and blackened timbers.

Out Market street as far as the eye can reach there was nothing but ruins. North to the bay, west to the Mission, nothing but ruins. The wholesale district was destroyed, the retail district was destroyed, the manufacturing district, the financial district, the water front section, all destroyed. The hills rolled to the seas as bare as when the pioneers landed in the days of '49. But the hills that welcomed them were shining in green and covered with grass and shrubs and trees, while now they are a blackened waste.

Instead of grass there are acres of ashes; instead of shrubs there are but twisted iron and steel, and instead of tall trees there rise but brick chimneys and ragged fragments of walls towering above the desolation that surrounds them.

I will not attempt any detailed description of this scene. I know that no description gave me the slightest understanding of what had occurred, and I do not believe that any words of mine could convey to a reader the slightest comprehension of this interminable area of wreck and ruin.

Indeed, to get any sort of accurate impression one must free the mind of the idea that there has merely been a fire, no matter how great, in San Francisco, and must realize that there has been a fire ᴏꜰ sᴀɴ ꜰʀᴀɴᴄɪsᴄᴏ, that the whole city has gone up in one mighty blaze that roared and raged and burned for three days and nights and left nothing standing but a fringe of houses along the southern and western limits....

The calamity seems overwhelming and yet the people are not overwhelmed. Everything has been destroyed except that indomitable American pluck, that unconquerable American spirit which will not be subdued.

–William Randolph Hearst, supplement to the San Francisco *Examiner,* May 13, 1906

85

86

86

Alcatroz [sic] *Island from Russian Hill—Looking Across a Sea of Ruins.* Keystone View Company's stereophotographer stood near the corner of Green and Taylor to capture this rare view. The house on the left was—and still is—on Taylor, between Green and Union. The diagonal street is Columbus. The cable cars are at Taylor and Bay. Fisherman's Wharf is at Taylor and Jefferson. "Fire engines were stationed along the eastern side of East street [Embarcadero] (the other side was too hot for them) and were wetting down the wharf buildings and ferry houses. The fire boats Active and Leslie, with several

thousand feet of hose, had come down from the Navy Yard at Vallejo, and were pouring salt water on the flames as fast as their engines could pump it.... The wharfage was in danger almost continually during the fire, but water and heroism saved it intact." –Aitken & Hilton, *A History of the Earthquake and Fire in San Francisco*, 1906

V iew west from Ferry Tower showing two piers collapsed by earthquake.

ACT II
WALKING THE RUINS

An imprint never effaced

"**B**OOKS <u>DESCRIBE</u> places, scenes, subjects,—but it is the mission of the stereograph to <u>reproduce</u> with absolute fidelity the thing itself, presenting the <u>reality,</u> not an imitation, so that the mind receives the same impression as in the bodily presence of the object,— an imprint that is never effaced."

–H. C. White Co., *Catalog of Stereographs and Lantern Slides,* 1907

Hawley C. White was born in Bennington, Vermont, in 1848. The stereoscope maker began manufacturing stereo views in 1899. By 1906, he had become one of America's premier manufacturers of both. His stereophotographer was on the scene within days of the Earthquake, documenting what White and many others called San Francisco's great "disaster."

H. C. White & Co. issued thirty-one stereo views of the aftermath of the Earthquake and Fire. Eighteen (numbered 8701– 8718) were released together as a set, depicting a walking tour of the devastation. They included timely—if not always accurate— descriptions on the back of each card. White promoted his "San Francisco Disaster Series" in his 1907 Catalog:

"Our history records no such complete destruction of a magnifi-

cent city with such big attendant losses as that which befell the metropolis of the Pacific Coast on the 18th of April, 1906. Without warning the all powerful elemental forces of Nature burst upon the doomed city. Thousands of families were made homeless in a night. Millions of dollars worth of property were destroyed. The whole world paused for the time aghast. The heart of its people was touched. Swift succor was hurried to the stricken people; the scenes of desolation were cleared away and a new city now looks out through the Golden Gate.

"Our Stereographs depict this most terrible catastrophe accurately, clearly and adequately. Scenes of desolation and destruction, awful rents in the earth's crust, street upheavals, twisted buildings, dismantled homes, magnificent structures gutted by fire, ruins of palatial residences, wrecked trolleys, suffering refugees,—all these and more form the permanent record of that awful 18th of April."

All eighteen cards and their original descriptions are reproduced in the following pages, along with related images and stereo views. Together, they vividly portray San Francisco before, during, and after the earthquake and fire that destroyed 508 city blocks and left 200,000 homeless.

*B*urned cable cars—looking E. on California St. [toward Hyde] over the terrible wreckage.

San Leandro April 18— We have just experienced a terrible earthquake. We are alive, but San Francisco, San Jose are wiped out. It is too awful for anything. I wish I could go back east. Fire started in the city and they are blowing the buildings up to keep it from spreading. Will send you reports later. Our chimneys fell. We are sleeping in tents. Hastily, Marcia

FERRY BUILDING, FROM THE BAY, SAN FRANCISCO, CALIFORNIA

8701. General view of burned area, (Market St. on left) from Ferry Tower, San Francisco Disaster, U.S.A.

"ON OUR WAY across the lovely Bay to this stricken city, we saw the hills on which it lies now as bare as they looked to the pioneers of fifty years ago, yet with a difference. Now, mounting to the tower of the Ferry building on the water-front, we stand fully 200 feet above the street to gaze upon this scene of desolation, stretching before us as far as the eye can see. Straight ahead lies the once busy thoroughfare, Market Street, now bordered by shattered ruins. The very tall domed building on the left is the sixteen story Call Building, and sweeping from it towards the right is a zone of great modern structures which escaped the total demolition of the older buildings near us. This was the Wall Street section of San Francisco, containing the largest banking-houses, the exchanges and banks; though all that we see

is the most important business part, filled with the great wholesale houses, and the leading business establishments. The large building right of the centre is the Merchant's Exchange, the outer walls intact, but completely destroyed inside [designed by D. H. Burnham & Co.'s Willis Polk in 1903 and rebuilt after the Earthquake]. It stands on California Street, which runs from its sharp angle with Market up the slope of Nob Hill, crowned by the enormous Fairmount Hotel [named for James Fair, the Fairmont, as it is now called, was under construction in 1906]. The nearer parallel street is Sacramento, and on the extreme right is Clay Street. The broad space in front is East Street [now Embarcadero] running along the Bay. Market Street was opened to the public only the day before, and though tolerably clear now, it had been piled high with debris from the wrecks. This was removed most expeditiously over tracks hastily laid from the Southern Pacific terminus several squares to the left." ▶

89

8701.
*G**eneral view of burned area,
(Market St. on left) from Ferry
Tower.* Foreground: East Street (now
Embarcadero); left: Market Street;
center: Sacramento Street; right:
Clay Street.

View west from Ferry Tower showing Nob and Russian (right) hills. Foreground: East Street (now Embarcadero); left: Clay Street; right: Washington Street.

8702. Great Ferry Building, showing damaged tower, San Francisco Disaster, U.S.A.

"NEAR THE FOOT of Market Street we are looking at the immense front of the Ferry Building, sweeping along the shore of the Bay for more than 800 feet. The stone-work on the lower part of the graceful tower has been shattered by the earthquake and has fallen away from the steel frame. The tower has been braced temporarily, but it has been pronounced unsafe and will be taken down [Arthur Page Brown and Edward R. Swain's masterpiece—originally known as the Union Depot and Ferry House—had opened in 1898 and was, of course, saved]. A most significant mark of the earthquake shows on the clock-face, whose hands stand at the moment, 5:16, when the shock stopped it. [The clock has maintained a long tradition of seismological stoppage, stopping at 11:19 p.m. on June 1, 1899 and 5:04 p.m. on October 17, 1989. On April 18, 1906, it was probably running fast—the quake struck at 5:12 a.m.] The marvel is that the building was not destroyed by fire. All about disappeared in the flames, and several times the wind seem [sic] to drive the conflagration towards it. A line of refugees is still on the way to the ferries by vehicles of many kinds; but for the first days after the calamity this spot was the scene of most fearful confusion. Thousands of terror-stricken people surged in a mob about the ferry. Some had struggled down Market Street over great piles of stones and bricks, and even over the dead; while many more were forced by fear of raging flames and falling walls to walk for miles around the north and east of the danger-zone. It took in some cases more than four hours to cover a few blocks on Market Street near the ferry. The throngs of refugees accumulated to thousands, fighting and pushing their way to the boats and safety. The condition was desperate. To the terror caused by the roar of the fire, the thunder of dynamite and crash of falling walls behind the fleeing multitudes was added the pangs of hunger and exhaustion. Hundreds were forced to spend the night here, some with no refuge but the pavements. For a time the only telegraph working in the city was operated in the Ferry tower and even that was finally abandoned."

The Union Ferry Depot where all passengers land. 1905

In September 2005 David Burkhart sat down with 1906 Earthquake survivor (Heimie) Herbert Hamrol. Herbert, the son of Jewish immigrants from Poland, was born in San Francisco on January 10, 1903. The quick-witted centenarian has had at least three loves in his long life: his wife, his work, and his hometown. He reminisced about Cecelia, his Irish wife of 40 years, with great warmth and devotion. When asked what has kept him going all these years, he described a rich variety of jobs, from meat market delivery boy to lamplighter to wholesale grocer.

Though he "retired" at age 64, Herbert still works a few days a week at Andronico's Market on Irving: "I walk around the store, and make sure the shelves look good. If someone takes a can out, I'll reach back in and put another one in its place and sorta make it look nice. It looks like you're not doing any business, but in reality it looks very good to see all the shelves in order. And then I sit down."

Herbert was just three years old when the big one struck: "All I remember, my mother carried me down the stairs. How do I remember that she carried me down on her left arm and on the right she held the banister? How do I remember that or am I imagining it? I don't know. But I tell people that's the way I remember my mother getting out of the house when the earthquake came. After the earthquake—we were living at 6th and Clementina—we slept in the park not too far away, about two or three nights at the most, and then we went back to Chicago where my father's family lived." They soon returned to San Francisco.

"Did I ever see any ruins of the earthquake? I don't know how old I was—ten, twelve—but I remember walking down McAllister Street. And I got down as far as

Hyde Street, and that's where I saw my first steel columns, sitting there, standing there, that used to be a building. And then I looked around and I saw other columns, where they had been burnt down, and broken down with the earthquake. The fire did more damage. South of Market was destroyed by fire. A lot of buildings were destroyed by fire. They had to dynamite certain parts of the city in order to stop the fire and that's the only way they could stop it."

8702.
Great Ferry Building, showing damaged tower.

Interview with Herbert Hamrol, continued:

DB: "What do you think makes San Francisco so special?"

HH: "Well, I think it's a cosmopolitan city. I've heard that name mentioned a long time ago. Different people of different races come here. It was a melting pot—it still is."

DB: "And everybody gets along."

HH: "They have to."

Refugees camping in front of Ferry Building.

DB: "Are you ready for the next big one?"

HH: "How can you be ready for an earthquake? If we're safe, you're going to be frightened to death. Is the building safe? It could tumble. So, it's hard to say how you're going to come out. You come out good, you're happy. Otherwise your life could be ruined."

Busy scene at the Ferry Building, saved by heroic effort from the great fire.

8703. Palace Hotel, undamaged by earthquake, interior burned out, San Francisco Disaster, U.S.A.

"LESS THAN A MILE up Market Street from the ferry, we stop to gaze at the empty shells of these great buildings, once the very centre of the public life of the gay, cosmopolitan city of San Francisco. Directly in front stands the windowless, floorless Palace Hotel, the largest and most popular in the city. The huge building [built by William C. Ralston, who drowned before its October 14, 1875, opening], capable of sheltering 1,200 guests, extends around an inside court. The yawning window-spaces were filled by a continuous line of bay-windows, which gave the hotel an appearance peculiarly characteristic. On the night of April 17th it was crowded to the doors with guests from all parts of the State, attending the opera season by the Conried Company of New York. The hotel was not injured by the earthquake, but before seven o'clock one of the fires, which broke out in many parts of the city from bursting gas-mains set blazing by electric currents, was within a block of the huge building. All escaped, but with enormous loss, and the flames rapidly devoured all but the brick walls. [It was rebuilt in 1909.] Next above stands the ten story [Meyer and O'Brien's 1906] Monadnock office building, hardly completed at the time of the disaster and but little damaged. Beyond that rises the tallest building in San Francisco, the huge Spreckels Building, better known as the Call, from the newspaper whose offices were located in it. This too was completely gutted by fire, though it had suffered little from the shock of the earthquake. Almost directly in the rear of the Call Building, on Mission Street, parallel to Market on the left, stood the Grand Opera House [where *Carmen* had been performed April 17], entirely destroyed by fire. None of these high buildings fell, so the street is perfectly clear at this point."

Palace Hotel, S.F. Interior View. This rare Carleton Watkins stereo view was published—uncredited—by Isaiah W. Taber. Ulysses S. Grant stayed at the Palace. His carriage entered the ornate interior court in 1879. Twenty-seven years later, Enrico Caruso became the last of the plethora of distinguished guests to lodge at the gargantuan hotel.

Knights Templars Passing Palace Hotel—President McKinley's Visit. San Francisco loves a parade, and McKinley's 1901 visit was a good excuse for one. In the foreground is Lotta's Fountain. Donated in 1875 by gold rush performer Lotta Crabtree (1847–1924), it became a popular rendezvous in 1906. On Christmas Eve, 1910, diva Luisa Tetrazzini (famous for her voice and an eponymous chicken dish) sang there. Every April 18, at 5:12 a.m., San Franciscans gather at the Fountain to commemorate the 1906 Earthquake and listen to the reminiscences of its survivors.

8703.

*P*alace Hotel, undamaged by
earthquake, Interior burned out.
Bounded by New Montgomery,
Market, Annie, and Jessie Streets.
Bank of California president William
C. Ralston did not live to see his posh
hotel open on October 14, 1875. An
avid swimmer, he mysteriously
drowned in the icy waters of the Bay
the previous August. Ralston had
outfitted his colossal hotel with state-
of-the-art fire protection. Most of its
water reserves were used up by the
time the flames reached the Palace on
April 18, however, and the venerable
inn succumbed to the conflagration.

8704. Great Call Building gutted by fire, San Francisco Disaster, U.S.A.

"WE ARE NOW in Newspaper Row in San Francisco [at Third, Kearny, and Market, near Lotta's Fountain], looking from the eighth story of the Chronicle Building on the north side of Market Street, across to the empty shell of the most imposing of her edifices [the Call Building—today, looking quite different, it is known as Central Tower]. The great dome, crowned by a lantern 315 feet above the level of the street, stood out conspicuous [sic] from every point of view near the city. Built within ten years, the huge steel framework was anchored firmly to a solid foundation of steel and concrete, and is said to be perfectly secure. Notwithstanding it stood almost unscathed by the shock, the relentless flames crept upon the building from the rear about 10:00 o'clock, breaking into the windows on the fourth floor. Then surging upward with a terrible fury, in what seemed to the watching crowds in the street but a second, the fire burst from the round windows of the dome in enormous waving streamers. All the polished wood and marble of the interior has vanished, the pale sandstone of the main part is blackened and the granite of the lower stories is chipped and marred. The Examiner Building, just below the Call, was dynamited, and men from both papers rushed to the Chronicle Building nearly opposite to get out their editions. But the fire soon drove them off [the April 19 *Call-Chronicle-Examiner* was printed in Oakland]. The new Chronicle Building, not entirely completed at the time of the disaster, was only slightly damaged, while the old [1889 Burnham and Root designed] building of this newspaper, beside it, was gutted [it was rebuilt after the Earthquake, and redesigned in 1962]. Next above on the extreme right we see part of the front of the United States Savings Bank [William Curlett's 1902 Mutual Savings Bank Building at Kearny and Market was rebuilt in 1906], a fine eleven story structure with a great mansard roof. Beyond the Call Building is the Kamm Building, which was badly wrecked; and further up Market Street, beyond the next cross-street, which is 4th, stands the ruin of the Emporium. In the back-ground we see the ridge of hills along the Pacific Ocean, and on the left of Market Street the burned Mission district sweeps far to the southwest."

The Call, New Era Edition; color lithograph on paper; H. S. Crocker Co., San Francisco, lithographers; December 19, 1897.

8704.

*G*reat Call Building gutted by fire. SW corner, 3rd and Market Streets. Erected in 1896, the 19-story Claus Spreckels Building was home to the San Francisco *Call* newspaper. Its height to the top of the main cornice was 210 feet; to the top of its dome, 310 feet. The purportedly fireproof structure, "constructed of marble," contained 272 offices.

H. C. WHITE CO., Gen'l Offices N. Bennington, Vt., U.S.A.
Branch Offices : New York, Chicago, London.

The "PERFEC" STEREOGRAPH. (Trade Mark.)
Patented April 14, 1903. Other Patents Pending.

(4) 8704 Great Call Building gutted by fire, San Francisco Disaster, U.S.A.
Copyright 1906 by H. C. White Co.

Market (left) and Post Streets, looking West. 1905. Before designing San Francisco's famous Ferry Building, Arthur Page Brown designed the Crocker Building on the gore at Market and Post. Brown's handsome flatiron survived the Earthquake and Fire, only to be replaced by the Aetna Life and Casualty Building in 1969. Behind the Crocker is the clock tower of Daniel H. Burnham's 1889 Chronicle Building, San Francisco's first iron and steel frame skyscraper.

The black trail of ruin and desolation, Great Earthquake, San Francisco. Note overhead trolley wires. The Chronicle Building fared better than it appears in this stereo view, and remains standing today, albeit with a very different looking skin. Behind it, at Kearny, is William Curlett's 1902 Mutual Savings Bank Building, also a survivor. James D. Phelan was the president of this bank.

16869. The black trail of ruin and desolation, Great Earthquake, San Francisco.

JAMES M. DAVIS, New York City, and St. Louis, Mo.

Copyright 1906, by B. W. Kilburn.

Chronicle Building; color lithograph on paper;
Dickman Jones Co., San Francisco, lithographers; early 1890s.

*P*ast Lotta Fountain to Palace Hotel. Ruins of Grand Hotel in distance. Lotta's Fountain, a gift to the city from Lotta Crabtree in 1875, became a meeting place for refugees. Today, it is the annual meeting place of 1906 Earthquake survivors and their admirers.

INTERNATIONAL STEREOGRAPH CO.
Photographers and Publishers

HOME OFFICE AND WORKS
Decatur, Illinois, U.S.A.

20636 Past Lotta Fountain to Palace Hotel. Ruins of Grand Hotel in distance. San Francisco, Cal., Disaster. COPYRIGHT 1906 BY C. L. WASSON.

"The Emporium," the great Market St. department store, after earthquake and fire.

8705. Wreck of interior of Emporium which collapsed after fire, San Francisco Disaster, U.S.A.

"HERE IS ONE of the most ghastly evidences of ruin from the double calamity of earthquake and fire. This confused mass of fallen and shattered steel beams and bare framework from which the walls have fallen, roofless and wrecked, was once the largest store in San Francisco, a huge department establishment, formerly thronged with eager crowds of shoppers. The upper stories were used by the State Supreme Court, but now all that remains in the least intact of the once handsome [Albert Pissis and Joseph Moore's 1896] Parrott Building [home of The Emporium] is the stone front on Market Street and that is badly cracked. Probably the intense heat of the fire softened the steel beams and they gave way at last beneath the heavy mass of wreckage from the upper floors. Now it will be a tremendous task to clear out the piles of debris before any new building can be started [the facade of The Emporium, and Albert Pissis's 1904 James L. Flood Building across the street, at Market and Powell, were saved]. The ruins of the Emporium were hardly cool, before the firm started business again in a dwelling-house on Van Ness Avenue [see page 207]. Near the Emporium on 5th Street, the next cross street on the west, stands the U.S. Mint [designed by Alfred B. Mullet, it opened in 1874 and still stands], the only building saved intact in a vast space south of Market Street. Fifty employees and ten soldiers fought the flames, which were completely enveloping the building, for seven hours and saved it. This was possible only because the huge granite building was almost uninflammable and an artesian well within the enclosure supplied them with water. Directly opposite the Emporium, Powell Street entered Market, and in this vicinity and over towards Union Square, only three blocks away, were a number of theatres, whose inflammable contents added a greater fury than ever to the devouring flames. Other steel structures withstood the fire far better than the Emporium, therefore it must have been structurally weaker or it would never have collapsed in this wholesale [and, in this case, retail] manner."

105

*E*mporium Bldg. The facade of
The Emporium was saved. The
James L. Flood Building, on the left,
across the street, was also saved.

105

52. Emporium Bldg.
Copyright by Tom M. Phillips, 1906.

105

8187-United States Mint, surrounded by the ruins of earthquake and fire San Francisco, Cal. Copyright 1906 by Underwood & Underwood. V-97113

*U*nited States Mint, surrounded by the ruins of earthquake and fire. Thanks to the efforts of Superintendent Frank Leach and 50 brave employees, the Greek Revival Mint building at 5th and Mission was saved. "Soon great masses of flames shot against the side of our building as if directed against us by a huge blow-pipe. The glass in our windows, exposed to this great heat, did not crack and break, but melted down like butter; the sandstone and granite, of which the building was constructed, began to flake off with explosive noises like the firing of artillery."– Frank A. Leach, *Recollections of a Newspaperman*, 1917

Central Theatre. On Market near 8th St. The show at the Central on April 17 was "Dangers of Working Girls," featuring vaudeville between acts and moving pictures. After the Earthquake, "the first new playhouse to arise over its former ruins was the Central Theater [sic], the old home of melodrama and sentimental plays. Here the old stock company had to appear under the shelter of a big circus tent.... The audiences of the Central Theater did not seem to care whether their favorite plays were presented under a roof or under canvas. The play was the thing, not the accommodations; so the great tent has been crowded night after night ever since it opened."–Edwin Emerson, Jr., *Sunset Magazine*, October 1906

14. Central Theatre.
Copyright by Tom M. Phillips, 1906.

From Howard and 7th Strs. over blocks of ruins to Post Office and City Hall, San Francisco, Cal. Copyright 1906 by Underwood & Underwood. U-61123

*F*rom Howard and 7th Strs. over blocks of ruins to Post Office and City Hall. On the morning of April 20, "the officials of the Post Office, the Railway Mail Service and the Inspection Division gathered to make plans for the rehabilitation of the Mail Service.… It was…decided to cover the camps with an outgoing service as quickly as possible, and automobiles were impressed for that purpose. I took one of them to cover the Presidio and Golden Gate Park and any intermediate gathering I could find, the plan being to inform the people that collections would be made from their camps in the afternoon and those that desired to communicate with their friends should be ready with their mail." [continued]

A crude post-office—reorganizing the mail service after the earthquake. "The Post Office would handle everything, stamped or unstamped, as long as it had an address to which it could be sent. When I went back in the afternoon…to collect the mail from the camps, the wonderful mass of communications that poured into the automobile was a study in the sudden misery that had overtaken the city. Bits of cardboard, cuffs, pieces of wrapping paper, bits of newspapers with an address on the margin, pages of books and sticks of wood all served as a means to let somebody in the outside world know that friends were alive and in need among the ruins."–William F. Burke, *The Argonaut*, December 18, 1926

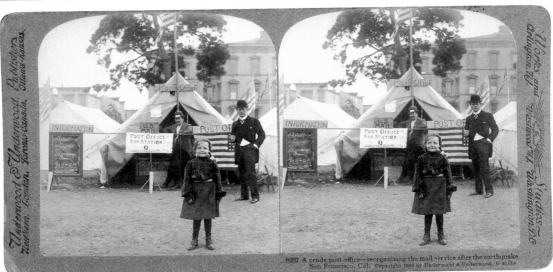

COURTESY OF JANE AND LARRY ROSEN.

8706. Post Street, once a busy shopping district, now a scene of desolation, San Francisco Disaster, U.S.A.

"WE ARE STILL in the heart of the business section, only a block or two from Market Street near the Call and Chronicle Buildings. No attempt has been made to clear away the wreckage in the street, so we see what was the aspect of most streets in the fire-swept region. The roadway is filled from curb to curb with bricks that have been shaken down, not so much by the earthquake, as by the repeated blasts of dynamite used in hope of staying the progress of the flames. Then on a level with the curious spectators is a tangled mass of charred wires, sagged down from their supports, and luckily dead in more than one sense. These were the danger-points of the disaster and the origin of most of the fires that broke out at once, as the electric currents ignited the escaping gas from bursting mains. Post Street formerly contained many shops, though none of the large department-stores, which were mostly on Market Street. It was becoming a favorite retail shopping district, particularly in the vicinity of Union Square, a short distance down the street behind us. In this square a great many took refuge, after leaving the Palace Hotel, and the entire space was piled high with trunks, rescued from danger. But when this was threatened, many dragged their trunks along the street over to the west, and the noise of their grinding and scraping added a mournful accompaniment to the awful concussions of dynamite and the roaring of the flames. The skyscraper in the background [Shea and Shea's steel-framed Whittell Building at 136 Geary Street] was in process of construction at the time of the disaster and was not injured either by the earthquake or the fire."

Jack London described April 18th's "caravan of trunks" in his *Collier's* article:

"The hills of San Francisco are steep, and up these hills, mile after mile, were the trunks dragged. Everywhere were trunks, with across them lying their exhausted owners, men and women. Before the march of the flames were flung picket lines of soldiers. And a block at a time, as the flames advanced, these pickets retreated. One of their tasks was to keep the trunk-pullers moving. The exhausted creatures, stirred on by the menace of bayonets, would arise and struggle up the steep pavements, pausing from weakness every five or ten feet. Often, after surmounting a heart-breaking hill, they would find another wall of flame advancing upon them at right angles and be compelled to change anew the line of their retreat. In the end, completely played out, after toiling for a dozen hours like giants, thousands of them were compelled to abandon their trunks."

110

Bound for the Ferry After the San Francisco Earthquake and Fire Disaster of April 18, 1906.

8706.

*P*ost Street, once a busy shopping *district, now a scene of desolation.* William and Frank Shea's steel-frame Whittell Building, at 136 Geary Street, was under construction before April 18.

*P*athetic evidence of misery wrought by earthquake and fire—Open air relief kitchen, foot of Dewey Monument. The remains of the Sutter Street Synagogue, a survivor of the 1865 and 1868 quakes, loom large above Union Square.

FRANCIS THE DOG'S 1906 EARTHQUAKE SURVIVAL STORY is inspiring. The line, "Whence all but him [sic] had fled" comes from "Casabianca," a poem written by Felicia Dorothea Browne Hemans (1793–1835). She was inspired by the poignant story of 13-year-old Giocante Casabianca and his father, a ship's captain. During the 1798 Battle of the Nile, his French ship, *L'Orient*, caught fire and exploded, killing both father and son. An excerpt:

The boy stood on the burning deck
Whence all but he had fled;
The flame that lit the battle's wreck
Shone round him o'er the dead.

Yet beautiful and bright he stood,
As born to rule the storm;
A creature of heroic blood,
A proud, though child-like form.

The flames roll'd—he would not go,
Without his Father's word;
That father, faint in death below
His voice no longer heard....

With mast, and helm, and pennon fair,
That well had borne their part—
But the noblest thing which perish'd there
Was that young faithful heart!

*S*hattered remains of the beautiful office of the St. Francis Hotel.

" Whence all but him had fled "

FRANCIS
Five days through fire and earthquake, without food, in the Hotel St. Francis wine cellars, San Francisco

8707. A fire engine caught and crushed by a falling wall, Post. Street, San Francisco Disaster, U.S.A.

"A LITTLE TO THE NORTHEAST, on the [far] right, we see the eleven-story [1891 Burnham and Root designed] Mills Building owned by D. O. Mills of New York, one of the finest modern structures in the city. [The cupola of the Merchant's Exchange is also visible.] The tall building on the left [Meyer and O'Brien's 1906 steel-frame Marston Building at Kearny and Hardie Place] was still under construction when the disaster came, and was only slightly damaged, as there was little for the flames to feed on. But an eloquent wreck directly in front of us tells what frightful dangers attended the desperate struggle of the firemen. Like many others, this engine had to be abandoned, because of the rapid advance of the flames. Although their work was perfectly [in] vain, the firemen clung so tenaciously to their duty, that only when exhausted and half maddened by smoke and escaping gas would they withdraw or be pulled back from their perilous positions. Bricks are piled about it, and even on top of its once brightly polished parts. And the flames, sweeping up the narrow streets, as along a horizontal chimney, have burned up all that was inflammable. The spokes of the wheels are gone, the tire is reduced to a charred mass, and the long spiral wire is all that remains of the rubber suction pipe. Within twenty minutes after the earthquake, one hundred fire-calls were given and the admirable force promptly responded, to find to their dismay that the hose could pump not a drop of water. The principal break in the pipes was down at San Mateo [County], which was almost flooded in consequence. To add to their despair, [Fire Chief Dennis T.]

Sullivan, the efficient head of the department, had been crushed in his bed by a falling building, and died without knowing there had been a fire."

A more accurate description of Sullivan's demise appeared in the 1908 *San Francisco Municipal Reports*: "Chief Sullivan and wife occupied quarters on the third floor of the building occupied by Chemical Company No. 3 on Bush Street above Kearny. The earthquake overthrew the high ornamental tower that surmounted the roof of the California Hotel, immediately adjoining and high above the quarters of the Chief, which, toppling over on the latter roof crashed through the building to the ground floor, going through the room occupied by Mrs. Sullivan and carrying her in her bed to the bottom floor. Meanwhile the Chief, who occupied the adjoining room, was awakened by the crash, and unmindful of anything but his wife's safety, rushed into the room occupied by her, and in the dim light fell through the opening in the floor made by the falling tower down to the bottom floor, receiving injuries that resulted in his death four days later."

Assistant Fire Chief John Dougherty took over the Sisyphean task of fighting fire without water.

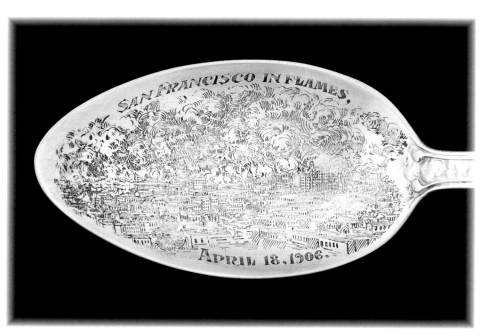

8707.

A fire engine caught and crushed by a falling wall, Post Street. Frederick H. Meyer and Smith O'Brien's steel-frame Marston Building (left), at Kearny and Hardie Place, was under construction before April 18. "While no means an alarmist, it was always Chief Sullivan's aim to be prepared for any exigency that might arise in fire protection matters, and as far back as 12 or 15 years ago, he earnestly advocated the establishment of an auxiliary high pressure salt water supply for this city, which undoubtedly would have proven of inestimable value during the conflagration of April, 1906." [continued]

*B*rave fire boys battling with flames among the ruins at Mission and Spear Sts. "Some 10 years ago [Chief Sullivan] also conceived the advisability of the establishment of a trained corp of engineers and sappers, well versed in the proper methods and application of high explosives as a preventative of the spread of a serious conflagration.… The only obstacle to the immediate putting into effect of these plans, was the providing of about $1,000 for the building of a brick vault in the [Presidio] reservation grounds for the storage of the explosives."–*San Francisco Municipal Reports*, 1908

Shaken by Earthquake and Gutted by Fire, [Darius Ogden] *Mills Bldg.* [on Montgomery] *From Bush and Sansome Sts.* Burnham and Root designed this steel-framed skyscraper. In early 1906, a seventh floor office was rented by Pacific States Telephone and Telegraph Company executive Theodore V. Halsey. There, he bribed members of the San Francisco Board of Supervisors to award his company the City's telephone franchise. He was unaware that the Supervisors were also taking bribes from the Home Telephone Company, through political boss Abe Ruef. Much to Halsey's chagrin, the Supervisors kept the money, and Home got the franchise.

8708. Wrecked Hall of Justice, seen from a street in Chinatown, San Francisco Disaster, U.S.A.

"CHINATOWN, that mysterious and fascinating quarter of San Francisco, has vanished. Nevermore will sight-seers as of old, turn towards that densely crowded district, to explore the narrow streets, lined with queer wooden dwellings, theatres and joss-houses, or here and there with tall tenements swarming with Chinese. No new Chinatown will probaly ever present the same weird, Oriental aspect, nor add the hidden mystery of those vast underground burrows, now for the first time laid bare. [In 1889, (Joseph) Rudyard Kipling (1865–1936) explored the Chinese tenements he called "icebergs,—two-thirds below sight level," yet their existence was as apocryphal as much of the rest of the Chinatown lore that fostered San Francisco's love-hate relationship with "the city of Canton set down in the most eligible business-quarter of the place."] The district was bounded approximately by Sacramento, Stockton, Pacific and Kearney [now Kearny] Streets, and we are standing in the heart of it on Washington Street, now filled with heaps of brick and iron beams that was once the front of a wrecked building. Down the street stands the Hall of Justice, with the steel frame of its cupola toppled over on the tower. Part of the ruin was caused by the earthquake, but the raging fire that swept this district cleaned out the interior. The scorched trees on this side of the building are in Portsmouth Square, bounded nearest us by Kearney Street. This was formerly known as the Plaza, and about it stood the original little Mexican settlement of Yerba Buena, found here by the pioneers of the early forties, and the actual starting-point of San Francisco. As the flames swept up from the Bay, a frenzied mob of Chinamen took refuge in the square, howling and fighting, and soon joined by excited crowds of Mexicans, Spaniards and Italians, from the Latin quarter, lying north toward Telegraph Hill. The troops were forced to quell the uproar with bayonets; and to add to the confusion, about a hundred prisoners were in jail within the Hall of Justice and had to be removed in irons to a place of safety."

118

Among the dens of Chinatown—ruins of the notorious 620 Jackson St. The Schmitz Administration was on the take from San Francisco's "municipal cribs," including Chinatown's most notorious assembly-line brothel at 620 Jackson Street. "For the late severe loss the city may find some compensations—as the cleansing effect of fire; much filth, material and moral, has been destroyed. Yet one is forced to observe that the precincts of Satan retain their land values equal to any other locality."–Hubert Howe Bancroft, *Some Cities and San Francisco, and Resurgam,* 1907

8708.

Wrecked Hall of Justice, seen from a street in Chinatown. The Hall of Justice was on Kearny at Washington Street.

9232—In " Chinatown," San Francisco, Cal., U. S. A.

*I*n *"Chinatown."* Sing Fat & Co., 614 Dupont Street (now Grant) at California, before the Earthquake. On the reverse: "The Chinese portion of the city of San Francisco, 'Chinatown,' of which our view shows the business thoroughfare, has always been, and we suppose always will be of great interest so long as it is inhabited by the Mongolian race. Here 40,000 Chinamen are huddled together in quarters which would not accommodate one fifth that number of Americans, and they have brought

with them all the habits and ways of life of the mother country. They have five theaters, joss houses, opium joints, and gambling houses, all conducted in the Chinese fashion."

*F*rom wreck of famous Chinese store, Sing Fat & Co., N.E. to Hall of Justice. *Sing Fat & Co. was rebuilt.*

H159

11659—Reading the War News—In Chinatown, San Francisco,
Cal. U. S. A.

Reading the War News—In Chinatown. By 1900, San Francisco's love-hate relationship with Chinatown was as passionate as ever. On the reverse: "See how intently these people are looking for news from the Boxer rebellion. In 1900, China-town was a part of San Francisco not far from the docks and near the business center of the city. It had shops and stores, restaurants, drug stores with amazing remedies, gambling dens and opium cellars, temples with incense burning before the gods,… more than 20,000 Chinese talking their own language and living their own life apparently untouched by American ideas. That was the trouble."

Chinese at Dinner. The total relief offered to San Francisco's Chinese was estimated at $10,000. Many fled to Oakland. Those that remained were forcibly relocated several times. Abe Ruef was chairman of the Committee that finally exiled them to Camp Number 3, a desolate, segregated spot near Fort Point. On May 9, opening day, the camp's population was at its peak of 186. By the time it closed on June 12, San Francisco's Chinese had won their fight against the relocation of Chinatown. Reconstruction was completed within two years.

8709. Looking down California Street, Ferry Building in distance, San Francisco Disaster, U.S.A.

"ON THE EASTERN crest of Nob Hill, where we are standing, one of the most determined fights was made to stay the advance of the conflagration, which was threatening the beautiful residence section lying back of us. By nine o'clock on the morning of April 19th, the fire was sweeping up this steep street. The only building that escaped destruction on the left side of California Street is the [1901 Percy and Polk designed] Kohl Building, several blocks down, near Montgomery Street. It is practically uninjured. Nearer this way, on the corner of Dupont [now Grant] Street, stands the ruin of [Old] St. Mary's Roman Catholic Church. Merely the tower and blackened walls remain [it was rebuilt]. From that point to the top of the hill the buildings were all rather low, not more than three stories. Directly across California Street, in line with our position, stands the beautiful Fairmount [its original spelling] Hotel, whose great shadow is cast on the street just below us. On the right side of the street stands the tower of Grace Church, one of the oldest of the Episcopal Churches in San Francisco. Like St. Mary's, nothing else is standing but roofless walls [Grace Church was rebuilt as Grace Cathedral, on the site of the decimated Crocker mansion]. In front of the church the slight break in the incline of the street marks Stockton Street, which on the left is almost indistinguishable under the rubbish. To the right of Grace Church tower we can see the rear of the Merchant's Exchange, a fine modern four-

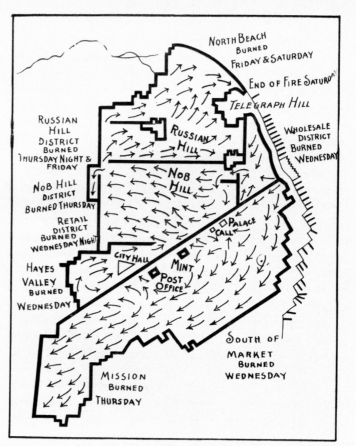

Map Showing Course of Fires

—Aitken & Hilton, *A History of the Earthquake and Fire in San Francisco,* 1906

teen-story building, fronting on California Street opposite the Kohl Building. In line with St. Mary's tower stands the Ferry Building on the waterfront. On the Bay, rather indistinct because of the smoke still rising from smouldering fires, several ferry-boats are crossing to the suburbs on the other side. Oakland lies directly in line with the Ferry tower, five miles distant; Berkeley lies a short distance to the left. Rather dim in the distant background stretches the long line of the Coast Range."

124

Stamped on the reverse of this card: *Views of California—St. Mary's Cathedral San F., corner California and Dupont* [now Grant] *streets. C. Beach Stationers and Bookseller, 34 Montgomery St., S.F.* [see page 73]. Chilion Beach's shop was at this address from about 1862 to 1870. Today, St. Mary's Roman Catholic Church is known simply as Old St. Mary's. Built of brick brought around the Horn and China-quarried stone, the 1854 landmark survived the earthquake. But it was ravaged by the fire on April 19. Old St. Mary's reopened June 20, 1909.

8709.

Looking down California Street, Ferry Building in distance. Right: Grace Church, at Stockton. Left: Old St. Mary's Church, at Dupont (now Grant); the Kohl Building, at Montgomery. Far right: the Merchant's Exchange Building, at Leidesdorff.

The "PERFEC" STEREOGRAPH. (Trade Mark.)

Patented April 14, 1903. Other Patents Pending.

605 California St, west from Sansome St., San Francisco, U. S. A.

Copyright 1900 by H. C. White Co.

California St. west from Sansome St. 1905. Note Old St. Mary's Church and the Fairmont Hotel on the right side of the street; Grace Church on the left, at Stockton Street.

127

*C*alifornia St. to Fairmount [its original spelling] *Hotel, great Merchant's Exchange on left.* The ruins of Grace Church are on the same side of California Street as Daniel Burnham's 1903 Merchant's Exchange Building. The latter, a steel frame building with a distinctive belvedere, survived. It still stands today.

California St., to Fairmount Hotel, great Merchant's Exchange on left, San Francisco Disaster, U. S. A.

8710. A desolate and forbidding scene—Telegraph Hill from Nob Hill, San Francisco Disaster, U.S.A.

"NO PART OF THE CITY has such an absolutely bare appearance as this northeastern section, because except in the blocks nearer us all the houses were of wood and were wiped out without leaving any trace of walls. We are looking from the ruins of a house on Mason Street, which marked the western edge of the burned district for about ten blocks to the north, that is at a right angle with the cross street in front, which is Clay Street. Then in a slanting direction the fire was headed off towards the east, eating its way at last to the Bay at North Point behind Telegraph Hill. On the extreme right we can about locate the northwest corner of Chinatown, and further on we see the very steep slope of Kearney [its original spelling] Street, as it ascends the rise of the hill. Near the slopes of Telegraph Hill was the Latin quarter, crowded with a great foreign population of Italians, Mexicans, Greeks and Japanese. As the fire swept from the slope near us in that direction, the firemen were able to get a stream of water from the Bay, by means of a hose a mile in length. Thus some houses on the hill were saved. But the wind turned and the flames soon were driven up to the top of the hill. The few houses that are still stand-

ing near the eastern slope were saved by the Italian residents of that vicinity, who soaked sacks and blankets in casks of wine from their cellars, covering the houses with them, and drenching the sides of their dwellings with the wine. In this appalling nakedness of the city we can see, as never before, the tremendous slopes of the streets. In the centre stands the Roman Catholic Church of St. Francis, on Broadway [sic—St. Francis of Assisi Church is at the corner of Vallejo and Columbus], the street by which thousands of terror-stricken refugees reached the Bay, while skirting the burning districts."

LA DOMENICA DEL CORRIERE

Anno . . . . NEL REGNO L. 5 — ESTERO L. 8 —
Semestre . . . . » 2,75 » 4,25

Si pubblica a Milano ogni Domenica
Dono agli Abbonati del " Corriere della Sera "

UFFICI DEL GIORNALE:
Via Solferino, 28
MILANO

Anno VIII. — N. 19.   13 Maggio 1906.   Centesimi 10 il numero.

L'incendio nel quartiere italiano di S. Francisco di California spento coraggiosamente col vino.
(Disegno di A. Beltrame).

8710.

*A desolate and forbidding scene—
Telegraph Hill from Nob Hill.*
North Beach's St. Francis of Assisi
Church, at Vallejo and Columbus, is
one of the few recognizable land-
marks in this desolate landscape. The
Norman Gothic church was dedi-
cated on St. Patrick's Day, March 17,
1860. After the 1906 Earthquake, it
was rebuilt within its original walls.
Today, it is known as the National
Shrine of St. Francis of Assisi.

130

*M*iles of Wreckage to Telegraph Hill from Chronicle Bldg. Looking up Kearney (now Kearny) Street.

43. Miles of Wreckage to Telegraph Hill from Chronicle Bldg., San Francisco, Cal.

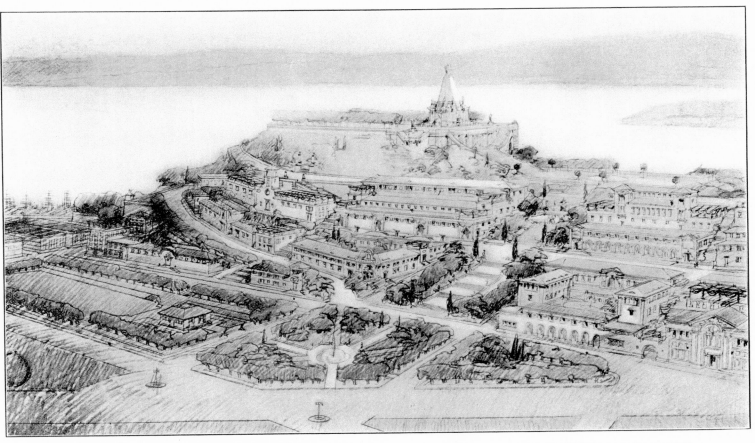

VIEW FROM THE SOUTHEAST, SHOWING THE TREATMENT OF TELEGRAPH HILL—THE PROMISED SAN FRANCISCO.
(Sketched by E. H. Bennett.)
Report of D. H. Burnham.

The Architectural Record, June 1906. In the original Burnham Report, the caption beneath this image described it more accurately: "Telegraph Hill, Looking East, Showing Suggested Architectural Treatment."

"The calamity that laid low two hundred and sixty-nine blocks, or nearly 3,000 acres of San Francisco, may be considered to some extent a blessing in disguise, because it gives us now the opportunity we have long sought to build by the Golden Gate a city which will be unexcelled throughout the world in the excellence of its plan and in its facilities for commerce and trade."–James D. Phelan, *The Present Situation*, 1906

FORMED ON JANUARY 15, 1904, James D. Phelan's Association for the Improvement and Adornment of San Francisco sought to promote "the beautifying of the streets, public buildings, parks, squares and places of San Francisco; to bring to the attention of the officials and the people of the city the best methods for instituting artistic municipal betterments; to stimulate the sentiment of civic pride in the improvement and care

of private property; to suggest quasi-public enterprises, and, in short, to make San Francisco a more agreeable city in which to live." Chicago architect Daniel H. Burnham was invited "to direct and execute a practical and comprehensive plan for the improvement and adornment of the city." His report, submitted to the Association on September 15, 1905, was well received. After the Earthquake and Fire, Phelan and his associates saw their earthquake-and-fire-razed San Francisco as the tabula rasa that would make Burnham's proposed Paris-izing possible. But as with other metropolitan fires—London in 1666 and Chicago in 1871, for example—big business wanted to get back to business ASAP. In San Francisco, public benevolence and noblesse oblige notwithstanding, Burnham's grand plans were largely ignored.

131

8711. Nob Hill and Fairmount [its original spelling] Hotel, Chinatown in foreground, San Francisco Disaster, U.S.A.

"FROM A HEIGHT of nearly 300 feet on Telegraph Hill, near the Bay, in the northeastern part of the city, we gaze upon a great sweep of desolate ruins, not altogether blackened, as one would naturally imagine; but covered with grey dust, and stained with a dull red, that adds a horrible ghastliness to the tortured fragments. On the level ground near the hill, the diagonal street on which a number of people are walking is Montgomery Avenue [now Columbus], running out almost to Fort Mason on the extreme right. Just beyond this street Chinatown begins, extending about three blocks to the south and two on the west. Far to the south we see the long slope of California Street, climbing Nob Hill. On the left stands the ruin of Grace Church, and on the crest of the hill, like a citadel, rises the magnificent Fairmount Hotel, which was scarcely completed at the time of the disaster. The marble walls are blackened by the flames in places, and the woodwork of the interior was burned

out, but the damage was not serious. The splendid building was erected at a cost of $2,000,000 by Mrs. Oelrichs, the daughter of James Fair [hence, Fairmount], one of the bonanza millionaires. Nob [short for Nabob] Hill took its name from the fine residences of the rich mining and railroad magnates of early San Francisco. Behind the hotel is the huge [James C.] Flood mansion [on California Street, designed by Augustus Laver, 1866, and today home to the Pacific-Union Club], the only one whose walls are now standing [and still stand today]. Opposite the Fairmount, on California Street were the Hopkins Art Institute [site of today's Mark Hopkins Hotel] and the Stanford house, both gone with valuable treasures. Further up all that remains of the Crocker residence is a chimney and the wrecked first story. The newer fashionable residences were further west along Van Ness Avenue and towards Pacific Heights."

THE ILLUSTRATED LONDON NEWS, MAY 12, 1906.—679

HOMELESS MILLIONAIRES: THE FLIGHT FROM THE FLAMES AT SAN FRANCISCO.

DRAWN BY W. RUSSELL FLINT FROM A SKETCH MADE FOR "LESLIE'S WEEKLY" BY GEORGE W. PETERS.

WHERE MONEY WAS USELESS: THE PLIGHT OF WEALTHY SAN FRANCISCANS DURING THE BURNING OF NOB HILL, THE FINEST RESIDENTIAL QUARTER.

On Nob Hill stood the mansions of the wealthy families of San Francisco, the Crockers, the Spreckels, and others whose fortune dates from the great gold rush of 1849. The whole district was destroyed, and the inhabitants had to flee at night in the very lightest garments. It was an extraordinary irony of circumstance to see those people, who the day before could have commanded anything, reduced to temporary destitution, and driven to realise for the first time in their lives that there are moments when money has no purchasing power. They fled to the parks and open spaces, where they bivouacked in what comfort they could, sharing misfortune with the poorest of their fellow-citizens. For the time all class distinctions were at an end.

"On the highest levels of this quarter stood the old show-houses of San Francisco, products of the bonanza wealth of the seventies. Here the Crockers, Fairs, Floods, Stanfords, and Mark Hopkins had erected huge family altars to their wealth, to be this day claimed and preempted from them by fire."

–Louise Herrick Wall, *The Century Magazine*, August 1906

133

8711.

*N*ob Hill and Fairmount [its original spelling] *Hotel, Chinatown in foreground.* Far left: Grace Church (consecrated 1862), on California at Stockton; far right: James C. Flood mansion, on California at Mason, home today to the Pacific-Union Club.

California Street Cable R.R. S.F. On August 2, 1873, at 5 a.m., Andrew Hallidie conducted his first cable car experiments on what would become the Clay Street line. The California Street line began operating on April 10, 1878. By that time, the weekly *Wasp* had already become "the first journal in the United States to print cartoons in colors. In addition to this feature the 'Wasp' made essays in the fields of light literature, but the columns to which its readers turned most readily were those devoted to showing up the foibles of prominent citizens."–John P. Young, *San Francisco*, 1912. San Francisco's most prominent cable car stop: Nob Hill.

*R*esidence of Mark Hopkins, Esq., *Cal. St. Hill* [today the site of the Mark Hopkins Hotel]. The song, "San Francisco," is from MGM's 1936 movie by the same name, set in 1906. Clark Gable plays Barbary Coast saloon keeper Blackie Norton, who falls for singer Mary Blake (Jeanette MacDonald). His romantic rival is Jack Burley (Jack Holt), the wealthy son of a Nob Hill matron (Jessie Ralph). After the quake, Blackie informs Mrs. Burley of her son's death. They watch in horror as her Nob Hill home—a scale model of the Hopkins home pictured here—is dynamited. On April 19, 1906, the real mansion was home to the Mark Hopkins Institute of Art—destroyed by fire, not dynamite.

Residence of Mark Hopkins, Esq., Cal. St. Hill, S. F.   3704

136

*R*esidence of Gov. Stanford,
California St. [at Powell] *S.F.*
Leland Stanford came to California
in 1852, becoming the Golden State's
Republican governor during the early
days of the Civil War. In *Builders of a
Great City*, his biographer writes that
in 1860, before becoming governor,
Stanford made the acquaintance of
Abraham Lincoln, "and voted for him
as Republican candidate for the Presi-
dency. He was in full accord with the
Union party, and it is worthy of note
that President Lincoln, with his
shrewd judgment of men, recognized
in him an able and trustworthy friend
of the Government."

Stanford was one of the "Big Four." His fellow railroad barons were Collis P. Huntington (friend of Carleton E. Watkins since boyhood), Mark Hopkins, and Charles Crocker. On May 10, 1869, Stanford attempted to drive the last spike at Promontory Summit, Utah, connecting the Union Pacific and Central Pacific Railroads. He missed.

Gateway to ruined Palace of Mrs. Leland Stanford on Nob Hill. Neither Leland nor his wife Jane lived to experience the 1906 Earthquake.

Residence of Chas. Crocker, Esq., California St. [between Taylor and Jones]. Railroad magnate Charles Crocker (1822–1888) and his family attended Grace Church, just down the street, at Stockton and California. This deceptively simple stereo view epitomizes the genius of stereophotographer Carleton E. Watkins. To Watkins, depth was something to be expressed more than exaggerated. Even the captured reflections in the windows of the 1876–77 Crocker home serve the quiet verity of Watkins's imagery.

*T*he Crocker residence and wrecked automobiles, ruined by earthquake and fire. Virtually all that remained of the magnificent Crocker mansion was its stone fence and wrought-iron railings. Charles Crocker's son, munificent banker William H. Crocker (1861–1937), donated the site of the demolished home to his local diocese. Today, the property is home to Grace Cathedral, completed in 1964. Portions of the original fence and railing remain, including a pylon near the Taylor Street garage entrance that shows spalling and blackening from the fire. The imposing Sacramento Street gate, which also survived, was originally the mansion's rear carriage entrance.

8712. Terrible destruction of City Hall (cost $7,000,000), from Market Street, San Francisco Disaster, U.S.A.

"THE MAGNIFICENT and costly City Hall, the pride of San Francisco, stands about a mile and a half from the Bay [where the San Francisco Public Library stands today], in a small triangular park, called Yerba Buena after the original Mexican settlement northeast of Market Street. Its once stately outlines can with difficulty be traced in the wreck, which less than a minute produced. For the destruction here was entirely the work of the earthquake. Fire added little to its mutilation, though the flames raged all about the vicinity. As we observe, even the palms in the oblong grassy plot around the "Pioneer Monument" [located today between the San Francisco Public Library and the Asian Art Museum] have not been consumed. Nothing in all the ruined city shows more vividly the awful force of the earthquake than this rent and shattered building. It is as if a gigantic hand had seized the great dome and shaking it violently had stripped it almost bare of the stately casing of row on row of encircling columns. Down in the mass of fragments piled high in the street below are the ruins of the larger columns which once enclosed the curving front of the main part, between the square projections. But the worst ravages are seen in the great wing over on the left, in shattered walls and great clefts, beyond which a solitary fragment stands as complete a ruin as some old temple of antiquity. On this Larkin Street side then walls were thrown down for several hundred feet, filling the street for two blocks with high piles of brick and cement. Only two blocks away on the left, at Van Ness and Golden Gate Avenues, the fire reached its western limit, though it burned through lower down."

140

The Damndest Finest Ruins

After Kipling's "On The Road to Mandalay"

Put me somewhere west of East Street where there's nothin' left but dust,
Where the lads are all a hustlin' and where everything's gone bust,
Where the buildin's that are standin' sort of blink and blindly stare
At the damndest finest ruins ever gazed on anywhere.

Bully ruins — bricks and wall — through the night I've heard you call
Sort of sorry for each other cause you had to burn and fall,
From the Ferries to Van Ness you're a God-forsaken mess,
But the damndest finest ruins — nothin' more or nothin' less.

The strangers who come rubberin' and a huntin' souvenirs,
The fools they try to tell us it will take a million years
Before we can get started, so why don't we come to live
And build our homes and factories upon land they've got to give.

"Got to give!" why, on my soul, I would rather bore a hole
And live right in the ashes than even move to Oakland's mole.
If they'd all give me my pick of their buildin's proud and slick
In the damndest finest ruins still I'd rather be a brick!

WORDS BY
LAWRENCE W. HARRIS

COPYRIGHT, 1906
LAWRENCE W. HARRIS

PUBLISHED BY
A. B. PIERSON
1539 VAN NESS AVE.
SAN FRANCISCO

8712.

*T*errible destruction of City Hall *(cost $7,000,000), from Market Street.* "Earthquakes uncover strange secrets. The ruins of our monster seven million dollar City Hall cried to heaven the shame of the men who built it."

–Mary Edith Griswold, "Three Days Adrift," *Sunset Magazine*, June–July 1906

16878. Main Front of the City Hall, just before the Earthquake, San Francisco.

Copyright 1906, by B. W. Kilburn.

Main Front of the City Hall, just before the Earthquake. "By 1870, a site had been chosen, plans drawn up and adopted, and a method of financing worked out…. A 'pay as you go' method of financing the new structure was adopted. This consisted of a special tax levy, the income from which was to be handled and expended by a City Hall Commission. In practice, the plan worked badly, for the cost far exceeded estimates, and construction frequently had to be stopped until additional funds became available. [continued]

"So long was it building that citizens began to refer to it as 'the new city hall ruin,'...a structure that defied [architectural] classification though it by no means stilled criticism."
–Byington and Lewis, *The History of San Francisco*, 1931

*E*nd View of the Magnificent City Hall Showing Wreck Caused by the Fire and Earth quake.

Ideal
Picture and Map
of
SAN FRANCISCO
CALIFORNIA
HEAVY LINES SHOW EXTENT OF THE
BURNED DISTRICT
AREA ABOUT FOUR SQUARE MILES
PROPERTY LOSS $300,000,000
APRIL 18TH, 19TH, 20TH, 1906

In the morning of thy splendor
Facing the rising sun
Thou art veiled by tried affliction
Lest Pride should say "Well done."

Those eyes now moist with sorrow
To me more beauteous seem
They glisten like the dewdrops
Which on lilies purest beam.

Oh lift thine eyes my Loved One
And let me see Thy soul
Effulgent in its beauty
Breathing life and making whole.

Oh lift thine eyes my Loved One
And lean upon His breast
Trusting Him supremely
Who doeth all things best.

COPYRIGHTED 1906, BY A. H. M. DAVIES, SAN FRANCISCO, CAL.

8713. Curious result of the earthquake—settling of houses on Howard Street—San Francisco Disaster, U.S.A.

"WE ARE NOW in the region of cheap lodging-houses south of Market Street, the part that suffered most from the earthquake and was almost completely wiped out by the fire. The low ground in this section was built over for miles with small, flimsy, wooden houses of two or three stories, generally of the kind we see here on Howard Street. This is one of the principal streets of this section, running from the Bay parallel with Mission and Market Streets, and then at 11th Street, turning in the same way as Mission quite sharply to the south. We are standing at a point below 15th Street, in the neighborhood where the shock wrecked so many houses, generally far more

seriously than those we are looking at. Many houses around here collapsed entirely, burying their inmates in the ruins and causing a large proportion of the deaths. It seems odd that these buildings escaped when the fire travelled along the eastern side of the street. Rushing like a terrible red billow [wave] along the south side of Market Street, the flames cut a swath about four blocks wide, sweeping this region almost bare, and over to the west as far as Dolores Street, where the fire was checked by some open spaces, which were being changed into a park. We can see how cheaply they were constructed from the flimsy brick foundation walls, and it is not surprising that they went like tinder. It seems there were about 50,000 frame buildings in the city, 90% of all; and these were largely in this district and that between Nob and Telegraph Hills, which now looks even barer than this Mission district."

144

8713.
Curious result of the earthquake—
settling of houses on Howard Street
[between 17th and 18th streets].

*E*arthquake effect on Mission Police Station. Built in 1902, the Mission Police Station, at 3057 17th Street, was saved. It still stands today.

*S*an Francisco Earthquake, April 18, 1906. Houses on Howard Street [between 17th and 18th streets] *after the earth quaked.*

5542 San Francisco Earthquake, April 18, 1906. Houses on Howard Street after the earth quaked.

"MORE APPALLING THAN the wrecked and shattered buildings in the stricken city are these ghastly signs of the terrible convulsion, which give a sense of sickening insecurity in what we think of generally as the solid earth. It was this neighborhood which suffered most severely from the earthquake, and if the large buildings had been here, far more awful scenes would have been enacted. Most buildings however in this Mission district were low wooden ones, and many were badly wrecked. The greatest disaster, the collapse of the Valencia Hotel, two blocks to the west of this point, caused the death of probably seventy-five persons, who were buried in the ruins. It appears that in that locality, Valencia and 18th Streets, there existed a geologic fault in the rocky foundation of the peninsula, which was the cause of the numerous marks of the violent action of the earthquake all about here. [Actually, this neighborhood—like San Francisco's Marina District, which suffered similarly in the 1989 Loma Prieta Earthquake—was built on "made ground." The site had once been a lake, the "Laguna de los Dolores" (later known as "Laguna de Manantial"),

near the banks of which San Francisco's Mission Dolores was founded in 1776—see page 152] At one point a crevice about six feet wide appeared in the street; in many places the ground sank four to six feet below the former surface. Car-tracks were pinched into sharp protruding angles and sometimes described large curves several feet above the asphalt. Here the fissure is not very wide, but the convulsion extended on all sides. Every stone on the sidewalk has been shaken and tilted out of position, and the asphalt looks as if it had been heaved to the left from the shattered curb, and then crumpled into great waves. Capp Street runs between Mission and Howard, beginning at 14th Street, south of Market. We are standing just below 18th Street and near the centre of the region most violently shaken. The fire advanced from Howard Street along 18th, but the houses in the distance ahead were saved by dynamiting."

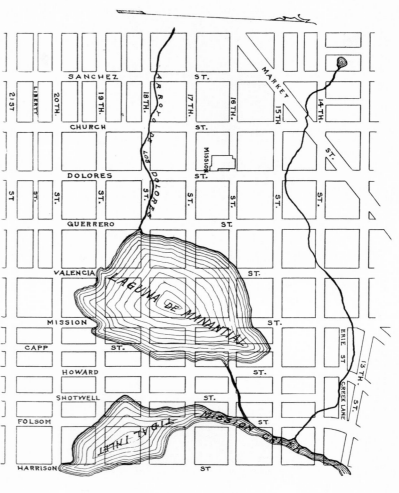

8714.
Great cracks in street and settling sidewalks, Capp Street [below 18th Street].

H. C. WHITE CO., Gen'l Offices N. Bennington, Vt., U.S.A.
Branch Offices : New York, Chicago, London.

The "PERFEC" STEREOGRAPH. (Trade Mark.)
Patented April 14, 1903. Other Patents Pending.

(14) 8714 Great cracks in street and settling sidewalks, Capp Street,
San Francisco Disaster, U. S. A. Copyright 1906 by H. C. White Co.

THE VALENCIA ST. HOTEL, on Valencia between 18th and 19th streets, was one of a number of low-rent boarding-houses South-of-the-Slot. It was built on "made ground" and—until April 18, 1906—stood four stories tall.

OFFICER H. N. POWELL, Mission Police Station, was on duty in the lobby of the Valencia St. Hotel when the earthquake struck:

"Valencia Street not only began to dance and rear and roll in waves like a rough sea in a squall; but it sank in places and then vomited up its car tracks and the tunnels that carried the cables.... The hotel lurched forward as if the foundation were dragged backward from under it, and crumpled down over Valencia Street. It did not fall to pieces and spray itself all over the place, but telescoped down on itself like a concertina [an early invention of Sir Charles Wheatstone, father of stereoscopy]."

–*The Argonaut*, October 16, 1926

As THE FIRE approached, Valencia Street's remaining inhabitants that could flee, fled. Former mayor James D. Phelan's home at 17th and Valencia was consumed by flame. So, also, were the ruins of the Valencia St. Hotel, where over 100 are believed to have died.

The fire stopped short of the Bancroft Library, which was at 1538 Valencia, near 26th Street. Twenty-five years earlier, prescient bibliophile Hubert Howe Bancroft (1832–1918) had moved his treasured collection away from San Francisco's fire-prone downtown. In 1905, the collection was sold to the University of California, Berkeley. After the 1906 Quake and Fire, the only large private library to survive was carted up and ferried across the Bay to the University of California's Berkeley campus, where it remains safely ensconced today.

Valencia St., which sunk four feet, breaking a great water main.

151

"Sunday dawned in San Francisco; Sunday in the camp of refugees. On a green knoll in Golden Gate Park, between the conservatory and the tennis courts, a white-haired minister of the Gospel gathered his flock. It was the Sabbath day and in the turmoil and confusion the minister did not forget his duty. Two upright stakes and a cross-piece gave him a rude pulpit, and beside him stood a young man with a battered brass cornet. Far over the park stole a melody that drew hundreds of men and women from their tents."

–Charles Morris, *The San Francisco Calamity by Earthquake and Fire*, 1906

8715. Curious wreck of Steiner Street Catholic church and settled houses, San Francisco Disaster, U.S.A.

"THE EARTHQUAKE played a fantastic trick on this church [St. Dominic's, at Bush and Steiner] as it rocked the building to and fro in the dawn of that April morning; so we shall pause a moment to look at the wreck. The stone-work of the spire on the upper end of the front has been shaken off the frame, but that is not as odd as the effect on the tower on this side. Here for about twenty feet the brick and stone have fallen out, leaving the wooden dome perched on the inside framework, like a huge liberty-cap upon a pole. No church in San Francisco suffered so great a loss by the disaster as did the Roman Catholic. It has been estimated that property valued at $10,000,000 has been destroyed. The most costly of these churches was the great Jesuit Church and college of St. Ignatius [where Louise M. Davies Symphony Hall stands today], the largest church in the city, on which $2,000,000 was spent, and now only a mass [no pun intended] of ruined walls; St. Mary's Cathedral on Van Ness Avenue has been badly damaged by fire; the church and convent of Notre Dame was destroyed in the Mission district fire, besides many other churches of less importance. It is reported that the Methodists lost ten churches, Episcopalians, five, Baptists, four and Congregationalists, three. On the right side of the street the small frame houses have settled down with a decided lurch toward the sidewalk. In other districts the settling was much greater. In some cases a three or four story dwelling sank until it was no more than one story above the ground. It was in such situations that most of the 500 who were *reported* [italics added] killed have perished. Up the street is seen the hill running up to the fashionable quarter, lying to the north. Steiner Street is about five blocks west of the limit of the burned district north of Market Street."

Sold only by *The Thomas Mfg. Co., Dayton, Ohio*

50. Mission Church, built 1776, San Francisco, Cal.

The Thomas Mfg. Co., Publishers Dayton, Ohio

Mission Church, built 1776 [sic], *San Francisco.* Although Mission Dolores was founded in 1776, the Mission Dolores pictured—and still standing today—was built in 1791. It has survived countless earthquakes since it was dedicated on a site near the Laguna de los Dolores (see page 148). "The stout adobe walls of the old church are not cracked, but beside them are the ruins of the great brick church which took the place of the adobe mission as the parish place of worship."–San Francisco *Bulletin*, April 30, 1906

8715.

Curious wreck of Steiner Street Catholic church and settled houses. St. Dominic's, at Bush and Steiner, was rebuilt. After the 1989 Loma Prieta Earthquake, flying buttresses were added.

E. C. WHITE CO., Gen'l Offices N. Bennington, Vt., U.S.A.
Branch Offices : New York, Chicago, London.

The "PERFEC" STEREOGRAPH. (Trade Mark.)
Patented April 14, 1903. Other Patents Pending.

(15) 8715 Curious wreck of Steiner St. Catholic church and settled houses, San Francisco Disaster, U. S. A. Copyright 1906 by E. C. White Co.

8716. Refugee Camp in Lafayette Square looking into city, San Francisco Disaster, U.S.A.

"HERE WE HAVE a glimpse of one of the saddest results of the disaster in the pathetic efforts of the thousands of homeless citizens to find a shelter in the public parks and squares. The greatest numbers fled to the Presidio and Golden Gate Park, both further to the west. But many took refuge in the small squares, which are rather numerous in the northern section. Lafayette Square is about two blocks square, lying about midway between Market Street and the Bay, and two blocks west of Van Ness Avenue. The fire came very near, only a block away, at the corner of Franklin and Clay Streets. The experiences of these refugees must have been terrifying during those dreadful days, for their position was perilous and for hours they could hear plainly the awful explosions of dynamite and the reverberations of the cannon blowing up the beautiful houses on Van Ness Avenue, during the desperate attempt to stay the advance of the fire towards the Western Addition. All danger is long since passed, but for many days these people have been living out-doors. The tents were supplied from the Government stores at the Presidio, but in many cases the people in the small squares had no better shelter than sheets of some slight covering, and suffered greatly during the heavy rains which followed. The wretched looking woman on the left is apparently in this case. In front of the tents on the pathway are two little fire-places made of a few bricks. These were seen all over the city, as no one was permitted to make a fire in a house; so that even those who were occupying their own houses were obliged to do their cooking in this way on the street. The food was distributed from the supply-stations, where rich and poor alike had to wait in line, sometimes in the days of the greatest need for hours at a time."

8285—Searching for family relics in the ruins of the dear old home—San Francisco, Cal. Copyright 1906 by Underwood & Underwood. II-91891

Searching for family relics in the ruins of the dear old home.

49C. Light Hearts and Heavy Burdens Leaving the Long Bread Line at St. Mary's Cathedral. After the San Francisco Disaster.

Light Hearts and Heavy Burdens Leaving the Long Bread Line at St. Mary's Cathedral [Van Ness at O'Farrell, where KRON's television studios are today]. *After the San Francisco Disaster.* San Francisco has had three "St. Mary's": "Old" St. Mary's Roman Catholic Church on California Street (1854–present), St. Mary's Cathedral on Van Ness (1891–1962), and the Cathedral of Saint Mary of the Assumption, AKA St. Mary's Cathedral, on Gough Street (1970–present).

8716.

Refugee Camp in Lafayette Square looking into city. Camp No. 17, at Lafayette Square (Washington, Gough, Sacramento, and Laguna streets) officially opened on June 2, 1906. As many as 622 people were "housed" there at one time. The Camp remained open until February 2, 1907.

*O*ver refugees' Camp Lake showing edge of unburned district. Burned area lies beyond (loss over $300,000,000). A hot-meal kitchen and a spectacular view drew refugees to Camp Lake. The aptly named camp was located near Laguna and Market. The white boardinghouse on the right still stands today, at the corner of Laguna and Hermann, near Market.

*T*he San Francisco Earthquake,
April 18, 1906. True Grit.
Ready for business at the old stand.
The northwestern end of the Ferry
Building is on the right.

5331 The San Francisco Earthquake, April 18, 1906. True Grit. Ready
for business at the old stand. Copyright 1906 by C. H. Graves.

*H*omeless among ruins of former wealth—crude shelters in Union Square. This old-timer was alive during the Civil War rallies that gave Union Square its name. Upper left: Ruins of the Union League Club Building.

A *band of little homeless refugees* [twins!] — *happy in spite of the terrible calamity.* The photogenic young lady in the pigtails also appears on page 109, in another Underwood & Underwood stereo view. Excerpts from San Francisco schoolchildren's Earthquake compositions: "They said San Fras. was going to be destroyed and so a volcano blew up and covered the city with lather." "They dinamited everybody's house up." "They are working hard to get the ruins finished."

–*The Argonaut*, May 12, 1906

34. Refugees' Camp, Showing City Hall in the Background, San Francisco, Cal.

Refugees' Camp, Showing City Hall in the Background. Far right: The Hall of Records was relatively undamaged by the Earthquake, but gutted by the Fire.

*F*un making by the earthquake refugee—a temporary home. Edith Wharton's book, *The House of Mirth*, inspired the occupants of this Jefferson Square dwelling. Camp No. 16, at Jefferson Square (Jefferson, Gough, Golden Gate, and Laguna streets), officially opened on June 2, 1906, remaining open until August 23, 1907. Its maximum population was 2,000.

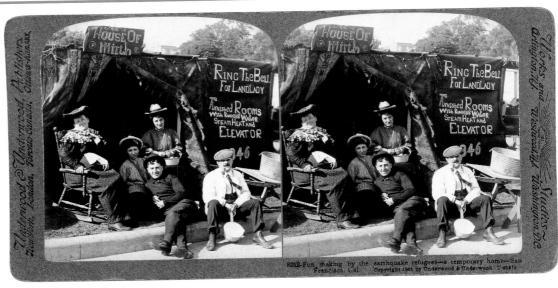

8211 Street kitchens jokingly named for famous hotels—after the earthquake.
San Francisco, Cal. Copyright 1906 by Underwood & Underwood. 8-51186.

*S*treet kitchens jokingly named for famous hotels—after the earth-quake.* Cooking indoors was strictly prohibited (and the ban strictly observed) until inspection of the City's thousands of chimneys could take place. Alfresco dining became de rigueur. "The preparation of the morning and evening meal—for San Francisco does not partake of more than that number at present—is one of the most picturesque sights resulting from the catastrophe. In front of every house there is a small improvised furnace or cook stove whereon the food is prepared. In some places the Chinese servants still remain faithful to their employers and to them the cooking is entrusted." [continued]

Cooking dinner in the street—after the great disaster.

"But it is no unusual thing to see the wives of men, who, a few days ago were the possessors of millions, stirring the porridge or deftly manipulating bacon and eggs [to be sure, more deftly than the breakfast preparation that ostensibly precipitated the so-called Ham-and-Eggs Fire in Hayes Valley on April 18]. The housewives enter into the spirit of the work with a zest and good nature that demonstrates the facility with which the average American adjusts himself of herself to the needs of the hour."

—The Argonaut, April 28, 1906

A restaurant kitchen on the street, outside the burned district. Western Addition Oyster & Chop House. Although restaurants were permitted to serve their patrons indoors, even those outside the burned district were required to cook on the street. Barbecuing became a San Francisco "tradition" within weeks.

The Presidio, 1907. By June 30, 1908, when the camps officially closed, the Department of Lands and Buildings had constructed 5,610 cottages. "For two years following the disaster most of the public parks were covered with the green shacks of refugee families. At the end of three years there was not a green shack left in any park. The shacks exist [some still exist today], but they are so changed, so disguised and expanded, that the stranger could never discover them at all. The refugee shacks literally [sic] took wings, flew away to pleasant hillsides in the outlying districts, and there were transformed into comfortable homes."

—Rufus Steele, *The City That Is*, 1909

8717. Dynamiting dangerous walls on Market Street, after the fire, San Francisco Disaster, U.S.A.

"BY APRIL 21st the fire was practically extinguished and the next day the work of cleaning up was begun. First of all Market Street was made passable, and for this work citizens of all classes were pressed into service by the military authorities, who were still the supporters of law and order. But when the debris had been cleared from the street, a great danger to pedestrians and traffic still remained in the shattered walls, which here and there were still standing in the most threatening condition. As the trade-winds began to blow in steadily and strongly directly after the disaster, a large number of dangerous walls were thrown down by the gales. But many remained, menacing public safety. We have now an opportunity to see the method used to destroy them. The dynamiting is being done under the direction of the Building Committee, a body of forty citizens appointed by Mayor [Eugene E.] Schmitz. [The first meeting of the "Citizens' Committee of Fifty" was held April 18, at 3 p.m., in the Hall of Justice, at Kearny and Washington. Schmitz was Chairman; former mayor James D. Phelan was elected Chairman of the Finance Committee. The Committee of Fifty disbanded May 5, having been replaced by the "Committee of Forty" or "Committee on Reconstruction" May 4. Phelan chaired the new sub-committee on Burnham Plans, continuing his pre-earthquake push for the adoption of architect Daniel Burnham's "City Beautiful" plans. But San Francisco was more interested in rapid "upbuilding," as it would become known, than gradual beautification.] Several members of the committee are in this automobile, watching the explosion several hundred feet down the street. It will be some time before the extraordinarily dense smoke, which has just risen in a compact mass, will clear away and show the gap that has been made. This work will have to be done all over the burned district, for most of the ruined walls can be handled only in this way. The noise of dynamite explosions became a familiar one in those days of horror, as building after building was blown up in the vain hope of arresting the fire. A general opinion decided that more harm than good was done, as the buildings were shattered and thus became an easier food for the flames."

166

A publication of the Southern Pacific Railroad. Cover art by San Francisco artist Maynard Dixon (1875–1946).

8717.

Dynamiting dangerous walls on Market Street, after the fire. "San Francisco's location on her great bay, facing the Orient, the gateway through which will pass the trade of this great land; San Francisco, the metropolis of the Pacific Coast, and backed by California's wonderfully varied resources, her people brave, undaunted, resourceful, and with the sympathies of all the world enlisted in her favor; San Francisco will rise again, regenerated by her baptism of fire."

—"Earthquake Governor" George Cooper Pardee (1857–1941), *Will San Francisco be Rebuilt*, in *The Story of the California Disaster*, 1906

Dynamiting unsafe walls left by the earthquake and fire. St. Mary's Cathedral, at Van Ness and O'Farrell, is visible in the distance. "The fire spread over three-fourths of the city and could not be controlled, no water to fight it, no light, and the earth still trembling. Building after building was dismantled to check the progress of warring, seething flames, but of no avail.... The fires blazed like volcanos, and all business houses, hotels, theatres, in fact, the entire business portion lay in ruins and also two-thirds of the residences; but I trust 'Frisco will rise a phoenix from

its ashes, that a new and more beautiful San Francisco will be born, and that the generous American nation will give it the support and financial assistance it so fully deserves." –Brewer Adolphus Busch, who was in the audience at the Grand Opera House on April 17, in *San Francisco's Great Disaster*, Sydney Tyler, 1906

Pulling down the walls of great business bldgs., ruined by earthquake and fire.

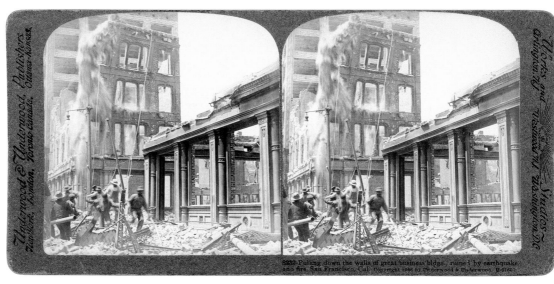

Opening safes from the great business buildings wrecked by earthquake. Charles Morris: "Out of 576 vaults and safes opened in the district east of Powell and north of Market Street, where the flames had raged with the greatest fury, it was found that fully 40% had not performed their duty. When opened they were found to contain nothing but heaps of ashes." Savvy San Francisco safecrackers heeded the spontaneous-combustion lessons learned in the Baltimore Fire of 1904. Upon the premature opening of a hot safe or vault, the rush of air often resulted in a quick, fiery end to its owner's hopes and valuables. Patience was more often richly rewarded.

Benjamin *Schloss Building.* 409 Market Street. "CRASHED! BUT NOT CRUSHED. OFFICE 514 DEVISADERO. ORDERS FOR CROCKERY, GLASS AND ENAMELED WARE TAKEN AND FILLED QUICKLY. SCHLOSS CROCKERY CO." By 1907, Benjamin Schloss had relocated his business to Beale Street, near Market, and his place of residence to Alameda.

40.   Schloss Building.
Copyright by Tom M. Phillips, 1906.

8718. Overlooking Kearney [now **Kearny**] *Street—lower burned area from Telegraph Hill—San Francisco Disaster, U.S.A.*

"FROM THE STEEP SLOPE of Telegraph Hill, so steep that one has the greatest difficulty in climbing it at this point, we see stretched before us the most important business section of San Francisco, wrecked and mute. The long street directly in front is Kearney Street, once a busy thoroughfare, lined with many of the best shops of the city. At the further end, where it runs into Market Street, stands the lofty Call Building, easily distinguished by its dome. Just to the left is the very tall, new building of the Chronicle, and somewhat below in the same direction we see the long outline of the Palace Hotel. The tallest building far to the left, with a cupola on the roof, is the great Merchant's Exchange on California Street; a modern steel building which cost $2,500,000. The rather lower, light colored building, standing to the right of the Exchange, is the huge Mills Building, on which $1,000,000 was spent, and between that and the Palace Hotel stands the tall Crocker Building. The most conspicuous ruin on Kearney Street is the Hall of Justice on the left-hand side, showing its high square tower resting apparently on a very slight connection with the main building. Opposite the Hall of Justice, across Kearney Street, we see the lower edge of Chinatown, which extended in our direction to the diagonal street, running to the right. The fire first attacked this district from below, along Sansome Street; then, checked for a time by the great buildings on the left, it spread gradually westward and by 5:00 o'clock in the afternoon reached the Hall of Justice, then leaped across Kearney Street into Chinatown."

Gone – Gone forever are the days of 49.

To my dear friend Frank Keenan from Homer Davenport 1906

Cartoonist Homer Davenport (1868–1912) left the circus in 1892 to join the staff of William Randolph Hearst's San Francisco *Examiner.* Hearst brought him to New York three years later. Dubuque, Iowa-born actor Frank Keenan (1858–1929) was actor Ed Wynn's great uncle and actor Keenan Wynn's great-granduncle. After the Quake, Hearst encouraged the sale of such prints to raise money for disaster relief.

8718.

Overlooking *Kearney* [now Kearny] *Street—lower burned area from Telegraph Hill.* In the foreground of this haunting image is the intersection of Broadway and Kearny. On the left side of Kearny, at Washington, is the ruined tower of the Hall of Justice. Political boss Abe Ruef's Sentinel Building— a flatiron on the gore at Kearny and Montgomery Ave. (now Columbus)—was under construction in 1906. Today, as the Columbus Tower, it is home to Café Niebaum-Coppola. After his parole from San Quentin on August 21, 1915, Ruef (1864–1936) maintained an office there. On his door, a brass plate proclaimed: "A. Ruef, Ideas Investments, and Real Estate."

8718 Overlooking Kearney St.—lower burned area from Telegraph Hill—San Francisco Disaster, U. S. A.

ACT III
WAS THERE AN EARTHQUAKE AT...?

SENATOR STANFORD'S FARM AT PALO ALTO, CALIFORNIA, AND THE PROPOSED UNIVERSITY.—[See Page 286.]

1. The Cactus Garden.   2. Senator Stanford.   3. The Senator's Home.   4. The Lake.   5. Palo Alto.   6. The Railroad Depot.   7. The proposed University Buildings.

COURTESY OF REID AND PEGGY DENNIS.

"Discouragement is an unknown idea in California. It is men, not buildings, which make a university."
—Stanford President David Starr Jordan (1851–1931), *Pacific Monthly*, 1906

JANE LATHROP STANFORD commissioned Stanford Memorial Church in memory of her husband, Leland. "While my whole heart is in this University, my soul is in this church." Designed by Charles Coolidge of Boston, the non-sectarian church opened on January 25, 1903. Mrs. Stanford died on February 28, 1905.

"The Leland Stanford Junior University is situated one mile from Palo Alto, in Santa Clara County, California; it was founded by Senator Leland Stanford and Jane Lathrop Stanford, in memory of their son Leland Stanford, Junior, who died at Florence, Italy, in 1884. The cornerstone of this magnificent institution was laid on the fourteenth day of May, 1887. The University was formally opened to students October 1st, 1891.... The past years of Stanford have been designated as 'The Building Stage; the Stone Age.' The buildings had almost reached the stage of completion [by 1906]."—Bertha Marguerite Rice, *Leland Stanford Jr. University Before and After the Earthquake*, 1906

San Francisco Earthquake, April 18, 1906. Memorial Arch, Leland Stanford [Jr.] University, Palo Alto.

ON APRIL 18, Stanford was on spring break. Unlike San Francisco, it suffered from neither fire nor dynamite. Two perished, a student and a fireman. "The dilapidated condition of the onetime splendid buildings of the Leland Stanford Jr. University as a result of the earthquake shock is the subject of uncomplimentary discussion by the members of the faculty. Some of the professors hint that the earthquake has shown that the buildings were inadequately constructed and give weight to a rumor current in Palo Alto during the past three years that the

specifications for the proposed magnificent buildings and arches were ignored in an effort to erect pretentious but in reality cheap and gingerbread structures."

–San Francisco *Examiner*, May 1, 1906

HARPER'S WEEKLY

JOURNAL OF CIVILIZATION

VOL. L.   *New York, Saturday, May 19, 1906*   NO. 2578

ALL THAT REMAINS OF THE ELABORATELY DECORATED CHAPEL
AT LELAND STANFORD UNIVERSITY

*R*uins of Memorial Church, Stanford University, Palo Alto, Cal. "The spire of wood weighted by tiles plunged through the nave of the church. The concussion of air forced off the church front with the great mosaic, 'The Sermon on the Mount.' The flying buttresses of the tower fell crashing through the apses. Otherwise the church suffered little. The bells and organ are unharmed, the steel-braced walls are perfect, and the mosaics and stained glass windows are mostly intact. The church will doubtless be at some time restored, but with a Spanish dome, rather than the spire and buttresses of its American prototype, Trinity Church in Boston."–Stanford President David Starr Jordan, *Pacific Monthly*, 1906

Sold only by Griffith & Griffith
Philadelphia, Chicago, London, Hamburg, Ger., St. Petersburg, Russia
Copyright 1906, by Griffith & Griffith

Geo. W. Griffith, Publisher
Philadelphia, Pa.

88. Ruins of Memorial Church, Stanford University, Palo Alto, Cal.

The Stanford Residence, Palo Alto, circa 1895. The Stanfords also maintained a residence on Nob Hill (see pages 136–137).

(see pages 136–137).

*R*esidence of Senator Stanford, *wrecked by the terrible earthquake Palo Alto, Cal.* Leland died in 1893. Jane died twelve years later, in Hawaii. Her obsequies were held in the magnificent "Stone Age" church that she had commissioned in her husband's honor.

Ruins of Leland Stanford [Junior] *University Library badly wrecked by earthquake, Apr. 18, 1906.* "The great dome [of the unfinished library] and its steel supports are unharmed; their swaying completely wrecked the rest of the building of stone and brick."–Stanford President David Starr Jordan, *Pacific Monthly*, 1906

"Angel of Grief," broken, amid ruins of the terrible earthquake, Stanford Univ. Mrs. Stanford commissioned the "Angel of Grief" in memory of her brother. On April 18, its cupola-like canopy collapsed. "We mourn our dead: Gleaming whitely,— kneeling low, amid the trees in its secluded spot, the 'Angel of Grief' breathes a prayer. Prophetic,—it has always been. Strangely symbolical it seems, now, in its attitude of intense sorrow."

–Bertha Marguerite Rice, *Leland Stanford Jr. University Before and After the Earthquake*, 1906

Ruins of Harmon Gymnasium completely wrecked by earthquake, Leland Stanford [Jr.] University. "The most interesting ruins are those of the Leland Stanford Junior University, at Palo Alto, 6 miles east of the fault line. These buildings were on a soft soil and were therefore subjected to the severest earthquake conditions.... The destruction was very great, most of the buildings being wholly or partially destroyed."

—Gilbert, Humphrey, Sewell, and Soulé, *The San Francisco Earthquake and Fire of April 18, 1906 and Their Effects on Structures and Structural Materials*, 1907

ICHTHYOLOGIST AND Stanford president David Starr Jordan (1851–1931) studied at Harvard with American-born Swiss naturalist Jean Louis Rodolphe Agassiz (1807–1873). Agassiz studied with German naturalist Friedrich Wilhelm Heinrich Alexander von Humboldt (1769–1859), in whose honor a county, a university, a current, and a squid have been named. He is familiar to astronomers as the "Humboldt" in the moon's "Mare Humboldtianum." On April 18, 1906, Stanford University's statue of Humboldt remained on its "tenure track." Agassiz, however, took a nose-dive, leading to the campus quip that the "head-foremost" scientist was "better in the abstract than the concrete." Agassiz was returned unharmed to his precarious perch. He and his mentor are still there today.

*R**uins of St. Agnes's* [Agnews] *Insane Asylum, Santa Clara, Cal.* In 1885, on Santa Clara Valley land purchased from Abram Agnew, the State established the California Hospital for the Chronic Insane. Soon, it became the State Insane Asylum at Agnews; in 1897, it became simply Agnews State Hospital. Like Stanford, Agnews suffered from neither fire nor dynamite. But the death toll was staggering: 106 patients and 11 staff members died. "In the gray light of dawn, the scene was terrible." Today, in the heart of Silicon Valley, the Sun Santa Clara Conference Center occupies the site of one of the Earthquake's greatest tragedies.

*R*uins of the First Presbyterian Church, wrecked by the earthquake, April 18, 1906, San Jose, Cal. Refugees, in their Sunday best, stop to view the damage. San Jose suffered from both earthquake and fire. Mayor George D. Worswick's "Proclamation!" was more temperate than his San Francisco counterpart's "shoot-to-kill" order, however. Worswick imposed a 7:30 p.m. curfew and admonished all persons to "remain away from that part of the business section now being patrolled. ALL LAWLESSNESS WILL BE REPRESSED WITH A HEAVY HAND."

186

Relief Line at Oakland. City Hall. "Each morning a line of about 2,000 men and women may be seen slowly winding in and out of the City Hall in Oakland, all waiting for a permit to go to the burned metropolis."–*The Signs of the Times*, Mountain View, May 23, 1906. Thousands fled to Oakland, many camping on the shores of Lake Merritt. Homeless "Celestials" filled Oakland's Chinatown to overflowing. Oakland Mayor Frank Mott worked with Governor (and former Oakland mayor) George Pardee, coordinating the receipt—mostly by rail—of relief supplies from all over the country, and their distribution throughout the Bay Area.

187

Wrecked by the Memorable Earthquake of April 1906, 1st Baptist Church, Oakland, Calif. This stereo view tells only the second part of 1st Baptist's earthquake story. The church's steeple was severely damaged by the earthquake, but somehow remained fixed in a perilously exalted position atop the church's entrance—until pulled down by the hands of man.

Wrecked by the Memorable Earthquake of April 1906, 1st Baptist Church, Oakland, Calif.

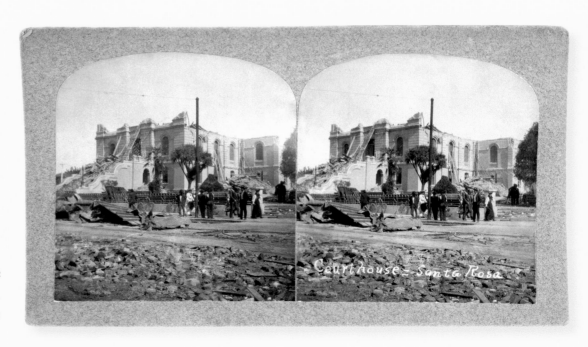

Sonoma County Court house. Santa Rosa Cal.
Dear Grandma.—This is the Court house
in S.R. [Santa Rosa] after the quake. Was
there an earthquake in Neb. [Nebraska] I
heard there was one. We felt another one
last night about 8:30.

by by Sadie H.

POSTCARD, addressed to Mrs. Laura Hansen, Fremont, Nebraska. Postmarked "Sebastopol, May 18, 1906." The severe earthquake to which Sadie is referring occurred at 8:21 p.m. on May 17, 1906. Felt throughout the San Francisco Bay Region, it was classified a **VI** on the **I** to **X** Rossi-Forel Scale. A **VI** indicated a "general awakening of sleepers; general ringing of bells; swinging of chandeliers; stopping of clocks, visible swaying of trees; some persons run out of building."

188

Court House ~ Santa Rosa.

THE EARTHQUAKE of April 18 was a **IX** on the Rossi-Forel Scale. Santa Rosa was decimated, her citizens unaware of the extent of San Francisco's tragedy until refugees began arriving from the City. "At Santa Rosa, the destruction was greater than in any other section affected by the earthquake, and the fire that followed wiped out the business section of the town, which suffered a greater proportionate total loss than San Francisco."–Gilbert, Humphrey, Sewell, and Soulé, *The San Francisco Earthquake and Fire of April 18, 1906 and their Effects on Structures and Structural Materials*, 1907

ACT IV
PUBLIC AFFAIRS FOR PRIVATE ADVANTAGE

Politics, *n*. A strife of interests masquerading as a contest of principles. The conduct of public affairs for private advantage.
–Ambrose Bierce, *The Devil's Dictionary*, 1911

"A SCHMITZ BUTTON on your lapel means that you are for government by grafters. It means that you want the Commissions to be run for private profit and not for public service. It means that you want the police force to continue to be what it is— a protector of criminals, a menace to the law-abiding and a tool for the use of the Mayor and the thieves who surround him. It means that you approve of the supremacy of Ruef in the City Administration and of his activity as a collector of "fees" in exchange for the exercise of the Mayor's power to enforce or suspend laws. It means that you are in sympathy with what all reputable men, of all parties, are battling against in the cities of America— corruption in government. So if you choose to wear a Schmitz button you have no more reason to resent being classed with the social dregs of the community than your choice for Mayor has to bleat for pity when he is confronted with the Grand Jury's report, which tells of his acts and holds him responsible for the corruption that rots this Administration."
–San Francisco *Bulletin*, October 12, 1905

Attorney Abraham Ruef and violinist Eugene E. Schmitz were both born in San Francisco in 1864. Ruef, after graduating from the University of California at 17, got involved in San Francisco politics, running North Beach for the Republican Party. Schmitz, a talented musician and composer, became the conductor of the pit orchestra at the Columbia Theater and the local musicians union's first president. In 1901, when Mayor James Duval Phelan became embroiled in a bitter labor dispute, ruining his chances for re-election, Ruef seized the opportunity. Rather than backing the Republican candidate, however, Ruef realized that it might be easier to win a three-way race by a plurality than a two-way race by a majority. For this, he needed a candidate who would appeal to labor, without threatening the status quo. What better choice than a union man in white tie and tails?

The violinist won, exactly as Abe Ruef hoped he would. Two elections later, on November 7, 1905, despite mounting legal troubles and the *Bulletin*'s vitriolic accusations, Schmitz won again, this time by a simple majority. And now, for the first time, Ruef and Schmitz controlled the Board of Supervisors, who had successfully ridden Schmitz's handsomely tailored electoral coattails into office.

189

by ex-Mayor Phelan (also on the dais). After Schmitz's reelection in 1905, all three became embroiled in the graft and corruption trials that cost Schmitz his job.

*P*resident Roosevelt at Unveiling of Navy Monument. Dewey Monument, Union Square, May 14, 1903. TR was introduced by Mayor Schmitz (left, in the wideawake hat*), who, in turn, had been introduced

*Mayor Schmitz was almost never seen without his trademark wideawake hat. The wideawake is a soft felt hat with a broad brim and low crown that got its name from the fact that it has no "nap."

TR: "It is eminently fitting that there should be here in this great city on the Pacific Ocean a monument to commemorate the deed which showed once for all that America had taken her position on the Pacific."

*S*t. Francis hotel, the interior of which was burned out. To the left of the hotel, in the middle of Union Square, is the Dewey Monument. As if by a miracle, Robert Aitken's bronze "Victory" (modeled after Alma de Brettville, who became Mrs. Adolph Spreckels) did not fall from the granite Corinthian column upon which she still balances today. Inscribed in the Monument's base: "Erected by the citizens of San Francisco to commemorate the victory of the American Navy under Commodore George Dewey [1837–1917] at Manila Bay, May first, MDCCCXCVIII" and "On May twenty-third, MCMI, the ground for this monument was broken by President McKinley."

*M*ayor Schmitz, on his rounds *of untiring labors to relieve his stricken city.* "All contemporary stories of the great fire concur in describing Mr. Eugene E. Schmitz, who was then Mayor of San Francisco, as one of the outstanding heroes of the catastrophe.... In such stark emergency it was reasonable for some to wonder if Mr. Schmitz would rise to the occasion. The first hour proved the man, and thereafter there was no shred of doubt as to the sterling worth of the service he had taken upon himself to perform."

–The Argonaut, January 15, 1927

*C*hief of Police J.F. Dinan, at
headquarters after the great disaster.
After the Earthquake and Fire, Chief
Dinan and his SFPD acquitted
themselves with aplomb. Later
allegations regarding their role in the
City's rampant graft and corruption,
however, were scathing: "The total
number of crimes for which indict-
ments were found by the Oliver Grand
Jury was 175, participated in by nearly
40 persons, representing practically
every walk in life. Not one of them was
unearthed by the Police Department of
San Francisco, and the Chief of Police
himself was indicted for perjury before
the Grand Jury and for conspiring to
prevent the detection of crime. It is

193

apparent that such a department must have been rotten to the core. As not a single officer or detective, commissioned or otherwise, has been removed for concealing or failing to discover any of the crimes, and as there have been practically no resignations from the department, it is apparent that its personnel is still of the same character. It would appear that another Schmitz-Ruef administration would find the same organized support standing ready to do its bidding."–William Denman et al, *Report on the Causes of Municipal Corruption in San Francisco*, 1910

*P*olice Headquarters in the ruined City—*St. Dominick's* [sic] *Church beyond.* Corner, Bush & Fillmore.

194

P-14061 Japanese Children Reading a Newspaper.

Japanese Children Reading a Newspaper. On the reverse: "Shall I tell you how these Japanese children learned to read? They went to school just as you do.... You read a line from left to right. You read a page from top to bottom. These children think that a topsy-turvy way to do. They read from right to left, from the bottom to the top, and their books begin on the page where ours end.... No other country has so many history stories about its heroes as Japan. The children must learn all these. This helps the boys to be brave. They, too, wish to be heroes." Had these Japanese children been living in San Francisco in the fall of 1906, they would have attended a segregated school.

Another Earthquake in San Francisco
(*From the New York World*)

more concerned with the risk of war with Japan than with being accused of municipal meddling, intervened. He invited Mayor Schmitz—who called the controversy "more of a tempest in a teapot than anything else"—and

195

ON OCTOBER 11, 1906, San Francisco's Board of Education voted to change the name of Chinatown's rebuilt "Chinese School" to the "Oriental Public School," mandating that Japanese children attend school there. Japan protested, catching the attention of President Theodore Roosevelt. TR,

members of the Board of Education to meet with him to resolve the matter. They traveled to Washington in February 1907, but TR prevailed and the discriminatory order was revoked. San Francisco's 93 Japanese schoolchildren were free again to attend the school of their choice.

B Y EARLY 1906, there was a new Poodle Dog in town, at Mason and Eddy. Gertrude Atherton, in her prolix 1907 novel, *Ancestors*, re-creates an evening there:

> The party of four entered The Poodle Dog—the socially successful offspring of the still enterprising and disreputable parent on the dark slope above…
>
> "I don't understand," said the bewildered Englishman. "Are we dining in a dive?"
>
> "Not quite, but almost!" cried Stone, refilling his glass from the large bottle in ice. "There is only one San Francisco! We have about six of these French restaurants—ever taste anything like these frogs in Paris? You scarcely ever see anybody in them at this hour with an 'all-night' reputation. There are plenty of other resorts, a good many of them under the sidewalks [the reference is to Chinatown], where the dinner is almost as good but where a man doesn't take his wife. And up-stairs—here—and in a few others—well, if a woman is seen entering by the side door she is done for. But then she isn't usually seen. Lord! If these walls could speak! The divorce-mills would explode. The waiters all invest in real estate. Policemen send their daughters to Europe, and the boss politicians get rich so fast they spend money almost like a gentleman."

Newspaper editor Fremont Older's San Francisco *Bulletin* crusaded against Mayor Schmitz, City Attorney Abe Ruef, Police Chief Jeremiah Dinan, and the Board of Supervisors. Their political peccadilloes were innumerable. And each was undoubtedly getting his slice of French restaurant pie: "The French restaurants were notified by the Police Commission that they would not get a renewal of their [liquor] licenses. Ruef stood up the restaurant men for a big 'fee' and immediately the threat of the Commission was forgotten and the restaurants got their licenses." Ruef then shared his so-called attorney's fee with his municipal cohorts.

During the 1905 mayoral campaign, Schmitz repeatedly denied Older's charges. "No graft," the mayor maintained, "has existed or does exist; none has been found or discovered, after the most microscopical examination by a boughten press, by a prostituted Grand Jury, by hired

detectives, by purchased assassins of reputation and character." After Schmitz's electoral victory, Older went to Washington to appeal to President Roosevelt for help in bringing political boss Ruef and the corrupted mayor to their political knees. Older enlisted the financial support of Rudolph Spreckels and ex-Mayor James Duval Phelan in his quest. Rudolph was the son of sugar magnate Claus Spreckels, who built the thirteen-story Call Building at Third and Market. It survived the Earthquake and Fire, unlike Phelan's father's eponymous Market Street edifice. Roosevelt put prosecutor Francis J. Heney and detective William J. Burns on the case.

Schmitz and Ruef were soon indicted for extorting money from the French restaurants. The restaurant keeper of the New Poodle Dog, Antonio B. Blanco, testified at Schmitz's trial. He was asked whether he gave money to Ruef because he was a city attorney or a political boss. "Well," he replied, "being a political boss we thought he had influence enough to get our licenses."

Mayor Schmitz's subsequent conviction in the French restaurant case was overturned on a technicality. The district court of appeals ruled that extortion, according to California law, must include the threat of *unlawful* injury. As it could find nothing unlawful about the withholding of a liquor license from a bordello, Schmitz was freed and similar charges against Ruef were dropped.

Poodle Dog Restaurant [Mason & Eddy], *James Flood Building and the Emporium—All Ruined by the Terrible San Francisco Disaster.* The Poodle Dog: "There have been no less than four establishments of this name, beginning with a frame shanty where, in the early days, a prince of French cooks used to exchange ragouts for gold dust…. On the ground floor was a public restaurant where there was served the best dollar dinner on earth…. On the second floor there were private rooms, and to dine there, with one or more of the opposite sex, was risqué but not especially terrible. But the third floor—and the fourth floor—and the fifth!"

–Will Irwin, *The City That Was*, 1906

88—Poodle Dog Restaurant, James Flood Building and the Emporium —All Ruined by the Terrible San Francisco Disaster.

HON. A. RUEF
ATTORNEY FOR THE MAYOR'S OFFICE

Take bribes from *both* of the telephone companies competing for the City's telephone franchise. In this case, members of the Board of Supervisors took bribes directly from one company, and indirectly—through Ruef—from its competitor. The latter won the franchise.

Take bribes to fix the gas rates of the Pacific Gas and Electric Company.

Take bribes from the United Railroads in exchange for permission to replace its pre-earthquake underground conduit and cable system with the post-earthquake overhead trolley system still in use on Market Street today.

By 1907, virtually every business in San Francisco, from the Poodle Dog to the Southern Pacific Railroad, knew that the way to get a leg up on the competition was to "retain" City Attorney Abraham Ruef. Although he maintained that the payments he received were attorney's "fees" from his clients, it is clear that he and Schmitz were involved in schemes to:

Extort money from the French restaurants in exchange for the renewal of liquor licenses.

198

Take bribes in exchange for the granting of prize-fight licenses.

Take bribes in exchange for the granting of an electric railroad franchise to the Parkside Company, a Sunset District real estate development company.

A Rift in the Earth— Deep crack in pavement on Mission St., showing half-burned street car.

"**M**ANAGER MULLALY of the United Railroads announces that cars will be operated to-day from the Ferry through the city to Turk, Eddy and Fillmore streets, and that within a few days the temporary service to be established would cover the greater part of the city. Transportation for all passengers and supplies will be free until conditions are relieved. Mayor Schmitz, in this connection, announces that he had guaranteed a temporary franchise for a trolley system down Market street, to remain in force until revoked."–San Francisco *Examiner*, April 22, 1906

The United Railroads (under the leadership of its president, Patrick Calhoun) forged ahead, despite newspaper editorials denouncing the "cold-blooded" corporation:

"You know that the Supervisors have passed to print an ordinance that aims to permit the United Railroads to operate permanently overhead trolleys on all of its lines. You also know that when this was suggested before the fire every organization that took any pride in the appearance of the city protested against San Francisco being turned into a trolley town…. The emergency that came with the destruction of the city gave the excuse for putting in overhead trolleys—they are the cheapest and quickest of construction—just as it is cheaper and quicker to erect temporary one-story sheds than to erect modern high-class business buildings. There is this difference, however: the sheds are frankly only temporary while the Supervisors propose that the dangerous, ragged, noisy trolley shall blemish our streets as long as the United Railroads runs cars….

"Mr. Abe Ruef has stated that the story that he had been retained as consulting attorney for the United Railroads was not the truth; so there must be some other reason for the giving of this franchise to the company. Why the company wants it is quite plain. It costs about ten times as much to construct the safe, clean, finished underground trolley system as it does the rattletrap, makeshift overhead system that contains a threat of death and destruction every time a wire snaps. The overhead trolley does well enough as a temporary expedient; it is the raw emergency machinery for getting around, but it has no more place in the streets of a beautiful, prosperous city such as San Francisco will be within a few years than the steam locomotives that will be run to carry off the debris."
–San Francisco *Examiner*, May 21, 1906

First car service after earthquake, rush to take advantage of trolleys.

UNDERWOOD & UNDERWOOD GLASS-PLATE NEGATIVE, THE KEYSTONE-MAST COLLECTION.
COURTESY, UCR/CALIFORNIA MUSEUM OF PHOTOGRAPHY, UNIVERSITY OF CALIFORNIA, RIVERSIDE.

Looking down Market Street to Ferry Bldg. from Call Bldg. Late afternoon, May 15 or 16, 1907. Less than a year after the Board of Supervisors permitted the United Railroads to build its trolley system, the carmen went on strike. Then Abe Ruef confessed. At the San Francisco *Examiner* newsstand, a torn sign announced the astonishing news: RUEF PLEADS GUILTY.

Ruef was one of the bribe *takers*. It was thought that his mea culpa would ignite a prosecutorial flame under the City's "real" criminals—the bribe *givers*—particularly those associated with the Southern Pacific and United Railroads. But in the end, it was Abe Ruef—part criminal, part scapegoat—who did the hard time.

A Short Talk on Advertising!

"The Examiner"
PRINTED
DURING THE MONTH OF APRIL
56,025 Inches
OF ADVERTISING
18,658 Inches or 933 Columns
More Than Any Other San Francisco Paper

AN AMERICAN PAPER FOR THE AMERICAN PEOPLE

San Francisco Examiner

REG. US. PAT. OFF.

THE WEATHER.
Forecast for San Francisco and vicinity: Fair Thursday; light north winds changing to westerly; fog in the morning.
A. G. McADIE.
District Forecaster.

VOL. LXXXVI   SAN FRANCISCO, THURSDAY, MAY 16, 1907.   No 136.

"I WILL TELL EVERYTHING"—ABE RUEF

Boss Ignores His Attorneys and Pleads Guilty to the Crime of Extortion!

SCENE in Judge Dunne's Court yesterday when Abe Ruef read the statement ending with his plea of guilty to the charge of extortion. Those in the picture, reading from left to right, are Attorney Murphy, Attorney Fairall, W. J. Biggy, Abe Ruef, District Attorney Langdon, Attorney Hiram Johnson, Detective W. J. Burns, Rudolph Spreckels (standing) and Francis J. Heney.

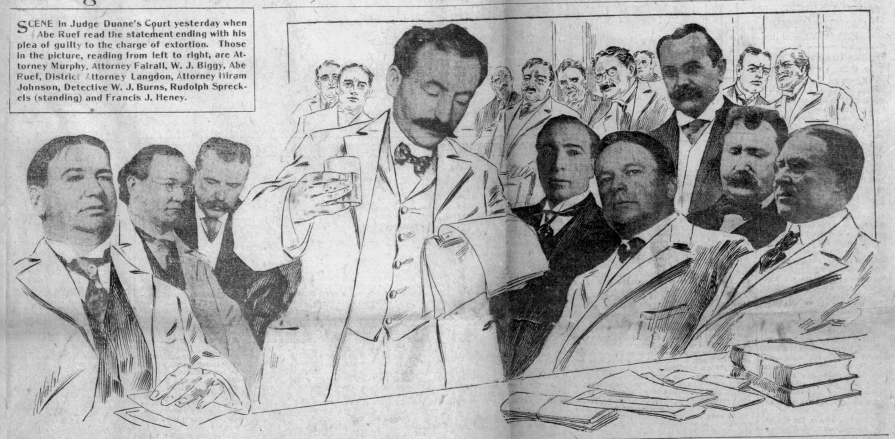

EXTRACTS FROM THE PLEA AND CONFESSIONS OF ABRAHAM RUEF

Former Boss of the City Tells Why He Confessed His Guilt and What He Now Intends to Do

"AS an earnest I have determined to make a beginning. I desire to withdraw my plea of not guilty heretofore entered, and to enter the contrary plea, and at the proper time submit to the court further suggestions for its consideration."

§ § §

"I have not been promised immunity, but I shall expect the leniency that is shown to men who have done what I have done and who do what I expect to do."

"I pleaded guilty to save the lives of those who are nearest and dearest to me on earth. If my father, my mother and my sister had been compelled to endure the strain of my trial, it would have cost their lives.

§ § §

"I will not say at the present moment that Mayor Schmitz is guilty of the charges that have been brought against him, or that he is innocent. I will say this: 'I wanted to break away from Schmitz before his re-election a year ago last November, and said to him, 'I am sick of the whole thing and I want to get out. I can't stand for all these bums you have gathered around you and will appoint. They would eat the paint off a house.' In answer the Mayor begged me to stay with him, and put up the argument that these fellows must be allowed their share or we never could hold the machine together.

"I don't feel that I am a criminal. I haven't criminal instincts. I am going to begin right away to build up my life again and to regain my position in the community."

INTENSELY DRAMATIC SCENE WHEN BOSS ABANDONS FIGHT

Weeps as He Admits His Connivance at Corruptions and Enters His Plea of Guilty

BY EDWARD H. HAMILTON

ONE Abe Ruef has pleaded guilty to the charge of extortion.

It looks very much as though the great bribe-givers and the great bribe-takers are at the sign post of the forking road, with one arm of that post reading "Honduras" and the other "San Quentin."

There are many heads usually held high that lay on restive pillows last night. The keystone of the arch of corruption is down. Now watch for the general smash. There is no telling where the revelations will stop now. Big and little, the rascals had better plead guilty and throw themselves on the mercy of the courts and the community.

Mayor Eugene E. Schmitz was jointly indicted for extortion with Ruef in exactly this case where Ruef has pleaded guilty. If Ruef was guilty Schmitz must be. The boss could have extorted nothing without the power of the Mayor to make the extortion possible. The case of the Mayor will be called for trial on Monday next. There seems no reason for further delay.

Heney has said all along that he can convict Calhoun, Herrin and the other big ones. He has made good with Ruef, and it looks very much as if he could make good all the way through. I take it for granted that Ruef will now tell all. So if Heney had a good chance to convict the great bribe-givers before, he has a certainty now. The day of San Francisco's deliverance

SCHMITZ DECIDES TO STAND PAT

MAYOR SCHMITZ, according to his friends, has decided to stand pat. He was informed of Ruef's determination to plead guilty on Tuesday afternoon, but, according to his confidants, sent back word that he could not help what Ruef did or intended to do, and that so far as he is concerned he is innocent and will face the music.

Yesterday afternoon Schmitz had a long conference with Attorney Joseph Campbell. They were together for a couple of hours. Then the Mayor sought the advice of his intimates.

He appeared to be greatly worried as a result of Ruef's attitude, but absolutely refused to make any statement for publication.

On Monday next Schmitz' trial for extortion will begin. The prosecution announces that its case against the Mayor is much stronger than the case against Ruef.

SCHMITZ LIVES IN A GLASS HOUSE, SAYS GALLAGHER

SUPERVISOR GALLAGHER commented briefly, but, in one respect at least, somewhat pointedly, on Ruef's plea of guilty and declaration of intention to confess. He said:

"I think that Mr. Ruef has done a wise thing—one tending to the benefit of the community. I think, too, that one immediate effect of his announced intention is to cause the Mayor to think he was rather tell all he knows will be to cause the Mayor to think he was rather hasty when he lately took it upon himself to animadvert from a standpoint of assured superior virtue upon the members of the Board of Supervisors.

"I don't object to being roasted by those who seem to have the right to roast me, but the throwing of stones by dwellers in glass houses is tiresome."

"I GAVE SCHMITZ $50,000 OF TROLLEY BRIBE," SAYS RUEF

Former Boss Collapses After Telling How Corruption Fund Was Divided

WHICH?

$200,000 WAS THE PRICE PAID FOR SUPERVISORS' VOTES AND INFLUENCE OF MAYOR AND BOSS

Grand Jury Hears Full Confession of the Deal Whereby San Francisco Was Sold to United Railroads.

RUEF TELLS HOW MONEY WAS PAID TO HIM IN THREE INSTALLMENTS BY FORD

FOR OVER an hour Abraham Ruef was before the Grand Jury yesterday and during that time San Francisco was on tip toe with expectancy. In many quarters this expectancy was heavily charged with dread, for it was known that Ruef was making his confession under oath, and that he proposed shielding none.

The wildest rumors disturbed the town—the evening papers lurid with headlines proclaimed the fallen boss's delivery of everybody who has been mentioned in the innumerable grafts. As a matter of fact, only Mayor Schmitz' and the United Railroads' group of bribers had definite cause to contemplate flight, for Ruef progressed no further than the overhead trolley bribery. He stated that the Mayor received $50,000 as his share of the bribe fund. The strain proved too much and he collapsed and was taken from the Grand Jury room by the elisor.

ATONEMENT

FORD SCHMITZ GLASS HERRIN CALHOUN

ALTAR OF JUSTICE

202

THE CARTOON ABOVE APPEARED in the May 16, 1907, *Examiner*. Center, kneeling: Abraham Ruef, San Francisco City Attorney. Offered up, left to right: Tirey L. Ford, Chief Counsel, United Railroads; Eugene E. Schmitz, Mayor; Louis Glass, Vice President and General Manager, Pacific States Telephone and Telegraph Company; William F. Herrin, Chief Counsel, Southern Pacific Railroad; Patrick Calhoun, President, United Railroads.

San Francisco's graft and corruption trials included the dynamiting of the home of one of the prosecution's star witnesses, Patrick Gallagher, the kidnapping of *Bulletin* editor Fremont Older, and the near-fatal shooting of chief prosecutor Francis J. Heney. The anticipated imprisonment of San Francisco's most powerful men never took place. Upon Ruef's conviction for extortion in the United Railroads case, San Francisco had its scapegoat. On December 19, 1908, *The Wasp* editorialized, "The conviction of Abe Ruef should silence the defamers of San Francisco, who have been loudly proclaiming for a couple of years that justice is powerless in our city and civic pride is dead." By then, San Francisco had grown weary of trials that dwelt on its past—the City's future was its focus, "upbuilding" its mantra.

In the end, it was Ruef who went to San Quentin. Fremont Older, who had once excoriated Ruef, atoned by becoming Ruef's apologist. With Older's help, on August 21, 1915—after serving four years and seven months of his 14 year sentence—the aging attorney was paroled.

O · GLORIOUS · CITY · OF · OUR
HEARTS · THAT · HAST · BEEN
TRIED · AND · NOT · FOUND
WANTING · GO · THOU · WITH
LIKE · SPIRIT · TO · MAKE
THE · FUTURE · THINE

–Inscription in the rotunda of San Francisco's new City Hall, which rose from the ashes of 1906

FROM A 1915 KEYSTONE VIEW COMPANY GLASS-PLATE NEGATIVE IN THE KEYSTONE-MAST COLLECTION.
COURTESY, UCR/CALIFORNIA MUSEUM OF PHOTOGRAPHY, UNIVERSITY OF CALIFORNIA, RIVERSIDE.

JAMES M. DAVIS,
New York City, and St. Louis, Mo.

Copyright 1906, by B. W. Kilburn.

16852. Amid the gray and blackened waste, Great Earthquake,
San Francisco.

*A*mid the gray and blackened waste.
This view is from the ruins of
Nob Hill. The old City Hall
remained standing long after the
Earthquake and Fire. The grim
reminder of San Francisco's tragedy
soon became a tourist attraction,
evocative of ancient Rome: "I went
over the city today. It is the Forum
and the Palatine Hill on a colossal
scale; miles of walls, arches, solitary
columns; hills that look like cemeter-
ies."

—Gertrude Atherton, *The Argonaut*,
May 19, 1906

FINAL CHORUS
THE CITY THAT IS

"WE WILL RESTORE THE CHIEF PORT OF THE PACIFIC."—Mayor Schmitz.
From the *News* (Detroit).

A<small>S</small> S<small>AN</small> F<small>RANCISCO</small> was being trans-formed physically and promotionally into "Greater San Fran-cisco," the phoenix of her flammable gold rush days took flight once again. In 1909, three years af-ter "The Fire," San Francisco *Call* editor Rufus Steele penned his resurrectional "The City That Is." It was written in an effort to supplant San Francisco *Chronicle-cum*–New York *Sun* reporter Will Irwin's eulogistic "The City That Was." The reverent Irwin had begun his 1906 tribute with the upbeat Willie Britt's "I'd rather be a busted lamp post on Battery Street in San Francisco, than the Waldorf-As-toria." But it was Irwin's succinct first sentence that caught everyone's atten-tion: "The old San Francisco is dead." Hyperbolist Steele, in an attempt at municipal transfiguration, countered with *his* first sentence: "The practical restoration of San Francisco within three years from the day the old city was destroyed be-speaks a constructive force that relegates the hammer of Vulcan to the limbo of inutile things." He contin-ued, "The San Fran-cisco achievement crowds back into his class the engineers of Babel, the pyramid builders, and a long line of wonder-workers…. Will Irwin may dry his tears."

In addition to the ubiquitous phoenix, early imagery of San Francisco's recovery ironically included the Romanesque ruins of City Hall, which became a popular stop on sightseeing tours of the burgeon-ing metropolis. By the time a souvenir City Hall coin was incor-porated into a souvenir fob, how-ever, the word "EARTHQUAKE" had been replaced with "DISASTER." After all, *any* city could suffer a disastrous fire. And so the "upbuilding" and pageantry began, along with the return of business—and customers.

205

The New San Francisco

TWO YEARS AFTER THE GREAT FIRE

IN 1907, TEDDY ROOSEVELT sent his proverbial big stick on a round-the-world tour, a sixteen-battleship traveling show of naval prowess designed to impress—if not intimidate—Japan. It also represented a show of support to San Francisco, Gateway of the Pacific.

"The arrival of the fleet at San Francisco on May 6 [1908] was characterized by such a demonstration of enthusiasm and an outpouring of the people as the country never saw before. Tens of thousands came hundreds of miles to see the entrance through the Golden Gate. Admiral [Robley] Evans, who had returned [from illness] to the command of his flagship [the Connecticut] the day before at Monterey, led the fleet into the harbor. The hills were black with spectators. The harbor was crowded with beautifully decorated shipping carrying thousands on the water to see the show. The Pacific fleet of eight armored cruisers and auxiliaries lay inside the bay. With the Battle Fleet was the torpedo flotilla that made the trip around South America at the same time that the Battle Fleet went around. The Atlantic and Pacific fleets joined in one and then Admiral Evans made a circle, nearly two miles in diameter, leading no less than forty-two men of war of the United States, the largest number of American warships ever assembled together since the civil war, and the most powerful fleet ever seen in the Western hemisphere, a fleet greater in size and power than any nation had ever gathered together before with the exception of Great Britain. Following the arrival of the fleet there was a great land parade in San Francisco, the next day, in which 6000 bluejackets [many of whom had landed near the still-standing Harbor Emergency Hospital] joined with the regular army troops and state national guard and other organizations. It was the largest parade of the kind since the great [Admiral] Dewey parade in New York ten years before.... The people cheered the bluejackets wildly, but they went mad over Admiral Evans. They made a hero out of him because of his persistent and plucky struggle with pain and disease.... His naval sun went down that day in a veritable blaze of glory. [Two days later, "Fighting Bob" Evans gave up his command,] declaring impassionedly that what this country needs 'is more battleships and fewer statesmen.'"

–Franklin Matthews, *With the Battle Fleet*, 1908

*T*he Pacific fleet (flagship Connecti-
cut in lead) steaming out to sea.
December 16, 1907. Bound for San
Francisco from Hampton Roads,
Virginia.

*S*an Francisco Bay During the Visit
of the Pacific Fleet, View from the
Call Building. This "Fleet Week" was
as much about San Francisco's pride
and rejuvenation as it was about
demonstrating America's naval
prowess. Note the results of post-
Earthquake "upbuilding" downtown.

207

*V*allejo's welcome to the fleet—
float built by workmen of Mare
Island Navy Yard. Note the temporary
"Emporium" on Van Ness Avenue.
The "Great White Fleet" returned to
Hampton Roads on February 22,
1909.

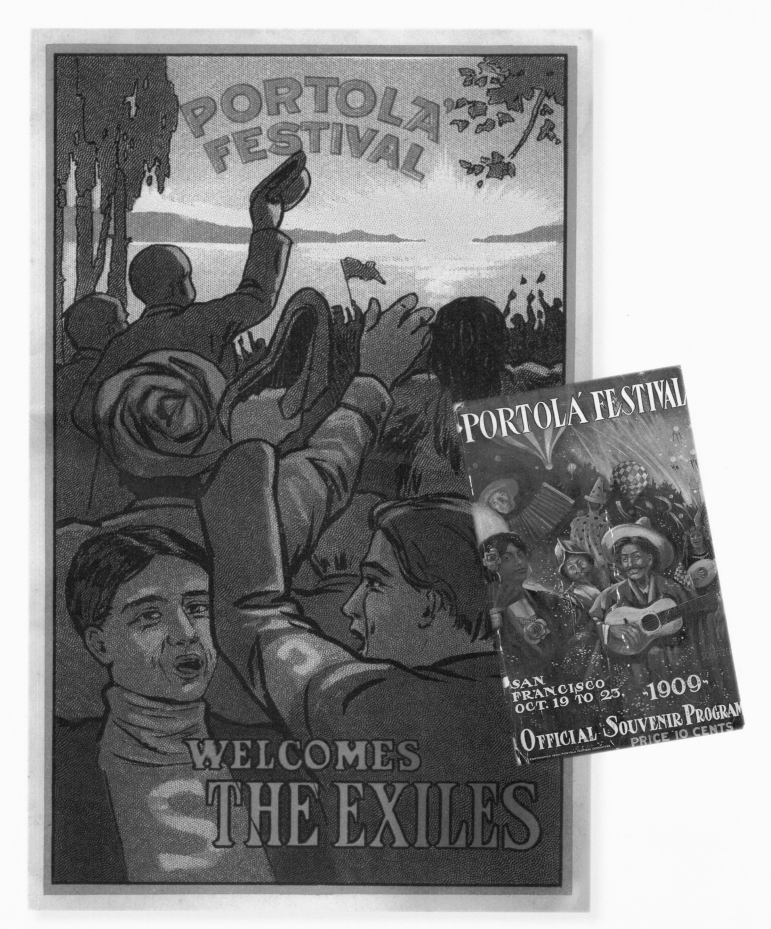

208

Published by the Portolá Festival Committee, whose offices were in the new Phelan Building on Market Street, the enticing *Portolá Festival Welcomes the Exiles* pitches the new San Francisco to the California diaspora, including Stanford and Cal students:

"Home hunger: Californians, wandering over the face of the earth, exiled for many reasons from 'your own, your native land;' have you felt it? San Francisco was the talk of the world three years ago when she hardly existed as a collection of houses; when fire swept over the city and consumed her. Yet the people by the Golden Gate were not destroyed. The hardy sons of pioneers, now pioneers themselves, rebuilt, and today present to the world a modern metropolis of steel and marble and granite, the like of which, for a three-year-old, is not recorded in history.… Exiles, hasten home. Come back. Be here October 19, and stay after October 23."

MORE THAN three years after the Earthquake and Fire—and 140 years after the discovery of San Francisco from high atop the Peninsula's Sweeney Ridge—San Francisco had an excuse for a party. The City's Portolá Festival was much more than a self-congratulatory celebration of history and recovery, however. It also served as both audition and dress rehearsal for an international event in San Francisco along the lines of the Chicago and St. Louis World's Fairs. Plans for such a fête had been fermenting since the Isthmanian Convention in Washington, DC, in 1903. By 1909, San Francisco was ready to strut her pre-Expositional stuff.

209

Portolá Festival. Civic, Industrial, and Fraternal Parade, San Francisco, October 22, 1909.

"**N**icholas A. Covarrubias [born 1839], of Santa Maria, who as Don Gaspar de Portolá, will reign as king over the Portolá Festival, October 19 to 23, is probably one of the most striking characters and dashing figures in the history of Southern California.... Cavalier in bearing, a magnificent horseman and daring rider, Covarrubias is the fiesta king *par excellence*. It is doubtful if California's first governor, the doughty old don whom he will impersonate, could be more dignified, or of more courtly and regal bearing."
—*Portolá Festival Program*, 1909

*P*resident Roosevelt discussing America's task with workmen at Bas Obispo, Panama Canal. November 1906. On the reverse: "This point in the 'big ditch' is near Culebra, about 12 miles from Panama; the cut whose ragged walls rise before and behind us is the second largest in the whole length of the canal." TR: "Of the success of the enterprise I am well convinced as anyone can be of any enterprise that is human.... They are doing something which will redound immeasurably to the credit of America, which will benefit all the world, and which will last for ages to come."

"One of the most attractive and beautiful features of this Exposition will be the electrical illumination. By an entirely new system of flood lighting a soft, restful, yet perfect light will pervade the courts at night, revealing in wonderful clearness the facades and walls of the palaces and the natural colors of the shrubbery and flowers. By peculiar and novel lighting devices the statuary and mural paintings will be made to appear with even heightened effect. Concealed batteries will project powerful yet softened rays of light that will cause tens of thousands of specially prepared glass "jewels," hung tremulously upon the towers, to flash and scintillate like great diamonds, emeralds and rubies. At a point on the bay shore will be erected apparatus that will weave in the night sky auroras of ever-changing color. Altogether the spectacle will be interesting and wonderful and never to be forgotten."

AFTER THE EARTHQUAKE, much of the rubble was transported to the Harbor View District (now the Marina) as landfill. In 1915, this "made ground" became the site of the Panama-Pacific International Exposition. On opening day, there were 245,143 visitors. 18,511,005 more would pass through the gates before they closed on December 4.

Neither the words "earthquake" nor "1906" appear in 1915's *Panama-Pacific International Exposition Program Booklet No. 1:*

> "On February 20, 1915—on time and minutely ready— the Panama-Pacific International Exposition will be opened at San Francisco. It will be the third exposition of its class held in the United States and the twelfth of its class held anywhere in the world. It is the official, national and international celebration of a contemporaneous event—the opening of the Panama Canal.... After much consideration Congress,

in 1910, entrusted the responsibility to San Francisco and the Panama-Pacific International Exposition represents the fulfillment of that national trust.... It seems fitting that the Exposition, which marks the beginning of a new era in commerce, should be held on the shores of the Pacific. California marks the limit of the geographical progress of civilization. For unnumbered centuries the course of empire has been steadily to the west. On the shores of the Pacific it finds itself still facing west, yet looking to the east; or, in [Walt] Whitman's beautiful phrasing:

> 'Facing west, from California's shores,
>
> Inquiring, tireless, seeking what is yet unfound,
>
> I, a child, very old, over waves, towards the house of
>
>   Maternity, the land of migrations, look afar,
>
> Look off the shores of my Western Sea—the circle
>
>   almost circled.'"

211

Destruction of San Francisco. Pavilion under construction at the 1915 Panama-Pacific International Exposition. Note the dome of the ruined City Hall. A very rare Keystone stereo view. Although the PPIE was ostensibly about the future, many of its eighteen million visitors were understandably fascinated with San Francisco's past.

Lagoon and N.W. Section of Columns of Fine Arts Palace, Panama–Pacific Int. Exp., San Francisco. On Bernard Maybeck's beaux arts oasis: "This palace faces upon a great lagoon of placid water which reflects its beautiful architecture. It is a fireproof structure."–*PPIE Program.* "There's a park on Jackson Street and we would look down at the 1915 Exposition and Lincoln Beechey was there (a very big attraction). He was the man that flew an airplane at nighttime, with lights on it, and it shone, oh, so pretty, and I think he did the loop-the-loop a couple of times. It was some sight to see."– Herbert Hamrol, 1906 Earthquake Survivor

Keystone View Company
Manufacturer Keystone View Co. Meadville U.S.A. *Publishers*
Copyright, 1915, by

Meadville, Pa., New York, N. Y., Portland, Oregon, London, Eng., Sydney, Aus.

17770—Lagoon and N. W. Section of Columns of Fine Arts Palace, Panama-Pacific Int. Exp., San Francisco, Calif.

16743 T *** Market Street—Twin Peaks in the Distance, San Francisco, Calif.

*M*arket Street—Twin Peaks in the Distance. THE CITY THAT IS. San Francisco's new Palace Hotel is on the left. Kirby, Petit, and Green's 1909 Hearst Building replaced Newspaper Row's old Examiner Building at the corner of Third and Market. Between the Palace and the Hearst Building is Meyer and O'Brien's Monadnock Building. After the Earthquake, the Call Building was refaced. The dome was later removed for another—far less successful—makeover in 1938. Today, as Central Tower, 703 Market Street at Third, it is almost unrecognizable. Past the Call Building, still on the left, stands Meyer and O'Brien's 1908 Humboldt Bank Building at 783–785 Market. In the foreground on the right

is the Crocker Building, torn down in the 1960s. Just past it is the Chronicle Building, minus its distinctive pre-Earthquake clock. In front of the Chronicle Building is Lotta's Fountain, where survivors still gather every April 18 to commemorate the Great San Francisco Earthquake and Fire of 1906.

View from Telegraph Hill, San Francisco, across bay to Oakland. The stereophotographer of this poignant view is unknown. We will never know whether his trench-coated subject is contemplating the City-By-The-Bay's past or its future.

SELECTED READING

"A man will turn over half a library to make one book."–Samuel Johnson

San Francisco/Earthquakes

Agee, James, and Walker Evans. *Let Us Now Praise Famous Men*. Boston, 1941.

Aitken, Frank W., and Edward Hilton. *A History of the Earthquake and Fire in San Francisco*. SF, 1906.

Atherton, Gertrude. *Ancestors*. NY, 1907.

Ayers, Colonel James J. *Gold and Sunshine: Reminiscences of Early California*. Boston, 1922.

Baird, Jr., Joseph Armstrong. *Time's Wondrous Changes: San Francisco Architecture, 1776–1915*. SF, 1962.

Baird, Jr., Joseph Armstrong, and Edwin Clyve Evans. *Historic Lithographs of San Francisco*. SF, 1972.

Bancroft, Hubert Howe. *Some Cities and San Francisco, and Resurgam*. NY, 1907.

———. *The Works of Hubert Howe Bancroft*. Vol. 19. SF, 1886.

Barker, Malcolm E. *Bummer & Lazarus: San Francisco's Famous Dogs*. SF, 2001.

———. *More San Francisco Memoirs; 1852–1899*. SF, 1996.

———. *San Francisco Memoirs; 1835–1851*. SF, 1994.

———. *Three Fearful Days: San Francisco Memoirs of the 1906 Earthquake & Fire*. SF, 1998.

Barry, T. A., and B. A. Patten. *Men and Memories of San Francisco in the Spring of '50*. SF, 1873.

Barrymore, John. *Confessions of an Actor*. Indianapolis, 1926.

Bean, Walton. *Boss Ruef's San Francisco: The Story of the Union Labor Party, Big Business, and the Graft Prosecution*. Berkeley, 1952.

Beebe, Lucius, and Charles Clegg. *San Francisco's Golden Era*. Berkeley, 1960.

Benemann, William, ed. *A Year of Mud and Gold: San Francisco in Letters and Diaries, 1849–1850*. Lincoln, NE, 1999.

Bierce, Ambrose. *The Collected Works of Ambrose Bierce*. Vol. 7, *The Devil's Dictionary*. NY, 1911.

Bizet, Georges. *Carmen*. NY, 1989.

Blake, Evarts I. *San Francisco and Its Municipal Administration, 1902*. SF, 1902.

Bolton, Herbert Eugene. *Fray Juan Crespi: Missionary Explorer on the Pacific Coast, 1769–1774*. Berkeley, 1927.

Bonnet, Theodore. *The Regenerators: A Study of the Graft Prosecution of San Francisco*. SF, 1911.

Bonnett, Wayne. *Victorian San Francisco: The 1895 Illustrated Directory*. Sausalito, 1996.

Bosqui, Edward. *Memoirs*. SF, 1904.

Brandt, Fred, and Andrew Y. Wood. *Fascinating San Francisco*. SF, 1924.

Brechin, Gray. *Imperial San Francisco: Urban Power, Earthly Ruin*. Berkeley, 1999.

Bronson, William. *The Earth Shook, the Sky Burned*. NY, 1959.

Brooks, George W. *The Spirit of 1906*. SF, 1921.

Brown & Paper Stationery Co. *Men Who Made San Francisco*. SF, 1915.

Browning, Peter. *San Francisco/Yerba Buena: From the Beginning to the Gold Rush, 1769–1849*. Lafayette, CA, 1998.

Burnham, Daniel H. *Report on a Plan for San Francisco*. SF, 1905.

Byington, Lewis Francis, and Oscar Lewis, eds. *The History of San Francisco*. Vol. 1. SF, 1931.

Caruso, Jr., Enrico, and Andrew Farkas. *Enrico Caruso: My Father and My Family*. Portland, 1990.

Chase, Marilyn. *The Barbary Plague: The Black Death in Victorian San Francisco*. NY, 2003.

Chastel, André, ed. *Leonardo on Art and the Artist: Leonardo da Vinci*. Mineola, NY, 2002.

Collier, Michael. *A Land in Motion: California's San Andreas Fault*. Berkeley, 1999.

Corbett, Michael R. *Splendid Survivors: San Francisco's Downtown Architectural Heritage*. SF, 1979.

Dalessandro, James. *1906: A Novel*. SF, 2004.

Dana, Jr., Richard Henry. *Two Years before the Mast: A Personal Narrative*. NY, 1964.

Davey, Frank. *Leland Stanford Jr. University, Palo Alto, California: Before and After the Earthquake of April 18, 1906*. San Jose, 1906.

Denham, William, et al. *Report on the Causes of Municipal Corruption in San Francisco, as Disclosed by the Investigations of the Oliver Grand Jury, and the Prosecution of Certain Persons for Bribery and Other Offenses Against the State*. SF, 1910.

Derleth, Jr., Charles. *The Destructive Extent of the California Earthquake*. SF, 1907.

Eddy, Elford. *The Log of a Cabin Boy*. SF, 1922.

Eldredge, Zoeth Skinner. *The Beginnings of San Francisco*. 2 vols. SF, 1912.

———. *The March of Portolá and the Discovery of the Bay of San Francisco*. SF, 1909.

Fracchia, Charles A. *Fire & Gold: The San Francisco Story*. Encinitas, CA, 1996.

Fradkin, Philip L. *The Great Earthquake and Firestorms of 1906*. Berkeley, 2005.

Frost, John. *History of the State of California*. Auburn, NY, 1852.

Genthe, Arnold. *As I Remember*. NY, 1936.

———. *Pictures of Old Chinatown*. NY, 1908.

Givens, J. D., and A. M. Allison. *San Francisco in Ruins*. Denver, 1906.

Hansen, Gladys, and Emmet Condon. *Denial of Disaster*. SF, 1989.

Harlow, Neal. *California Conquered: The Annexation of a Mexican Province, 1846–1850*. Berkeley, 1982.

Harte, Bret. *The Complete Poetical Works of Bret Harte*. Vol. 8. NY, 1902.

Hemans, Felicia Dorothea. *The Poetical Works of Mrs. Felicia Hemans*. London, 1836.

Hibler, Harold E., and Charles V. Kappen. *So-Called Dollars: An Illustrated Standard Catalog with Valuations*. NY, 1963.

Hichborn, Franklin. *The System: As Uncovered by the San Francisco Graft Prosecution*. SF, 1915.

Hittell, John S. *A History of San Francisco and Incidentally of the State of California*. SF, 1878.

Hjalmarson, Birgitta. *Artful Players: Artistic Life in Early San Francisco*. Los Angeles, 1999.

Holliday, J. S. *Rush for Riches: Gold Fever and the Making of California*. Berkeley, 1999.

———. *The World Rushed In: The California Gold Rush Experience*. NY, 1981.

Hughes, Edan Milton. *Artists in California, 1786–1940*. 2 vols. Ann Arbor, MI, 2002.

Irwin, Will. *The City That Was*. NY, 1906.

Jordan, David Starr. *The California Earthquake of 1906*. SF, 1907.

———. *Life's Enthusiasms*. Boston, 1906.

Keeler, Charles. *San Francisco and Thereabout*. SF, 1903.

Kemble, John Haskell. *San Francisco Bay: A Pictorial Maritime History*. Cambridge, Maryland, 1957.

Kennedy, John Castillo. *The Great Earthquake and Fire: San Francisco, 1906*. NY, 1963.

Kipling, Rudyard. *From Sea to Sea: Letters of Travel*. 2 vols. NY, 1899.

Kowalewski, Michael, ed. *Gold Rush: A Literary Exploration*. Berkeley, 1997.

Kroeber, A. L. *Handbook of the Indians of California*. Washington, 1925.

Kroeber, Theodora. *Ishi: Last of His Tribe*. NY, 1973.

———. *Ishi in Two Worlds: A Biography of the Last Wild Indian in North America*. Berkeley, 1961.

Kurzman, Dan. *Disaster! The Great San Francisco Earthquake and Fire of 1906*. NY, 2001.

Langellier, John Phillip, and Daniel Bernard Rosen. *Historic Resource Study, El Presidio de San Francisco: A History under Spain and Mexico, 1776–1846*. SF, 1992.

Lavender, David. *Nothing Seemed Impossible: William C. Ralston and Early San Francisco*. Palo Alto, 1975.

Lawson, Andrew C., et al. *Atlas of Maps and Seismograms Accompanying the Report of the State Earthquake Investigation Commission upon the California Earthquake of April 18, 1906*. Washington, 1908.

Leach, Frank A. *Recollections of a Newspaper Man: A Record of Life and Events in California*. SF, 1917.

LeBaron, Gaye, and Joann Mitchell. *Santa Rosa: A Nineteenth Century Town*. Santa Rosa, 1985.

Lee, W. Storrs. *California: A Literary Chronicle*. NY, 1968.

Leonard, Zenas. *Narrative of the Adventures of Zenas Leonard*. Chicago, 1934.

Linthicum, Richard, and Trumbull White. *San Francisco Earthquake Horror*. Chicago (?), 1906.

Lloyd, B. E. *Lights and Shades in San Francisco*. SF, 1876.

Longstreth, Richard. *On the Edge of the World: Four Architects in San Francisco at the Turn of the Century*. Berkeley, 1983.

Mack, Gerstle. *1906: Surviving San Francisco's Great Earthquake & Fire*. SF, 1981.

Margolin, Malcolm. *The Ohlone Way: Indian Life in the San Francisco-Monterey Bay Area*. Berkeley, 1978.

Martin, George. *Verdi at the Golden Gate: Opera and San Francisco in the Gold Rush Years*. Berkeley, 1993.

Matthews, Franklin. *With the Battle Fleet*. NY, 1908.

McCawley, William. *The First Angelinos: The Gabrielino Indians of Los Angeles*. Novato, CA, 1996.

Miller, Warren, Charles A. Smallwood, and Donald P. DeNevi. *The Cable Car Book*. Millbrae, CA, 1980.

Mordden, Ethan. *Opera Anecdotes*. NY, 1985.

Morris, Charles. *The San Francisco Calamity by Earthquake and Fire*. N.p.: W. E. Scull, 1906.

Morris, Edmund. *Theodore Rex*. NY, 2001.

Murray, W. H. *The Builders of a Great City*. SF, 1891.

Myrick, David F. *San Francisco's Telegraph Hill*. Berkeley, 1972.

Nelson, Kevin. *The Golden Game: The Story of California Baseball*. SF, 2004.

Norris, Frank. *McTeague: A Story of San Francisco*. NY, 1903.

O'Connor, Charles J., et al. *San Francisco Relief Survey: the Organization and Methods of Relief used after the Earthquake and Fire of April 18, 1906*. NY, 1913.

Older, Fremont. *My Own Story*. NY, 1926.

Olmsted, Nancy. *The Ferry Building: Witness to a Century of Change, 1898–1998*. Berkeley, 1998.

Pacific Art Company. *San Francisco: Greetings from California, 1904–1905*. SF, 1905.

Paddison, Joshua, ed. *A World Transformed: Firsthand Accounts of California before the Gold Rush*. Berkeley, 1999.

Pan, Erica Y. Z. *The Impact of the 1906 Earthquake on San Francisco's Chinatown*. NY, 1995.

Pardee, George C., J. C. Branner, David Starr Jordan, James D. Phelan, Van W. Anderson, Benjamin Ide Wheeler, Frederick Funston, et al. *The Story of the California Disaster*. Portland, 1906.

Peters, Harry T. *California on Stone*. Garden City, NY, 1935.

Pliny the Younger. *Letters of Gaius Plinius Cæcilius Secundus*, trans. William Melmoth, revised by F. C. T. Bosanquet. NY, 1909.

Potter, Elizabeth Gray, and Mabel Thayer Gray. *The Lure of San Francisco*. SF, 1915.

Rathmell, George. *Realms of Gold: The Colorful Writers of San Francisco, 1850–1950*. Berkeley, 1998.

Rogers, Fred Blackburn. *Montgomery and the Portsmouth*. SF, 1958.

Roosevelt, Theodore. *An Autobiography*. NY, 1913.

———. *California Addresses, by President Roosevelt*. SF, 1903.

San Francisco. MGM, 1936. VHS.

San Francisco Board of Supervisors. *San Francisco Municipal Reports: Fiscal Years 1905–6 and 1906–7*. SF, 1908.

Schussler, Hermann. *The Water Supply of San Francisco, California: Before, During and After the Earthquake of April 18th, 1906 and the Subsequent Conflagration*. NY, 1906.

Scott, Michael. *The Great Caruso*. NY, 1988.

Searight, Frank Thompson. *The Doomed City: A Thrilling Tale*. Chicago, 1906.

Secrist, William B. *When the Great Spirit Died: The Destruction of the California Indians, 1850–1860*. Sanger, CA, 2002.

Shakespeare, William. *Romeo and Juliet: The Arden Shakespeare*, Brian Gibbons, ed. London, 1980.

———. *Romeo and Juliet: A New Variorum Edition*, Horace Howard Furness, ed. NY, 1963.

Smith, Donald Eugene, and Frederick J. Teggart, eds. *Diary of Gaspar de Portolá during the California Expedition of 1769–1770*. Berkeley, 1909.

Soulé, Frank, et al. *The Annals of San Francisco*. NY, 1855.

Stark, Sam, ed. *Early Theatres of California*. SF, 1974.

Starr, Kevin. *Americans and the California Dream, 1850–1915*. NY, 1973.

———. *Inventing the Dream: California through the Progressive Era*. NY, 1985.

Steele, Rufus. *The City That Is: The Story of the Rebuilding of San Francisco in Three Years*. SF, 1909.

Steffens, Lincoln. *The Shame of the Cities*. NY, 1904.

Stetson, James B. *San Francisco During the Eventful Days of April, 1906*. SF, 1906.

Stevenson, Robert Louis. *From Scotland to Silverado*. Cambridge, MA, 1966.

———. *The Works of Robert L. Stevenson*. Vol. 2. London, 1906.

Sutherland, Monica. *The Damndest Finest Ruins*. NY, 1959.

Taper, Bernard, ed. *Mark Twain's San Francisco*. NY, 1963.

Taylor, Bayard. *Eldorado: Adventures in the Path of Empire*. NY, 1850.

Teggart, Frederick J., ed. *The Portolá Expedition of 1769–1770; Diary of Miguel Costanso*. Berkeley, 1911.

Thomas, Gordon, and Max Morgan Witts. *The San Francisco Earthquake*. NY, 1971.

Thomas, Lately. *A Debonair Scoundrel*. NY, 1962.

Tinkham, George H. *California Men and Events: Time 1769–1890*. Stockton, CA, 1915.

Todd, Frank Morton. *Eradicating Plague from San Francisco*. SF, 1909.

Twain, Mark. *Early Tales and Sketches; Volume 2, 1864–1865*. Berkeley, 1981.

———. *Roughing It*. Hartford, CT, 1872.

Tyler, Sydney. *San Francisco's Great Disaster*. Harrisburg, PA, 1906.

United States Geological Survey. *The San Francisco Earthquake and Fire of April 18, 1906*. Washington, 1907.

Watkins, T. H., and R. R. Olmsted. *Mirror of the Dream: An Illustrated History of San Francisco*. SF, 1976.

Wheeler, Richard S. *Aftershocks*. NY, 1999.

Wilson, James Russel. *San Francisco's Horror of Earthquake and Fire*. N.p.: Memorial Publishing Co., 1906.

Winchester, Simon. "A Crack in the Edge of the World: America and the Great California Earthquake of 1906" (manuscript, HarperCollins, NY, 2005).

Young, John P. *San Francisco: A History of the Pacific Coast Metropolis*. 2 vols. SF, 1912.

Zeigler, Wilbur Gleason. *Story of the Earthquake and Fire*. SF, 1906.

Numerous periodicals, including *The Argonaut*, *The Wasp*, SF newspapers, and the *Bulletin of the Seismological Society of America*.

Stereoscopy

Benton, Stephen A., ed. *Selected Papers on Three-Dimensional Displays*. Bellingham, WA, 2001.

Bowers, Brian. *Sir Charles Wheatstone*. London, 1975.

Brewster, Sir David. *The Stereoscope: its History, Theory, and Construction*. London, 1856.

———. *A Treatise on the Kaleidoscope*. Edinburgh, 1819.

———. *A Treatise on Optics*. London, 1831.

Crain, Jim. *California in Depth: A Stereoscopic History*. SF, 1994.

Darrah, William Culp. *Stereo Views: A History of Stereographs in America and Their Collection*. Gettysburg, 1964.

———. *The World of Stereographs*. Nashville, 1977.

Euclid. *Optics*. Trans. Harry Edwin Burton. *Journal of the Optical Society of America*. Vol. 35. 1945.

Galen. *On the Usefulness of the Parts of the Body*. Trans. and ed. Margaret Tallmadge May. Ithaca, NY, 1968.

Gill, Arthur T. *Early Stereoscopes. The Photographic Journal*. Vol. 109. London, 1969.

Gordon, Margaret Maria. *The Home Life of Sir David Brewster*. Edinburgh, 1869.

Harris, David. *Eadweard Muybridge and the Photographic Panorama of San Francisco, 1850–1880*. With Eric Sandweiss. Montreal, 1993.

Henfrey, Arthur, ed. *The Journal of the Photographic Society of London*. Vol. 1. London, 1854.

Holmes, Oliver Wendell. *Soundings from the Atlantic*. Boston, 1864.

Jenkins, Harold F. *Two Points of View: The History of the Parlor Stereoscope*. Elmira, NY, 1957.

Laval, Jerome D. *Images of an Age: San Francisco*. Fresno, CA, 1977.

Leonardo da Vinci. *A Treatise on Painting*. London, 1796.

Mabie, Roy W. *The Stereoscope and Stereograph*. NY, 1942.

Mayo, Herbert. *Outlines of Human Physiology*. London, 1833.

Nickel, Douglas R., and Maria Morris Hambourg. *Carleton Watkins: The Art of Perception*. SF, 1999.

Osborne, Albert E. *The Stereograph and the Stereoscope*. NY, 1909.

Palmquist, Peter E. *Lawrence & Houseworth/Thomas Houseworth & Co.: A Unique View of the West, 1860–1886*. Columbus, OH, 1980.

———. *Carleton E. Watkins: Photographer of the American West*. Albuquerque, 1983.

Solnit, Rebecca. *River of Shadows: Eadweard Muybridge and the Technological Wild West*. NY, 2003.

Wade, Nicholas J., ed. *Brewster and Wheatstone on Vision*. NY, 1983.

Waldsmith, John. *Stereo Views: An Illustrated History & Price Guide*. Iola, WI, 2002.

Wheatstone, Sir Charles. *The Scientific Papers of Sir Charles Wheatstone*. London, 1879.

White Co., H. C. *Catalog of Stereographs and Lantern Slides*. North Bennington, VT, 1907.

Wing, Paul. *Stereoscopes: The First One Hundred Years*. Nashua, NH, 1996.

Zeller, Bob. *The Civil War in Depth, Volu II: History in 3-D*. SF, 2000.

Numerous periodicals, including *Atlantic Monthly*, *The Philadelphia Photographer*, and *Stereo World*.

Powell, Mason, Tailor [sic], *Stockton, Dupont* [now Grant], *Kearney*
[now Kearny] *and Montgomery Streets, Great Earthquake, San Francisco.*
Lower left: Hibernia Savings & Loan (corner, McAllister & Jones streets).

3-D VIEWER INSTRUCTIONS

1. The enclosed 3-D viewer may be used with or without eyeglasses. If you are very nearsighted or farsighted, it is recommended that you keep your glasses on. If you use bifocals or progressive lenses, it is recommended that you look through the upper part of your eyeglass lenses.

2. To clean the viewer's lenses, moisten a lens tissue with eyeglass lens–cleaning fluid, or exhale onto the lenses' surface. Clean gently as you would clean a pair of eyeglasses.

3. Never put liquid lens cleaner directly onto the lenses.

4. Never wipe the lenses with a dry tissue, as it may scratch their surface.

5. The 3-D viewer itself is water resistant, but not waterproof. To clean it, simply wipe it off with a soft, clean cloth.

6. To learn about "freeviewing," see pages 7-9.

7. For more information, or to purchase additional viewers, visit www.1906quake.com.